W9-CFL-299

DOWN TO EARTH

DOWN TO EARTH

WISDOM, WIT AND GREAT ADVICE FROM A CONNECTICUT GARDENER

REA LUBAR DUNCAN

CONNECTICUT MAGAZINE
BRIDGEPORT

For my husband Ken Duncan:
Not without you

Copyright© 1995 by Rea Lubar Duncan

All rights reserved. No part of this book may be reproduced in any form
(except for review purposes) without permission from the publisher. Requests for permission should be
addressed to CONNECTICUT Magazine, 789 Reservoir Ave., Bridgeport, CT 06606.

All the contents of this book first appeared in CONNECTICUT Magazine.

Library of Congress Catalog Card Number: 95-74863
ISBN 0-9648033-0-5
Manufactured in the United States Of America
First Edition

CONTENTS

FAMILY PLANNING

LANDMARKS & BEAUTY MARKS

PREFACE

*D*o you *know* the people who read your articles?"
It was Kathleen Nelson on the phone barely a week after my column on her Gaylordsville nursery appeared in the October '94 CONNECTICUT Magazine.

Sure, I know 10, maybe 20, all personal friends in whose highly biased opinion I am the William Faulkner of garden literature. But no, I don't really *know* the people who read the articles.

"Well, *they know you*," Mrs. Nelson expostulated. "The first person who called me—the very same day the magazine arrived in the mail—said, '*Rea said* her white coneflowers are always sickly compared to her pink ones and your whites are wonderful. Do you have some now?' I thought she was a personal friend of yours, but then a man called and said, '*Rea said* the grass Little Bluestem will grow in poor, dry soil. That's what I have. Is this the time to plant?'" (At this writing Mrs. Nelson has received more than 300 inquiries from the column.)

"It finally struck me that these people *feel* they know you personally," she said. "They identify with you. It's remarkable."

It's more than remarkable. It's wonderful! (My column on Chinese tree peonies drew 1,300 visitors to Cricket Hill Garden in Thomaston!) But it doesn't go to my head because the reason for this heartwarming empathy is not that I'm a great gardener but that I'm *not*. It's that I'm an amateur, a dirt gardener, one of those people who "like to get down on their knees and grub," as we were described by Katherine S. White, author of the famed-and-feisty review of garden catalogs, *Onward and Upward in the Garden*.

I owe a deep thank you to CONNECTICUT Magazine for giving me the platform from which to share my garden joys and sorrows. My very special thanks go to Michelle Bodak, who, in editing this book, lovingly but sternly made me hew the line about consistent nomenclature, and gave days upon days to the proper indexing of every blooming sprout and tree.

More than 70 columns have appeared since 1983, 40 reprinted in this book that was compiled *at the request of readers*. Isn't that nice? An attorney from West Redding wrote that although he'd saved all the columns he'd read, he was afraid he'd missed some. Could they be reprinted in a book? A gentleman in Roxbury wrote, "Rea Duncan's garden articles are pure poetry." A woman in Sherman said, "Every scoop of earth in Rea Duncan's delightful gardening articles bears her particular creative lilt." (I'm blushing.) And a reader in Avon considers my CONNECTICUT columns "a perk" she gets for her $35 membership to Connecticut Public Television.

But readers have also written to tell me off. "It's not Grüss an Achen, but Gruss," I was advised. *Danke.* And there was the anonymous would-be murderer who threatened to shoot me if he or she ever saw me near his or her property picking wild daylilies.

I've tried to group the columns by broad overall subject: First, "How-tos"—what to plant when, where, why and how; second, "Theme and Variations"—groups of plants related thematically (flowering shrubs, blue-blooming perennials, climbers, ground covers); third, "Family Planning"—individual families of plants (iris, phlox, clematis, even delphiniums, those devils); fourth, "Landmarks and Beauty Marks"—outstanding Connecticut gardens.

But just as some of my border plants rambunctiously spill over, so do some columns. And others don't fit in anyplace—but I stuck 'em in anyway. Although the magazine's turf is the state of Connecticut and environs, most information about plants and growing conditions holds true for pretty much all the Northeast, the cooler regions of the Southeast, the temperate Midwest and Far West.

Inevitably, some things have changed since I wrote the columns. Sadly, Dan Arje, he of the "spendid color irritant" in "Living Color," and Jan Carlson of Carlson's Gardens in South Salem, N.Y., have both died. Joe Cicio sold his castle in Cornwall after restoring it to Renaissance glory. The young buck in our family of white-tailed deer used our golden chain tree to rub the velvet off his antlers—and killed it. Our two fringe trees shimmy and shake no longer—they perished in the bitter cold of winter '94.

Also, I've learned that the "yellow double herbaceous peony" Lady Drummond grew in her Sissinghurst garden was, in all likelihood, a Chinese tree peony raised from seeds sent her from China. Hybridizers have still not bred a true yellow double herbaceous type.

On the other hand, some things *don't change* and bear repeating. Daffodils, peonies and coneflowers, among others, are glorious year in, year out. So forgive me if I've gone on about them more than once.

The good news is that the Japanese weeping cherry we bought as a skinny young thing has grown to 20 feet and is hung with ravishing pink blossoms in May. The Red Jade crab apple is, as promised, covered with white blossoms in spring and red berries in winter. And my husband bought me the pricey, but gorgeous, daylily, Prairie Blue Eyes, for our 30th anniversary.

About the photographs. I, personally, took most of the pictures of my garden and, plainly, Robert Mapplethorpe I'm not. But I wanted to *show it* as well as tell it like it is. There are no hidden stakes supporting droopy stems, no regrouping of plants for design improvement. In short, nothing has been added or subtracted, not even weeds. What you see is what I've got, a dirt gardener's garden as is.

My deepest gratitude goes to my husband, Ken Duncan, an architect—and magician. Thanks to him, all of us who live on Turtle Pond consider ourselves blessed. Today there are four houses here; when Ken and I bought the land in 1973, there were none. Magically, he blended houses (he designed three of them), land and water, and wound a road among them, yet managed to preserve, five minutes from downtown Danbury, a pastoral landscape with 80-foot pines, hemlock and spruce, a great meadow, tumbling brook and luminous pond.

I'm sharing all this with you, dear readers, because, although I don't know you personally, I, too, feel a warm kinship and thank you for your welcome and friendship. May all your trees be lush and green and all your flowers—bugless, of course—in bloom from first thaw to hard frost. Mine, too.

Rea Lubar Duncan

NICHOLAS JACOBS

WHY I GARDEN

$\mathcal{I}$t wasn't until about 10 years ago that I first put a plant in soil, and gardening seized me." So wrote A.M. Rosenthal in his moving article on newspapering, "Learning on the Job," an ode to freedom of the press that appeared in *The New York Times Magazine* in December 1984, when he retired after 40 years at the *Times*.

Why did gardening seize him? Mr. Rosenthal added only, "I have learned that if you plant flowers, you see the world more clearly. I don't know why. I am not a philosopher."

Earlier gardeners were not always so terse. Dating back almost to the beginnings of civilization, when men and women first gardened, they have felt compelled to excuse, explain and justify the joyful seizures of gardening with lofty, sensible or otherwise socially acceptable reasons.

And such reasons! Religious. Romantic. Financial. Self-aggrandizing. Mind-expanding. Body-building. Liver-rejuvenating. Demon-expelling. Life-extending. Sexual.

Like all works of art, gardens take their shape from the relationship of man to his physical surroundings and his society. Over the centuries, therefore, styles in gardening have varied widely. But the reason people garden has remained the same. Glimmering through all the noble and pious talk, the true motivation has always been: *the pleasure gardening gives the gardener.*

It was thus of the Persians and their voluptuous, walled-in gardens, with their canals, avenues of plane trees, dovecotes, fountains and magnificent flowers (the word, paradise, derives from the Persian, *pairidaeza*); of the Chinese and their fantastic artificial landscapes symbolically representing the natural world; of the Japanese and their ritual compositions of stone and sand; of the Renaissance Italians and their imaginative reconstructions of classic tree-filled groves ornate with statuary and fountains; of the French, notably Le Nôtre's masterpiece at Versailles, "a theatre of greenery" extending the grand salons of the Sun King into the open air.

It was thus, too, of the English and their contrived "landscape" style that started in the 18th century and has been a dominant theme ever since; of the English "peasant" or cottage gardens, which, it is said, were begun by a Yorkshire sign painter who "jumped the wall" and let nature in; of the informal flower borders with which Gertrude Jekyll forever uncorseted English—and American—gardens.

Though the idiom has changed from place to place and from one period to another, the pleasure remains. As the Chinese proverb goes, "If you would be happy for a week, take a wife; if you would be happy for a month, kill a pig; but if you would be happy all your life, plant a garden."

Today, of course, thanks to Freud, society accepts pleasure as sufficient reason for gardening or, for better and worse, for virtually any other human activity. But in other times and places, pleasure for pleasure's sake was sinful at worst, shallow at best, so proper justification had to be contrived.

In the 17th century, one gardened to gain re-entry into the Garden of Eden—or at least to get as close as possible. "All bliss/Consists in this/To do as Adam did," wrote one seer, and his thoughts are echoed in virtually every gardening book of the period. Oh, how men longed to return to that first garden, and oh, how hopeful they were that gardening could get them there. In her captivating book, *Men and Gardens*, Nan Fairbrother quotes one gardener who explained virtuously, "It is impossible for us, Adam's posterity, ever to make a Garden as fair as Eden, yet doubtless by Industry and Painstaking in that lovely, honest and delightful Recreation of Planting, we may gain some little glimmering of that lost Splendour, although with much difficulty."

Another enthusiast even called in the angels: "I little doubt, that if Angels were confined to these lower regions, they would seek the Retirement and Pleasure of a Garden, as most agreeable to their heavenly disposition."

Ah, come off it! Angels would surely fear to tread in the summerhouse gardens of the Chinese princes, which were designed solely for dallying with their concubines, or, as Nan Fairbrother relates, those Persian bath gardens described by Vita Sackville-West "with a kind of central throne on which some nineteenth century Shah might sit, attired in the minimum of clothing, while the ladies of his harem, similarly attired or unattired, slithered down chutes from an upper gallery straight into the embracing arms of their imperial master." Or the English garden where Chaucer's heroine in "The Merchant's Tale" trysted with her lover above the head of her blind and jealous husband in the branches of a pear tree.

Among the funniest reasons for gardening—or so it seemed on first reading—was to have a polite topic of dinner conversation. Consider "how difficult and dangerous a thing Conversation has now become," Mrs. Fairbrother quotes a 19th-century gardener as saying, with "politics dangerous, religion unprofitable," and "to talk of the Weather . . . low, mean and peasantly."

On reflection, it's not so funny. Talk of politics can still lead to guests stalking from the table. Religion? Oh, my God. Even mention of the weather conjures up doomsday predictions of the end of our planet.

I do, however, take issue with the Tudor gentleman who equated a tidy garden with a tidy housewife.

"Husbands," he wrote, "used alwayes to judge that where they founde the garden out of order, the wyfe of the house (for unto her belonged the charge thereof) was no good hswyfe."

Phooey. The reason my garden is out of order at this writing is that I was so busy last fall keeping my house spiffy that I never got around to cutting down the yellowed stalks of daylilies or the standing corpses of phlox, perennial aster and coneflowers. And in summer, ah, in summer, when my garden will be a delight—weeded, cultivated and mulched—my house will be a mess.

An 18th-century clergyman recommended gardening for exercise, urging his fellows to dig till they glow but not till they sweat ("ad Ruborem" though not "ad Sudorem"). A hungrier chap advised that "if a man want an Appetite to his Victuals, the smell of the Earth new turned up, by digging with a Spade will procure it, and if he be inclined to a Consumption, it will recover him." And 200 years before the cholesterol frenzy, gardening was seen as an aid to digestion in that the fruits and vegetables we grow were considered more wholesome than "a Table loaded with Flesh and Pudding."

Regarding the fair sex, Mrs. Fairbrother quotes one 18th-century gent, "Gentlewomen, if the ground be not too wet, may do themselves sych good by kneeling upon a Cushion and weeding. And thus both sexes might divert themselves from idlenesse and evill Company, which often is prove the ruine of many ingenious people." "The Ladies," wrote another self-styled expert on women, "would soon think that their vacant hours in the Culture of the Flower-Garden would be more innocently spent and with greater Satisfaction than the common Talk over a Tea-Table, where Envy and Detraction so commonly preside."

Gardening has also been praised as a way to lengthen life, for "the spirits are still kept in a cheerfull temper and condition, and so work powerfully on the grosser parts of the body, conducive to Long-life." Practically speaking, gardens have long provided a source of income. One farsighted father planted a tree when each of his daughters was born and chopped it down to sell for a dowry when she married. Honey as well as fruits and vegetables have made gardening commercially viable. (Were earlier gardeners immune to poison ivy? They seem to have cultivated it so bees might feast on the nectar in its blossoms.)

Religion has planted many a garden. The followers of Zoroaster believed that all gardeners go to heaven. Buddhists went even further. "Herbs and trees, stones and rocks shall all enter into Nirvana," they wrote. Along with the gardener, one supposes.

And love, don't forget love as a reason for gardening. The Hanging Gardens of Babylon, one of the seven wonders of the ancient world, are said to have been built by Nebuchadnezzar to please his wife, who longed for the hills of her home. In a mammoth undertaking, he planted 3 acres of ground in the city, with 16-foot-wide terraces supported by arches placed on 4-foot-square hollow pillars, so trees could spread their roots through them. And of the Taj Mahal, the 17th-century garden tomb of Mumtaz Mahal that her husband built for love of her, Edward Lear noted in his diary of Feb. 16, 1874, "What a garden! What flowers! Henceforth, let the inhabitants of the world be divided into two classes—them as has seen the Taj Mahal; and them as hasn't."

SO WHY DO I GARDEN?

The opening sentence of Miles and John Hadfield's enchanting book, *Gardens of Delight*, tells me, "Fundamentally, all gardening is the transference of a vision into a touchable and seeable reality." Okay, I'm transferring a vision—untroubled, I would add, that I lack the artistry of Monet or Michelangelo or Le Nôtre. We gardeners are mostly flower growers, not garden designers. No matter that we're not great artists, we know what we like. Plain or fancy, it's our vision we're transferring.

But why, why, is transference of that vision so overriding a force in my life, worth spending far more money than we could afford to buy a piece of Connecticut land, worth the aching back, broken nails, blackened hands, even a hernia (from transplanting a 100-pound lilac bush)?

Gardens soothe the senses and sway the spirits to peace, one devoted 19th-century gardener wrote. Another, describing his time (and ours), noted that, "The chief flower in [the] Garden is Hearts-Ease because it is very scarce in the world."

Agreed. And yet, none of these reasons was, for me, the keystone that holds all the others in place. And then, I found it in a chance rereading of *Ring of Bright Water*, Gavin Maxwell's gentle, soul-lifting, heart-breaking recounting of 10 years spent on the remote northwest coast of Scotland in a landscape of sea and stony hillside. The book is best known for its enchanting tale (published separately) of two otters that were, all too briefly, Maxwell's pets. But the whole book is not to be missed for its philosophical yet lyrical study of man's relationship to nature and its creatures, including, in spite of Maxwell himself, mankind.

In the foreword, Maxwell wrote a passage that seized me:

> *For I am convinced that man has suffered in his separation from the soil and from the other living creatures of the world. The evolution of his intellect has outrun his needs as an animal, and as yet he must still, for security, look long at some portion of the earth as it was before he tampered with it.*

For me, Maxwell's words set off waves of explanations—explanations of me to me. It explained why, when my husband, who is an architect, asked me what kind of house I wanted, I replied, "A house that brings the outside in and the inside out." It told me why I will do office work till dawn so that we can arrive in the country before dark—to do nothing but look at the land. It made clear why we never invited back a gardener of note who advised us to clear the wild woods of our hillside and plant it entirely with Exbury azaleas. It clarified why I prefer swimming in our mud-bottom pond to a swimming pool, and why I have even made peace with the resident water snake who suns himself on our dock. And it revealed why my favorite shrubs and plants are not tetraploid daylilies, gorgeous as they are, but the swamp azaleas, ferns and Jack-in-the-pulpits I have transplanted from the wild.

It also explains why I cannot wait to put my ungloved hands in the newly soft earth in spring. It even explains why I no longer shudder at putting all of me in the earth, and why, after years of condemning burial as barbaric (cremation being "civilized"), I have begun to think it wouldn't be so bad to lie, as Keats put it, with "the flowers growing over me." And, on the subject of Keats, it explains why he said to a friend that the "intensest pleasure he had received in life was watching the growth of flowers."

Like the 17th-century gardeners who knew they could never recapture Eden, I know that, by gardening, I can never recapture the earth as it was before man tampered with it. But it is the closest I can get.

HOW-TOS

MASS IS MORE
MARCH 1987

$\mathcal{G}$ ive me broad strokes, no dits and dats," the late, great Dorothy Shaver, president of Lord & Taylor, would command. With those broad strokes, she transformed the store from a solid, stolid purveyor of humdrum staples to a glittering fashion leader drawing throngs of visitors from around the world to her dazzling Fifth Avenue windows and interior settings. As *Vogue* magazine said, "Dorothy Shaver made 'store biz show biz.'"

That was way back in the late '40s and early '50s, when I was a green kid in my first big job. But I still hear—and heed—her words, both professionally and as a gardener. This time of year especially, when digging through garden books is the only digging we can do and planning rather than planting must content us, I try to envision broad strokes in my garden.

Admittedly, I'm a dirt gardener, not a landscape designer, and I feel a bit presumptuous stepping on design turf. But from long experience, much of it bitter, from years of reading about gardening, from visiting other people's gardens—some famous and far away, others just next door—and from observing nature's show-biz tricks, I've picked up a few "broad strokes" that help show off flowering plants to their best advantage.

My two basic tools for broad strokes are color and mass or, more accurately, color used en masse. It's nature's technique. In spring in Portugal, a scarlet coverlet of wild poppies stretches for miles over the fields. In France at the end of May, yellow broom ribbons the roadways from Paris to Provence, gilding even the garbage dumps. In Connecticut, on Route 84, an undulating stripe of golden black-eyed Susans brightens the center island and a white fretwork of Queen Anne's lace delicately trims the roadsides. Stealing from nature, Geraldine Stutz borders the Shepaug River along her Roxbury property with thousands of orange daylilies.

True, all these involve more mass and color than most of us can manage, financially or spatially. But we can learn from them. We can create a miniversion of Ms. Stutz's daylilies with six plants, all in one color, grouped at waterside, around a tree or even in the border. We can set off fireworks in our garden with just three scarlet Oriental poppies. Or we can illuminate the dark edge of woods with a burst of several black-eyed Susans. The point is: Always use at least three plants of one color—more, if possible—that clearly proclaim yellow, orange, red, white.

At the rear of my lily bed, I leave three monkshood plants unstaked to arch over gray boulders. One would be pretty, but it would be a "dit" compared to the blue cascade that flows over the rocks in August. Just three low-growing saponarias can create a pool of pink. When we built the slate terrace of our second house in Danbury, we left two 2-foot squares of dirt unslated for planting, one on either side of the living room's slid-

15

ing glass doors. For dimensional interest, we grouped three irregularly shaped rocks in each square of soil, then planted around them with three saponaria. In May, a billowing tumble of pink eddies at either side of the doors.

In my opinion, lilies *must* be planted in blocks of one color for full exposure. Although individual blooms are huge and exotic, the air space between them dilutes their punch and you get dits and dats. Six Red Jamborees, each with six to eight blossoms, make a razzle-dazzle broad stroke. Paler and less flamboyant, Pink Rhapsody is charming solo, but what a color chorus a sextet makes. And a trio of heavily blooming Sunray is enough to simulate sunspots in your garden.

With flowering shrubs, the whole can certainly be more than the sum of its parts—*when the parts are all the same color*. Three lilacs that curve around the crest of my upper lawn drape a luxurious purple swag in late May. Three white lilacs set a backdrop for early daylily foliage and low green juniper mounds.

As for trees, why not a grove? Well, a *little* grove. Not a forest of towering horse chestnuts, but perhaps a small copse of dogwoods. Last spring, I splurged on three white dogwoods for our meadow, two little fellows and one spreading 10-footer. That was all the budget would allow. With 12 feet of growing space between, they're far from a grove now, but someday they'll unfurl into the great white fan I dream of.

For a different, perhaps more painterly effect, try plants in different monochromatic tones of the same color. In Kent, England, at historic Penshurst Place, Lord and Lady De L'Isle started planting rose-colored peonies in 1966 and now, 20 years later, have 110 yards of peonies in every conceivable shade of pink to rose. Now that's a broad stroke! I'd settle for six peonies in a long bed, perhaps two blush Nick Shaylors, two clear pink M. Jules Elies, two rosy Sarah Bernhardts. More would be better, of course, but if you zigzag the plants rather than setting them in a straight line, you'll get more depth and denser color from both flowers and foliage.

Or you might wind iris through your border. A one-color block of bearded iris—any color, just so there are at least three of a kind—makes an exclamation point. But for a broad stroke, make a ribbon of light-to-dark varieties—lavender to amethyst to purple, or azure to sapphire to midnight blue, or lemon to buttercup to chrome.

Azaleas and rhododendron lend themselves to one-color blocks and, if you have the room, to wondrous monochromatic drifts. The range might be mauve to purple, or petal-pink to raspberry, or cream to yellow. Do be careful how you use those vibrant fuchsias, oranges and stinging reds. By themselves, they're gorgeous; mixed haphazardly with other colors, they're garish.

Different plant varieties with blooms in the same color family give the garden both heightened visibility and unity. In my July-August border, mauve-pink coneflowers (three make a fat clump) mix with phlox ranging from pale Fairy's Petticoat to bright Dodo Hanbury-Forbes (three of each, please) and with Jamboree lilies (ditto) and pink mallows (double ditto because their spires are skinny).

For a blue study, try diminutive Chinese delphiniums with taller hybrids, softened with bell-shaped *platy-codon* (balloon flower) and spiked with blue Veronica. Edge them all with ground-hugging blue campanula.

I doubt I'll ever achieve a one-color garden. I'm too easily seduced by an enticing new color, even when it upsets my color plan. About three dozen yellow to peach-toned gold daylilies circle a giant maple at the far end of my border. Well, last July I spotted some low-growing daylilies in glorious deep ruby-red. You know what happened. Two ruby clusters now glow like jeweled brooches in front of the taller yellows.

The all-white garden that Vita Sackville-West built at Sissinghurst Castle in Kent, England, is legendary. Deservedly so. Actually, it's silver to gray to white. Among the special effects are almond trees that flank the center walk and bloom white in early spring, then seem to bloom again when a white climbing rose festoons the trees with June blossoms. A silvery willow-leaved pear bends gracefully over spreading foliage plants in tones of gray, white and silver-green. Madonna lilies, iris, delphiniums, roses and phlox paint a wash of white from spring to fall.

I would have to have several gardens if one were to be one color. (Indeed, Sissinghurst does.) My husband, the architect and interior designer, chose neutral beiges to soft brown for the interior of our home. I'm forever messing things up by bringing in a red, yellow and black mask from Venice or a Swahili necklace in beaded orange, red and bright green. Truth is, Ken approves. The neutral base is a foil for these contrasting accent points.

Which brings me to what most gardens are all about—contrast—not only in color but in form, shape, height and density. The flowing blue monkshood I mentioned sets off upright pink lilies. The pink phlox, coneflowers and mallows alternate with spiky blue Veronica and floaty white and mauve cosmos. Earlier, bursts of white phlox Miss Lingard are interspersed with big plantings of yellow evening primrose.

Contrast can, of course, be sharp and bold—red and white peonies, yellow and purple tulips; or it can be soft and subtle—pink and white poppies, blue and white columbine. It's your choice. Last June I saw an unforgettable study in contrast, yellow and white daisies solidly massed in a long bed about 12 by 4 feet. It was on the tiny island of Torcello off Venice, in the rather elaborate garden of the famed Harry's Cipriani Restaurant. But you and I could do it easily—in fact, I plan to next summer—with yellow anthemis and coreopsis and white Shasta daisies.

Obviously, color masses do not a garden make. You must be sensitive to space, to contours of the land, to environmental mood. But those are in the realm of landscape design, which I have assiduously tried to steer clear of—or as clear of as possible. The fact is, it's impossible to isolate plants from landscape. Those purple lilacs I mentioned crown a curving slope of land. The monkshood spills over boulders; the saponarias, over small rocks. The white dogwoods are a focal point in a big meadow. The daylilies encircle a thick-trunked maple.

But, still trying to stick solely to heightened flower effects, I quote Vera, the noted print designer whose vibrant floral scarves, sheets and table linens have brightened fashion and home furnishings for two generations. Essentially a shy, private person, she once begged off from making a speech by saying, "Color is the language I speak best."

Happily, it's an easy language for gardeners, too. But broad strokes, please. No dits and dats.

REA LUBAR DUNCAN

LOOKING EAST

JUNE 1991

*V*isiting the glorious landscaped grounds of the fabled Gold Pavilion in Kyoto, I was so dazzled that I was barely able to murmur to my husband, "I think this is the most beautiful garden I've seen in Japan."

"I think this is the most beautiful garden I've seen in my life," he replied.

Of course, Japan's ancient gardens—whether the spare ritual compositions of the Zen Buddhist monks or the lavish symbolic landscapes of the imperial gardens—bear heartening witness to the human ability, and need, to create beauty.

But so do the gardens of today's Japanese people, not Shoguns or Samurai princes but working people like thee and me. Tiny gardens, some of them only 6 feet square, grace virtually every Japanese house—even in the big industrial cities—and they are *tiny*. Japan's preeminence on the world scene makes you forget, at least made me forget, what a very small island it is and how many millions of people are crowded onto it. Literally every inch of land is precious—and staggeringly expensive.

Nonetheless, the Japanese *will have* their gardens, which, despite their minuscule size, are works of art. I learned a lot looking at those humble gardens, whose simplicity belies the creative wizardry that goes into them. Shape, I think, is the secret of their success—shapes, actually. There is the shape of the chosen plant material—often there are only two plants set in stones, sometimes just one; the shape of other materials used, a small piece of sculpture, for example; the rocks selected as stepping-stones or for decorative accents; the pebbles that form the base of the garden; the overall shape of the plot, the house, even the street. And, most important of all, how each relates to the others and to the whole. As in a haiku, each phrase, even each syllable, has its unique beauty but must fit into the harmony of the whole.

When I came home, I looked with new eyes at my garden (my gardens, actually, although that sounds too grand because some are just patches) and at the whole configuration of house, lawn and perennial border. Especially the border, which I thought could be made infinitely more interesting—in bloom and out—by adding or substituting shrubs and small trees Japanese style to create aesthetic variety through shape. My border is some 75 feet long and from 6 to 12 feet in depth. But even if yours is smaller, a single shrub or small tree can serve as a focal point and add some drama.

What small shrubs and trees? Well, how does your garden grow? If it has a built-in backdrop—a wall, perhaps, or a hedge, existing big trees, a deck, or your house itself—then you need shrubs and trees that fit, artistically as well as in size, smack in the border along with your perennials. So they should be small or smallish. If it's a freestanding border, as mine is, then bigger shrubs and trees can be placed behind it so that it has a seemingly natural setting and isn't so naked and contrived. In their tiny gardens the Japanese often use a rounded rhododendron of the evergreen *yakusimanum* species ("yaks" like it in Connecticut and are increasingly available at nurseries here) or a thickly branched *kurume* azalea (ditto), both of which grow only to 4 feet.

For contrast in contour, the Japanese might choose a taller, but still dwarf, columnar evergreen, perhaps one of the slender *hinoki* false cypresses (members of the *chamaecyparis* family), which also get only to 4 feet. Examples are the daintily needled *obtusa gracilis* or *obtusa crippsii*, whose needles are golden when new and then turn dark green. Both are at home here in Connecticut and available at many nurseries. The rhodies and azaleas bloom in May and June, generally in the pink family, so put them with perennials that flower in compatible colors: pink, white, blue, purple. Their round forms contrast handsomely with slender, spired shapes—delphiniums and iris, for example; the conical shrubs contrast well with round poppies and peonies. Both give substance and solidity and lasting green to the border.

A beautiful tree small enough for placement within the border—although it also makes an eye-catching specimen planted alone—is a dwarf, red-leaved Japanese maple. In the garden of an *udon* (noodle) restaurant in the heart of the business section of Kyoto, a red maple was the only living thing. It had been artfully placed against the building so that its branches curved forward over the pebbles beneath to greet the visitor. A stone lantern, to one side, was the only other decoration.

These cut-leaved maples are expensive—a 2-foot young'un can cost upwards of a hundred dollars—but even when midgets, they're exquisite in form and color. I got a bargain at a nursery for a "deformed" specimen, but 'tweren't deformed to me. Its so-called problem was that its backside was bare and all its branches arched in one direction—forward. Of course, it was exactly what I wanted for the back of the border, where its rear could not be seen and its front formed a fountain of finely cut, burnished copper leaves like a parasol over the border from spring through late fall. (I prune it to keep it "deformed.")

One of these maples can take up 5 feet in width so leave room, but small plants that will bloom in the dappled shade of its overhanging branches can be planted beneath for charming effect: crocus, miniature daffodils and primrose in early spring; iris *cristata* and candytuft a bit later; the garden pink *Dianthus deltoides*, which comes in a white-and-red form and needs only half a day of sun for showy bloom through June and July; and, of course, all the shade-loving ground covers—lamium, myrtle, pachysandra, minihostas—as well as shade-tolerant annuals. Incidentally, there are glorious green-leaved varieties of this Japanese maple, the foliage so fine it has a feathery look. They are expensive, though.

Another lovely deciduous tree for within the border—or just behind it—is the weeping Japanese dogwood, which is rarely used in Connecticut. In my border it has grown only to 4 feet in four years, with slim branches that curve gracefully outward, then downward, from its standard. The white blossoms are regular dogwood-size, lots of them, and ample sunshine gets through its airy foliage to low-growing perennials below. Something special happened in our weeping dogwood two years ago. A family of robins made a nest in the flat spot just where the branches start to grow from the standard. We were delighted to watch the hatching and rearing of the fledglings at eye level, but I don't think the robins were. Last year they made their home higher up in a nearby white pine.

The fringe tree *(chionanthus)* is another that can be charmingly used within the border; it can also be kept to whatever height you choose. Mine is now about 8 feet tall, but since leaf growth generally starts high and the branches and foliage are light and delicate, there's plenty of sunshine for healthy perennial growth underneath. Like dainty streamers, the long white tassels come in July and shimmy and shake with the slightest breeze. Fringe trees leaf out very late, so don't think they've been winter-killed. And they like a lot of water—don't let them dry out in midsummer heat.

Another deciduous tree that I favor mightily for the border is the weeping pussy willow. Angela Cummings, the noted jewelry designer (and expert gardener), has one weeping over a small bed of perennials just outside her house in Greenwich. It grows only to about 6 feet in height and has long, slim, pendulous branches that are clothed in silvery gray—fat, furry catkins, much bigger and longer than those of our ordinary pussy willow. These turn to yellow as they ripen and hang around as welcome guests half the summer. Cummings found her tree almost at its present height at a Greenwich nursery. The one I ordered from Wayside Gardens is what they call a "whip"—in other words, a skinny 2-foot whippersnapper. But even so, it came with a few pussies on it, and I have high hopes. (Like all willows, it likes a lot of water.)

The ravishingly beautiful wisteria tree is too big to be contained within most borders, but it would be a knockout at the far end, gorgeously marking off the boundary. (One at either end of the border could be spectacular.) I planted a small, white-flowering one seven years ago at our second house in Danbury. It is now 15 feet high and some 5 feet around. When in May-June bloom, it must have 300 snowy foot-long, fragrant racemes hanging from its branches. I also planted two lavender-flowering wisteria trees at our first house in Danbury back in 1974. These haven't done as well. Nearby pine and a Norway spruce have grown so tall that they keep the wisteria in almost constant shade. (I was a beginning gardener then and never expected everything else would grow. Live and learn.) Still, both trees throw some lovely amethyst blooms every spring.

A few words about the idiosyncrasies of wisteria. In its natural form, wisteria is a vine, which it never forgets. The trees are man-made by grafts to a standard. By the time you buy even a little tree, most of the vines sprouting from the root have been done away with, but that doesn't stop the would-be climber from sprouting vines from its branches. You have to prune ruthlessly or they will soar to the rooftop. Don't be frightened. Just prune as soon after blooming as the vines start sprouting, and continue to snip off particularly vigorous shoots all summer long.

Also, it's best to set a strong metal stake deep in the ground at planting time and lash the tree to it with strong twine, leaving a 6-inch space between stake and tree. The stake should be taller than the tree at the outset, providing room to grow on. In due time, leaves will veil the stake. Wisteria now comes in pink, white, light blue and purple shades. I find the pink the least floriferous and, even though I'm a pink freak, the least attractive—the shade is a bit washed-out. The whites and blues are heavy bloomers, the whites perhaps the most spectacular.

Many, many small evergreens—the broad-leaved types such as rhododendrons, azaleas and mountain laurel as well as needled conifers—can serve as accent points in the garden, separating drifts of flowering plants, introducing diverse shapes, and adding solidity where needed among wispier plant foliage. If you have room, the native rhododendron *maximum* stays exceptionally green and full all winter and blooms late (July) for a rhodie, with big, pale pink blossoms. But it needs space, 5 to 6 feet. And it gets tall—I've seen it flourishing at 8 feet. You can prune it, but as with all rhododendron and azaleas, do so just after it blooms, taking care to cut new growth only where you don't want it. (You might as well snip off dead blossoms at the same time. Otherwise, the plant works overtime, setting seeds you don't want.)

The smaller rhodies are easier (the nurseries and catalogs are full of them) but they bloom earlier. Do try the "yaks" I mentioned earlier. Some are not only small in overall size, but also have narrow leaves that are appropriately delicate in the perennial border.

Some of the newer mountain laurel hybrids, almost all developed by Richard Jaynes in Hamden, are ideal for the border. They run smaller than our native *Kalmia latifolia*, which is our state flower, and don't get as leggy. Elf is the smallest of the dwarfs. A little beauty, it gets only 3 feet high and has light pink buds that open to white blossoms. Snowdrift, with pure white flowers, gets taller, but is still far shorter than our 8-to-12-foot mature natives. It also has a dense growth habit so there are no spindly legs.

Besides Elf, I have two other hybrid laurels to the rear of my border next to a big rock. One is Ostbo Red, with showy, bright red buds that change to pale pink; the other is Pink Frost, with large, deep pink buds that open silvery pink for a glistening frosty look. In bloom, of course, they're a glory, but the glossy green foliage is welcome all year, softening the cold surface of the stone. And the loose, globular shape makes what interior decorators call "a green statement." Laurel, incidentally, will take more shade than rhodies, but does need morning sun, at least, to bloom well.

Among the many dwarf-needled evergreens that are small enough for the border, the weeping blue juniper is particularly suitable. It stays slim, with soft, delicately needled boughs in close to the trunk, and serves as a vertical landmark. It casts little shade, which means that perennial plants can be planted beneath and around it. Prune as desired.

The skinny Skyrocket juniper is another straight-up variety that enhances rounded garden shapes. I planted one because it was the closest I could get to the dark green Italian cypresses that march up and down the hills of Tuscany. It will get big if you leave it to its own devices, but I prune the sides to keep it skinny and the top to keep it short.

The weeping white pine, which is not a true dwarf but is still a midget compared to the full-size 50-foot giants, has a graceful loose form with soft, big-needled sprays rather like feather boas. It can be pruned, I read, but as I look at mine, which is now 10 feet tall, I don't know where to attack. Every branch seems to belong where it is. Best to leave space.

And don't forget the *chamaecyparis* family, some of which I mentioned early on. These small trees make charming grace notes in the border. *Plumosa aurea* grows slowly to 6 or 8 feet, is golden in the spring, green in summer and winter. *Tetragona aurea* is a most unusual fellow with pale yellow-to-golden foliage.

For globular shapes, try the beautifully blue spruce *(Pungens globosa)* or the cushion-shaped spruce *(echiniformis),* whose needles are a striking purple-green. The pyramidal cedar *(Cryptomeria taxodiaceae)* is native to Japan, where one sees it often in gardens large and small. The dwarf form *(Japonica cristata)* is rarely seen in the Northeast yet adds a beautiful Oriental touch to the border. It has an attractive striated trunk and irregular branches banded with bright green cockscomblike growth. Its ultimate height is 6 to 8 feet, but it takes many years to get there.

In brief, I'm advocating small shrubs and trees to enhance the look of your flower border by adding diversity of form and color—and some refined pizzazz. Now is a good time to plant—the earlier the better, so do visit a local nursery that features both evergreens and deciduous types. There's a wealth of beauty out there I haven't even touched on.

LIVING COLOR

AUGUST 1991

*M*y friend, Dan Arje, is noted for the beautiful window displays he designs for, among others, Bonwit Teller and the French Tourist Board, and for his equally beautiful showroom presentations of designer clothes and home furnishings. But sometimes, *sometimes*, the colors he puts on his back are beyond me. *Wild.* Like the day he wore a sizzling red-and-green plaid shirt with a scalding orange-saffron-and-acid-green plaid tie. "Danny, those plaids are terrible together," I berated him, just as the fabrics editor of *Mademoiselle* magazine chanced to come by. "Danny, what a splendid color irritant," she cooed.

In the garden, too, one man's—or woman's—color horror is another's splendid color irritant. Of course, tastes change, indoors and out, even for the same man or woman. Me, for example. Long ago I started out decorating my home with only the purest of the pure Early American furniture. Then I softened to French country pieces. Later I switched radically to stark contemporary. Now? Well, a kind description would be "an easy mix."

I've mellowed as a gardener, too. Early on, I had a rigid notion of color patterning with one hue dominant— *pink.* The only other touches I'd allow in were pale yellow, soft blue and white. Orange? Heaven forfend. Bright red? Never! Hot purple? Ugh. So look at me now. I've fallen head over heels in love with those new luscious apricot iris, orange-red penstemons, scarlet-and-yellow bicolored daylilies, hot purple delphiniums, crimson cardinal flowers, and even with the weedlike red monarda (bee balm) that spreads (and *spreads,* watch out) into sweeping drifts. What have I got now? Again, a kind description would be "an easy mix."

Pink is still my favorite color, however, and from June on, it dominates the border (except when the yellow evening primrose ribbon their way through the whole garden). But while I used to mix in other colors sparsely—only to heighten, by contrast, the effect of the pink—now I've succumbed to big bursts of orange and gold daylilies, orange-red phlox, wine-red peonies, burgundy sweet William, low mounds of purple asters, flaming penstemons, even once-spurned orange poppies.

Sure, one-color gardens are still something to dream on, but those who have them generally have big estates with several different gardens. But I have only one main garden, although I do have flowering shrubs here and there to add color as I need it. (I'll talk about those as I list color possibilities by month.)

I also have several lesser flower groupings scattered about, but they're hardly gardens. A small clump of blue-and-white Siberian iris flourish in a swampy spot where little else will grow. And rimming the rocks and boulders that we've used as landscaping accents are flowering ground covers: around one group, dense mats of dark green, shiny-leafed myrtle, with its solid coverlet of little periwinkle-blue cups in May; apple-green *alchemilla* (lady's mantle), with yellow flower spikes in June; and the variegated lamium, Silver Queen, with white tapers in May and June. Plus, I have a separate bed filled only with hybrid lilies that grow from a ground cover of myrtle to mask their leggy stalks. Even with the lilies, I've become shockingly—for me—eclectic in color choice. Used to be I'd have only pink or pink-spotted white-blossoming types. But Sunray is too dazzling and free-blooming a yellow to keep out because of color prejudice. And orange Enchantment, which I resisted for years because of advertising hyperbole, may be, as the ads say, the best hybrid of the century.

In my main border, I now welcome many colors other than pink, but not one here, one there, in "spatterdash" fashion. I adamantly insist on large clusters of the same color, generally the same variety—for example, three to six yellow iris in one bunch. I set these off from those delicious apricot varieties by putting a foil of blue or white flowers between—other iris, perhaps, or early-blooming blue-purple Chinese delphiniums. We all have our idiosyncrasies. One of mine is not to group bright yellows and oranges together, although God knows I've seen some ravishing gardens that do. Maybe yours?

Nor will I combine vibrant reds, blues, purples, hot pinks and oranges, although some of the greatest gardeners mass them gorgeously for a riot of color, Gertrude Jekyll among them. Who knows? Maybe next year I'll be among them, too. Anyway, here's how my garden works colorwise. This season, at least.

The closest I come to a one-color garden is first, in April and May, when several thousand daffodils drape a golden sash through the border, with big, arching forsythia bushes nearby extending the golden glow. (Please, *please* don't manicure forsythia into neat mounds. Let them grow as God wants them to, into a golden fountain.) Even then, the garden is not really one color, because the daffodil cups range from pure white to chartreuse to bright orange to near red. And there's a lot of blue in between, because the daffodils are interspersed with enchanting Virginia bluebells that, once planted, reseed generously in soft and charming contrast.

The second one-color show is in late June and July, when the yellow evening primrose form massive clumps that virtually blanket the full 75 feet. Yep, they are invasive—Attila the Hun could have learned from them—and must be rooted out by the dozens, but *after* their blooming show.

In between the daffs and the first-blossoming perennials, I look to trees and shrubs for color fill-in. In early May, there's azalea *schlippenbachi,* a heavy name for a graceful shrub with big pale pink blossoms as light as moth wings. One of the grace notes of spring, it requires only a once-a-year dose of Holly-tone to make an airy 5-foot shrub. Another standout May bloomer is the silvery, bright pink, small-leaved rhododendron Pioneer Silvery Pink, which I use in the foundation planting in front of the house, along with an early-blooming large-leaved rhodie, my favorite of all, Mist Maiden. This is a "yak" variety, with a downy underside to its leaves, that doesn't get more than 4 feet tall. Buds are an exquisite deep rose-pink, and blossoms are flesh-pink, almost white. Both adorn the shrub at the same time and the effect is sheer magic. For all its delicacy of look, Mist Maiden has Japanese ancestry and is very hardy. Give it the Holly-tone treatment, mulch it with pine needles, and you'll have 30 many-petaled blooms, each as big as your cupped hand, on one shrub in two years.

Also in May come two of my favorite crab apples. At the top of the list is the perfectly fan-shaped, never-fail Sargent's crab that gets only to 6 feet and almost smothers itself with pink buds that open white. Red berries follow that last through winter. If I could have only one flowering tree, this would be my choice. The other crab apple is Red Jade, which grows to only 10 feet and has widely arching branches and apple-blossom-pink flowers. This variety is even more famous for its red berries than for its blossoms. For winter color in the garden, it's a standout, its red brilliant against a snowy landscape. Red Jade's one shortcoming is that it gives you lavish bloom every *other* year. In between years, it's stingy with flowers.

Lilacs. Lilacs! They're a glory in May, even—especially—the common purple-blue lilac *vulgaris* of Connecticut's highways and byways. Try them with primroses underneath—any color—for a delightful look. The dwarf Korean lilac *palibiniana* is a particular favorite of mine. It blooms a week or two after its American cousins, with blossoms that are very dark in the bud, lighter when open. And the fragrance is heady. It grows to only about 8 feet but can get that wide—and wider—in time.

Now comes June splendor, when a glory of flowers are in bloom together; to name three of my most beloved: bearded iris, Oriental poppies and peonies. Iris was the name of the Greek goddess of the rainbow

23

and a rainbow of colors is yours for the choosing—blue, purple, white, pink, yellow, apricot, deep red, mahogany, near black, plus bicolors and dappled blends. Mix and match as you will. All I ask is that you make an aesthetic statement by grouping several of one color together.

Oriental poppies? These easy-to-grow beauties—the clumps get bigger every year—give you giant cups of pale pink to watermelon, snowy white, blue-purple, scarlet, flame, most with decorative black stamens at their heart. Each clump is an eye-stopper by itself. Group several together for drop-dead effect.

As for peonies, what's your choice? Vivid red, a dozen shades of pink, golden orange, wine, pure white? Tightly petaled doubles or silky singles? Dig in half a pound of bone meal when you plant them and repeat early every spring. Each plant will become a bush in time, so leave room.

A June bloomer that's not so frequently used is the coppery red *helianthemum* Fire Dragon, only 10 inches high but spreading to 20 inches. It's a nice up-front plant for tall blue, purple or white delphiniums, or if you favor a hot-color mix, with yellow, orange and red-toned bloomers.

The queens of the June garden, delphiniums, are tough to grow but worth the effort—and more. Their tall blue, purple or white spires—*in clusters, please*—seem to soar skyward, lending regal height to the garden. Space 'em between your peonies or iris or poppies for high drama. (You can't overfeed delphiniums; I give them heavy bone meal treatments in early spring, early summer and midsummer for repeat bloom.)

Now the midsummer stars begin to shine. Among the pinks: phlox (both the early phlox *carolina* and the later phlox *paniculata),* coneflowers in vivid pink with mahogany center cones (they bring the butterflies), *Malva fastigiata* that have hollyhocklike blossoms all up and down their tall stalks, and the heath, *erica* George Fraser, with muted grayish green foliage and rose-pink flowers all summer long.

Among the eye-stopping reds and red-oranges are the scarlet spiky cardinal flower (domesticated from the wild, it likes a damp spot and a winter mulch); crimson monarda, with its pungent-smelling, tufted flowers that bring the hummingbirds; and penstemon, commonly known as beard tongue, in a flaming variety called Prairie Fire with tubular flowers close to the 2-foot stem.

Among the purples, purple *liatris* or gayfeather has fuzzy spires that lure butterflies. Blue Lagoon is a subtly toned lavender-blue phlox. Lobelia *vedrariensis* is a tall good-looker with lovely spiky blooms that's not used often enough in Connecticut gardens. The lupines, in all colors (not only blue), are spectacular. When I lamented in a column once that I had trouble getting them to come back every year, a reader wrote me to explain that they have a biennial habit (the catalogs don't say so) and that if I'd just let them go to seed, I'd have new plants every year. She was right. Remember, they're English immigrants and need lots of water.

Among the best blues for me are *platycodon* or balloon flowers, with colored bells that bloom all summer; the petite campanula *carpatica* that gets only 8 inches high, and the tall campanula, Telham Beauty, with big blue bells on 3-foot stalks. Among my favorite whites are the early-blooming phlox *carolina* Miss Lingard, for its enormous shining white clumps and its extra advantage of being mildew-resistant; the snowy Rembrandt phlox *paniculata;* double and single Shasta daisies, lots of them; and *eryngium* or sea holly, a little-used plant with serrated leaves and thumb-sized blossoms not unlike white clover.

Among the yellows, daylilies—yes, *daylilies*—offer blossoms that are palest lemon to burnished gold; frilled, ruffled, crimped or smooth; day-blooming, night-blooming; from the lemon lilies in May through the multitude of July, August, September and October blooming varieties. In the border or on their own, they give their all in flower number and beauty.

For harmonious landscaping, summer-blooming shrubs and trees can be brought in to provide touches of interest outside the border. They include the delicately tasseled white fringe tree; the blue-blooming butterfly bush *(buddleia)* that has l-o-n-g spires that keep coming—and coming; the pink-flowered beautybush *(Kolkwitzia)* draped to the ground with blossoms; and the white-flowering dogwood, *kousa,* that starts blooming in June, can keep its flowers all through the summer, and has wine-red fall leaves and big, bright red berries that cling bravely all winter.

So now we're into August, September, October. For beautiful pinks—yes, I am still a pink freak—there are two outstanding perennial asters (called Michaelmas daisies in England) that grow into massive clumps. The first to bloom is Alma Potschke, a funny name for a great lady whose yellow-centered rich pink blossoms start in August and last until hard frost. The last to bloom for me is a lighter pink, Miss Harrington, with small blossoms in such numbers that they veil the 3-foot plants with pink. Another handsome pink late bloomer is *physostegia* or false dragonhead, with flowers on tall terminal spikes from July into October. These grow into such big clumps they can be divided every two or three years.

Among the late-blooming yellows, the *altissima* strain of daylilies (5 feet tall!) give welcome masses of blossoms when you no longer expect them. The perennial sunflower (*helianthus)* bears bright yellow sprays of double flowers on 6-foot stalks (flowers are long-lasting when cut); bold-colored *gaillardia* or blanket flower looks like oversize double daisies with yellow tips edging the coppery petals; and *chrysopsis* Golden Sunshine, rather meanly known as hairy goldaster, has elegant star-shaped flowers that appear at the top of 4-foot stems and bloom from August through October. Try it. You'll like it.

A particularly charming blue for late summer into fall is *catananche* (Cupid's dart) that ancient Greek women are said to have used in love philters. Be that as it may, it has dainty cornflower-blue double flowers that stand 2 feet above rosettes of leaves and make lasting indoor bouquets that, in fact, dry prettily into everlastings.

Ah, chrysanthemums, those mainstays of the fall garden. They come in myriad sizes, shapes and colors: from little buttons to giant football mums; single and double, flat and cushioned, narrow and broad-petaled; frosted and matte-finished; in white, yellow, pink, rose, near red, wine, bronze, terra-cotta, purple, mauve—and more. Most are hardy. In fact, you can double and triple your starting number by dividing plants every spring. Just feed the babies and keep them well watered for each to give you a robust new plant. Pinch them early in the season for bushy growth and give them some all-purpose plant food midsummer for generous fall bloom.

It's said there's always an exception that proves the rule. With me, chrysanthemums are that exception. They're the one flower I like boldly mixed together in every which color for a fireworks effect that seems to bring nature's fall foliage carousel into the garden. Visiting with us in Danbury last fall, a friend from California who's always touting the scenic wonders of her state finally confessed that something was lacking there. "What we don't have," she admitted ruefully, "is your *glory of the colors*. You're blessed." Amen.

NICHOLAS JACOBS

STRICTLY ORNAMENTAL
SEPTEMBER 1991

*A*bout 10 years ago our house in Danbury was broken into and ransacked. Astonishingly, nothing was taken, but every bed, cupboard, closet, candy dish, bottle, pot and pan was stripped, opened, emptied or otherwise scrutinized. Yet the only thing broken was a small stone frog that the vandals used to smash the glass sliders and get in.

I loved that frog. A gift from a friend who bought it from a North Carolina quarry, it welcomed us from our top front step, where it watched over our foundation planting of dwarf evergreens. A Michelangelo it wasn't, but it had a droll and charming character. Now one leg was gone, and its skull was fractured.

When the insurance investigator saw my sorrow, he kindly volunteered, "If you find out its value, we'll reimburse you for it." So I told my friend the story and said, "I'm embarrassed to ask you, but how much did the frog cost?"

"I'm more embarrassed to tell you," she answered. "Seventy-five cents."

I tell the story now to make the point that attractive garden ornaments need not be costly genuine antiquities, as those Nancy McCabe of Salisbury uses in her acclaimed landscape designs, nor contemporary sculptures by such masters as Claes Oldenberg and David Wynne, as at the Pepsico Garden in Purchase, N.Y. Taste, not price, is the determining aesthetic factor—taste in the choice of the object, in its suitability for its setting, and in its placement.

Personal preference comes first. After all, it's your garden. So what do you like? Statues of pagan deities in the classical style, like those that have graced Italian, French, German, English, and even American gardens since the Renaissance? Perhaps chastely draped Diana, or naked Cupid with bow and arrow, or macho Hercules?

Or maybe you favor Victoriana—the familiar, much copied, white cast-iron trellises, chairs, tables and plant stands intricately carved with twining ivy or other swirling motifs, which, for better or worse, seem to be experiencing a revival. Controversy about them has raged since the 19th century, when the casting process was developed. A dead-white ornament in the garden is too obtrusive, some garden designers complain, calling attention to itself rather than the setting. Others laud it as a luminous accent against a dark green hedge or in a shadowy grove. My only advice is: Don't overdo it. One piece of Victoriana—well, maybe a small grouping of table and chairs—is enough.

Perhaps you love animals? You're in good company. Animals have been residents of gardens since Roman times. Sometimes they dominate a grand layout, other times they're just incidental details—the owner's whim—like my frog. Visualize the larger-than-life "Lion Attacking a Horse" in the famous gardens at Rousham in Oxfordshire, England. Copied from a Roman model, it dominates a green expanse in front of the mansion house from atop a massive stone pillar.

Haven't got the spot—or inclination—for that? Well, would you prefer a fantasy Renaissance chair carved of two stone winged lions, as at the Villa Garzoni in Tuscany, the back formed by their outspread wings? Or a pair of graceful, wrought-iron, leggy cranes (reproductions, both good and bad, abound), as in the Chinese garden at Whatton House, Leicestershire? (Cranes augur long life in China.) Or the mean-looking gnarled monkey, half-hidden among weathered stones at Veithochheim in Bavaria? Or two merry stone squirrels, frolicking on a pillar at Meadowbank Farm in Pennsylvania?

You need not go the animal route. The most popular garden ornaments are actually urns, tubs and pots. They're also the most versatile of garden ornaments, combining decorative style with practical purpose. It was the Greeks who discovered that plants can be forced in pots, which we've been doing ever since. But even earlier, in ancient Egypt, simple earthenware vases were planted with small trees and shrubs. During the late Renaissance, the Italians gussied them up with elaborate carving. In the 16th and 17th centuries, the French brought them to new artistic heights, as at Versailles and Vaux-le-Vicomte, by placing them in sweeping architectural rows, often alternated with statuary. In 18th-century England, classical urns were vastly admired, even revered. And in the 19th century, Keats immortalized them with his ode "On a Grecian Urn."

We still use urns today. Nancy McCabe favors antique French terra-cotta "cloches"—from which the hats got their name—and English "forcers," pots that were placed upside down over rhubarb and sea kale. But every gardener knows that even the humblest pot or tub can be beautiful, with graceful vines tumbling over its sides and a crown of blossoms.

The history of garden ornament is fascinating. As George Plumptre writes in his comprehensive book *Garden Ornament* (Doubleday, 1990), which I treasure for its information about gardens both grandiose and humble, contemporary and historical, and for its bounty of beautiful photographs, "Gardens have evolved from two essential elements: plants and ornaments. Of the two the plants have a longer history . . . because man has always needed to grow food . . . . When he has not been preoccupied with the struggle for existence, *man has been a creature of aspiration and herein lies the impetus for garden ornament.*" The late Russell Page, one of the greatest landscape architects of our time, refers to ornamentation as "humanizing the garden."

The mainstream of ornamental gardening originated in ancient Mesopotamia and Egypt. Although we know little about the early gardens of Mesopotamia, we do know about Egyptian gardens from the hieroglyphics that endure. The gardens were formal, geometric and orderly, with water contained in pools and canals of key importance, as it has been ever since in arid countries. They were built around the temples, royal palaces and homes of wealthy Egyptians. Slaves tended them. Don't we still? As Kipling later put it, ". . . gardens are not made/By singing, 'Oh, how beautiful!'/And sitting in the shade."

Egypt and Mesopotamia were conquered by the ancient Persians, whose gardens were the basis for the glorious Islamic gardens incorporating exquisite architectural ornament, most notably the ravishingly beautiful Taj Mahal.

But the origin of ornamental gardens as we have known them in the West for the past 400 years lies in the Italian Renaissance, part of the creative flowering in all the visual arts. The Medici gardens around Florence are their prototypes, a wondrous unity of flowers, trees, statuary, terraces, balustrades and fountains.

If you visit Italy, a few—just a few—of the other dazzling gardens to see are the Villa d'Este in Tivoli, where the spectacular channels, fountains, water-steps and cascades remain unsurpassed; the Villa Garzoni at Collodi in Tuscany, with its terraced shrub-flanked staircases leading to an unexpectedly charming and intimate enclosed flower garden; and for high drama, the baroque Orsini garden at Bomarzo, in which Renaissance themes are taken to nightmarish limits with monstrous figures—a dragon attacking lions, a giant menacing tortoise, and a cave entered through the open mouth of a savage face. (You couldn't pay me to go inside.)

Inspired by the Italian Renaissance, the royal French gardens of the 17th and early 18th centuries transcended it in grandeur. The supreme examples, both designed by André Le Nôtre, acclaimed as the greatest landscape designer of any time, are Vaux-le-Vicomte, his first and greatest masterpiece, and Versailles, which Louis XIV, the Sun King, jealously commissioned later. The genius of Le Nôtre's achievement lies in the perfect balance and unity of both gardens' many component parts and in his absolute control of every detail, from flights of shallow stairs and water cascades linking different levels and parterres to the symmetrical placement of statues, urns, shrubs, trees and flowering plants.

In the 18th century, the style of Versailles was emulated by royalty across Europe who coveted the Sun King's position. But reaction was setting in, particularly in England, where the English instinctive love of the countryside rejected grand formality. Instead of trying to control nature, English gardens showed nature unspoiled. Well, almost. Although architectural ornament was shunned, and sheep and cows were encouraged to graze almost to the front door of the stately homes, landscapes were still manicured.

It was England's Gertrude Jekyll who uncorseted garden design in the early 20th century, bringing flowers into their own by using them in great and artful drifts, as English and American gardens have done ever since. Yet ornaments figure importantly in her designs. Together, she and architect Edward Lutyens created landscapes in which plants and flowers and architectural and decorative ornament synergistically enhanced each other.

Garden ornament today is hardly on the grand scale of the past. How many of us have the budget or space for an allée of fountains or a series of statues atop a stone balustrade or a Greek temple? And how many of us would want them even if we had the wherewithal?

All the same, *we will have our ornament*. According to Litchfield resident Joe Cicio, vice president of visual merchandising for all Macy's stores, garden statuary, pots and furniture are the biggest sellers in Macy's antiques departments. And Thomas Woodward, a leading antiques dealer at the prestigious Winter Antiques Show in New York, reports, "Garden ornaments are one of the hottest areas of collecting today." Certainly, the roadside garden-ornament and furniture shops along the highways in Connecticut draw crowds.

The final section of the book *Garden Ornament* pictures some 500 different examples of antique ornaments, some of which are available in the original and all in reproduction. They include wrought-iron gates, birdbaths, sundials, grotto fountains, bronze, marble, lead, stone and plaster statuary, and urns and vases.

There are eight pages of urns and vases, I'm happy to say, picturing about 50 different pieces. Some are a bit fancy for my taste—an overfussy Victorian cast-iron urn with grotesque fishlike handles, for example.

But others, ah! A simple, handled, terra-cotta jar of the kind still used to store olive oil in Tuscany and Provence cries out to me for a cluster of geraniums and trailing ivy. A long stone trough, carved with fruiting vines, from the Istrian peninsula in Yugoslavia (I think they trampled grapes in it), would be right at home in my Danbury garden filled with floppy petunias or small bushy azaleas. A classically shaped urn formed of flaring stone leaves would nicely house pansies for me, or perhaps marigolds or a favorite rose bush.

Among the other pictured decorations I covet is a small Japanese bronze gateway, shaped like a torri gate, which would work well at our contemporary house. But in contrast, so would a slim Victorian cast-iron lamp post or a painted wood English "dog gate" criss-crossed in Chinese Chippendale style, or a Japanese bronze toad that looks wart-covered and oh, so lifelike when wet.

As I think back over the garden ornaments I have seen that have given me the greatest, and most lasting, pleasure, both in far-off places and close to home, I realize it's a motley assortment. The most pleasure is in the seeing and remembering. From a Kyoto garden, there's the airy cage of bamboo stalks circling the trunk of a flowering cherry tree. The enchanting peaked birdhouse made of thatch on a plain pole in the gardens of Peale House in Wiltshire. The mother turtle with a young'un on her back clambering up a rock pondside at my neighbor Ben da Silva's house in Danbury. The giant cut-out metal abstractions hanging like silvery foliage from the trees surrounding the house of sculptor Tim Prentice in West Cornwall. The breathtaking statue by David Wynne, "Boy with Dolphin," set within a circular fountain of sunlit spray at Pepsico Garden, which captures the instant in time when the boy dives into the pool and the dolphin leaps up to meet him. The charming statue of a young man awkwardly holding on to his foot, which has just been bitten by a crab, in a shady "outdoor room" in landscape architect Wesley Rouse's Pine Meadows Gardens in Southbury.

Not to mention the stuff at my place. There's a 6-foot metal sculpture by David Edelman of Ridgefield that graces a grassy island in front of the house. Although it's a pure abstraction, I call it "Big Bird" because it stands on a single long "leg" and arcs into a curved "body," outspread "wing" and pointed "beak." And our two bird-feeder holders, also by Edelman, that look rather like Calder stabiles, with metal arms at different heights that hold three plastic feeder tubes. And of course, our stone frog (our friend gave us another).

So where do you buy garden ornaments? In antiques shops, of course, and stores and stands specializing in garden ornaments. But look around elsewhere. In pottery kilns, flea markets, even hardware stores (our son, who lives in West Cornwall, found a winning terra-cotta chicken in one). The flower district in New York, centered on 28th Street and the Avenue of the Americas, abounds in garden-ornament stores. Pots and urns overflow onto the sidewalk. So do sculptures ranging from life-size horses to tiny butterflies.

Plainly, you pays yo' money and you takes yo' choice. Just remember that the purpose of garden ornament is to enhance the natural scene, not overpower it. Yes, you can mix periods, but don't make your garden what Russell Page calls a "ragbag" of fences and furniture, animals and angels, posts and pots. Study your particular scene long and carefully, then determine what you want to play up—and maybe just as importantly, what you want to play down. Finally, *experiment* with its placement. ("Big Bird" was in three places before he finally alighted.)

"I have experimented endlessly," writes Russell Page in his not-to-be-without book, *Education of a Gardener*. "Awareness of the interplay between objects, whether organic or inorganic, is of major importance if your garden is to be a work of art."

REA LUBAR DUNCAN

ROYAL SUCCESSION
SEPTEMBER 1992

$\int$ uccession of bloom. I'm asked so often how to achieve it that I realize it's as crucial to gardeners as succession of rule is to royals. "The king is dead; long live the queen," translates into "The poppies are gone; long live the phlox." Or, "The daylilies are gone; long live the mums."

It doesn't take a Gertrude Jekyll to figure out that the way to get continuing bloom spring to hard frost is to plant species that will bloom in chronological order April through October. I'm talking about perennials, although even the greatest gardeners (Jekyll among them) have admitted to filling in with annuals when in need. I haven't had that need this year. Almost everything matured on schedule and in order thanks to the cool weather that lasted till mid-July (some years, 90-degree May days have brought everything out at

30

once)—lushly, too, from all the spring and early-summer rain. The only bloomless time for me was a week after the daffodils. That will be remedied next year with dwarf iris that blossom in early May, several weeks ahead of their taller cousins. Someone gifted me with two plants last year that produced glowing yellow blossoms about May 10. That's not enough to make a show, but I've just set nine more plants—three groups of three, all yellow—along the front of the border, which should provide golden sunspots until the main events later in May and June.

I'm also going to divide my one clump of Jacob's ladder *(polemium)*, which covers itself in early May with intense blue flowers. It's been there in the border for years, bursting into blue every spring although I do nothing for it. I'm always charmed by its little shrublike look and blue blossom coverlet, then forget about it. It's big enough to divide into three good clumps and the blossoms will make a lovely contrast with the yellow iris.

The timetable that follows reflects major comings and goings in my garden. I don't have the space to discuss lesser lovelies, what I call grace notes in the garden (bleeding heart, blue flax, sweet William) nor even other important perennials. Read your catalogs, haunt the nurseries, follow your heart. I've a passion for coneflowers; you may prefer Shasta daisies. Do it your way. And remember, everything doesn't have to be in one border, probably can't be unless it's a mile long. Small garden beds, artfully placed, give you room for more as well as setups for special effects.

Also, don't overlook flowering trees and shrubs. I haven't discussed them here but they open up a whole other category of choice for a continuing flower show.

MARCH, APRIL, EARLY MAY

The show started at our place in early April from bulbs: crocus, then daffodils in different varieties that lasted through mid-May. Snowdrops will give you even earlier bloom—a balmy day in February will bring up their nodding white heads. Ditto winter aconite *(Eranthis hiemalis)*, those enchanting little buttercuplike flowers frilled with green collars that bloom late February or early March. Happiest in shade, they're perfect for under evergreens. All the above should be planted in September and October, except for aconite stubs (that's what the bulbs look like), which should go in as soon as possible.

Crocus and daffodils will come up forever and ever, more and more of them every year. I couldn't be without them. A labor-saving trick is to drop a daff bulb in a 6-inch hole, cover it with 2 inches of soil, then drop in a crocus bulb, mix in half a trowelful of bone meal and fill the hole. Just don't fail to plant daffodils. Nothing, but nothing (well, maybe forsythia) gilds the bleak April-May landscape as they do. Even one clump of six will brighten the scene and the spirit. (Over the years I've planted thousands. And I've another hundred on order.)

MID-MAY THROUGH MID-JUNE

Here they come, some of the crown jewels of the Northeast garden: iris, Oriental poppies, peonies. Iris rhizomes should be planted in early August. You can stretch the iris display into a month if you plant early, mid-season and late-blooming varieties. Sapphire Hills, a gorgeous many-flowered blue, is the first to bloom for me; Ermine Robe, a ruffled white, starts midseason, lasts late. In between are pinks, yellows and amethysts. Plant them in full sun, in well-drained soil, in groups of three. Just a glance will tell why the Greeks named these beauties for the goddess of the rainbow, Iris.

Put in poppy plants as soon as the nurseries have them for sale. Poppies die to the ground after they bloom in late May, then come back with little green cushions of growth. Pick their locations carefully so they're there to stay (they have a long taproot that doesn't like to be disturbed). And plant them deep enough—shallow planting is the main cause of death.

Despite their spectacular appearance, poppies are easy to grow. Lots of sun, please, and a dose of bone meal in early spring. It takes a couple of years for a little plant to grow into a great clump, but it will happen. My Helen Elizabeths, a salmon-pink, give out with a dozen or more striking cup-shaped blooms per plant. Showgirl, a delicate pink-and-white, is not quite as floriferous, but still a standout. Ditto Watermelon. One of the loveliest features of poppies is the transformation from bud to bloom. The blossom is totally enclosed in

31

an outer green calyx that bursts, *pop*—if you're nearby, you'll hear it—and falls to the ground. There, with petals still pleated and furled like Fortuny silk, is the exposed bud, which slowly opens to cup size and reveals curly black stamens within. Just one of those miracles nature regularly pulls off.

Peonies? If you're planting tubers, they must go in the earth in fall. Potted plants can be set in spring or fall, but I recommend fall planting for bigger plants and more bloom next year. As with iris, you can get a long period of bloom from early, midseason and late-blooming varieties. They start the first of June and can keep coming all month.

What's your choice? You can have them single or double—the singles have great cushions of curly yellow stamens at their heart, the doubles are formed of hundreds of petals tightly incurled. Choose pink, white, red and mixes of all. For yet other colors, dazzling yellows and mauves, try tree peonies. These shrubs will grow to 5 feet, in time bear up to 50 (!) silky, enormous flowers. *Don't* cut them back as you do the herbaceous types. And don't be stingy feeding them. They'll enjoy a pound of bone meal every spring.

This is delphinium time, too, their tall spires in graceful linear contrast to the rounded shapes of other blossoms, but for me, they're toughies to keep coming. If I get two years from a plant, I'm happy. Still, ever hopeful I put in a couple of deep blues or purples every spring. The Round Table series produces the tallest and showiest, with the Blackmore and Langdon strain in close competition. Trouble is that delphiniums like cool soil and cool nights and we can't guarantee that in Connecticut. Not as tall or fat, the species delphiniums are easier and longer-lasting: blue *belladonna* and *bellamosa*, white Casablanca.

Roses? As a weekend gardener, I find them hard to keep healthy. Still, what would June be without roses? So I have two stalwart plants, both marvelous, that veil the railing of our back deck. The old-fashioned shrub Gruss an Achen that buds shell-pink and blooms white, and an old rose dating back to the early 19th century, Louise Dodier, with deliciously fragrant, deep pink quartered blossoms. Each lavished me with a hundred blooms in June and a few more all season long.

Late June Through July

Now come those two marauders, bee balm or monarda, and yellow evening primrose *(oenothera)*. I used to think the evening primrose was the most greedily territorial, but monarda is worse. It's actually choking out the primrose. Just four plants of the red variety I put in two years ago have become a drift of a hundred plants and have also popped up everywhere in the border, even among the mountain laurel 75 feet away. I pull 'em out ruthlessly—but not till after they bloom, not only for their looks but also because they bring the hummingbirds. We had two pair of the ruby-throated wonders hovering over the red spiky blossoms all of July. It gave me a chuckle, however, to read in a catalog that evening primrose readily forms "handsome colonies." Colonies, hell, it takes over.

Through July we had the show of shows from the combination of red bee balm and feathery white astilbe. Do plant astilbe. It grows into graceful clumps of slender ferny plumage and bears exquisite 2-foot tapered flower plumes. There are pink and reddish varieties, but I like the white best for the pristine touch it lends the garden. It divides easily, too, to give you more of its charming self.

Early July gave me two happy surprises. The daylily, Stella de Oro, burst into golden bloom well ahead of other daylilies. This is the third year I've had Stella, which, despite rave reviews, only squeezed out a blossom or two for me before. This year she's as touted, covered with seemingly never-ending blossoms. A shortie as daylilies go—16 inches—she's delightful in front of her tall brethren.

The other surprise was the tall white spires of snakeroot *(Cimicifuga racemosa)*, which deserves a better name. It bears no resemblance, in any way, shape or form, to snakes. Snakeroot generally comes in August, but here it was, in full bloom, beginning about July 8, and it's still going strong. Snakeroot is said to like shade and that's where I used to have it. But not only did it bloom later, it flopped over. Now in the sunshine, at the far end of the border, it stands tall and beautiful, its long spires turning white from the bottom up, eye-catchers in the garden.

Phlox Miss Lingard, the early-blooming phlox *carolina*, was also in full white glory by July 10. This is an 80-year-old girl who is ever young. She rarely gets mildew like the later-blooming phlox *decussata* (formerly called *paniculata*) and grows into showy 36-inch-tall clumps. If you cut faded blossoms, she'll give you new, shorter blooms from side shoots. Altogether, she's a welcome addition either in the perennial border or, in a cluster of two or three, as a handsome solo specimen.

Do you do lilies or are you afraid of the deer? A deer repellent keeps them away, or has so far. Called Ro-Pel, it's a fungicide that's absorbed by the plant so it lasts and lasts.

You can have lilies in bloom beginning in late June, when the charming Asiatic hybrids come into yellow, pink, white or red bloom, through August and September, when the huge, spectacular Oriental hybrids take center stage. Some die off, but others are as lasting as daffodils, and they'll give you a bounty of fragranced blooms outdoors and heavenly bouquets indoors.

Lilac-pink coneflowers *(echinacea)* and light pink *Malva fastigiata* both started to bloom the first week in July and haven't stopped yet. Coneflowers are a particular pet of mine. Their burnt-orange center cones have some seductive substance that brings butterflies en masse. Flowers last beautifully, then dry to delicate mauve-y pink. And they generously reseed to provide small new plants to place where you will.

Malva fastigiata, the so-called hollyhock mallow, does, indeed, look rather like a delicate hollyhock, with open-petaled pink flowers up and down its many long stems, which grow from a thick crown base and have pretty veined and lobed foliage. They, too, reseed generously.

July Through August

In my garden, pink and white phlox and pink boltonia were—still are—the stars of the midborder, with yellow, orange and pink-toned daylilies far left and right. For color contrast as well as textural diversity, indigo-blue monkshood *(aconitum)* arches its delphiniumlike foliage over the garden. (The deer would eat the phlox and daylilies but not the monkshood. Too smart—they know it's poisonous.)

Far right, the daylilies circle a huge tulip tree, some 30 or 40 plants that have grown into great clumps that resemble small green fountains. They include old-fashioned Hyperion and new-fashioned diploids. The Sweet Autumn clematis climbs 12 feet up the tulip tree, her thousands of tiny white flowers creating a snowy backdrop for the lilies in August and September. I planted her three years ago, cut off dead twigs every spring, give her some bone meal at her base—and let her rip. She's a joy.

Phlox *decussata* will bloom into September. I have short ones and tall ones, deep pink and pale pink, pure white, pink-eyed whites, lilac. Love 'em all.

Boltonia? Yes, boltonia! How's for thousands of pink daisylike flowers that started to bloom in mid-August? This is the first year I've had them so I don't know how long this splendor will last, but there's no sign of a letup yet. Three feet tall now, the plant will grow to 5 feet in three years.

September Into October

An *altissima* strain of daylilies has just started blooming and will go well into September. Called Autumn Minaret, it's gotten taller every year, now stands 6 feet and is loaded with yellow flowers dusted with luminous brown sprinkles.

The summer phlox keep going with second-time, shorter bloom. A red phlox appropriately called Fall Days has started to bloom and should last through September. And the magnificent spotted pink-and-white speciosum lilies continue their spectacle.

But the stars of my September-October garden are perennial asters. The low-growing Alma Potschke is already in bloom, and her rich red, yellow-centered blossoms will last into October. Miss Harrington is just beginning to set buds. She's a big girl who covers herself with small pink daisylike blooms till hard frost strikes her down. In fact, she's so weighted down with flowers, you may have to support her with tall stakes circled with twine. She's worth the trouble.

I don't have chrysanthemums (they take up too much room) but they do lend glory to the late garden. Choose from yellow, white, pink, red, bronze, purple, wine; buttons and big guys; curly-petaled and flat-outs. I settle for a couple of pots for the deck that I can't resist. You might consider buying blooming plants to set in the garden for color. I won't tell.

SINGING THE BLUES
MAY 1993

I could never have a one-color garden, not even a pink one—and I'm a pink freak. As the song goes, "I fall in love too easily," even with brash orange types I once shunned as vulgar. The open-faced blossoms, for example, of the *lychnis* Vesuvius (the name tells all) just plain seduced me. Ditto Hot Shot, a fiery orange evergreen azalea that got to me last May when it exploded into bloom at a nursery I frequent.

I've even lost my head to magenta—magenta!—once reviled as muddy and mundane. Let me tell you there's nothing mundane about that aristocrat of rosedom, the centifolia rose Tour de Malacoff, which I've just discovered although it's been around since 1856. And magenta loosestrife *(lythrum)* brings up the rear of my border in softly shaded, unmuddy fashion.

Oh, how wantonly I lose my heart. The daylilies circling a tulip tree at the far west of my border started out to be a subtle monochromatic study in yellow, shading from creamy tones to lemon to buttercup. Subtle, my foot. How could I resist the bold new tangerine beauty Heaven's Trophy, or even the wild double orange daylilies that I mooch from friends, or the brick red Admiral Nelson—not to mention the host of pink hybrids to which I am in thrall?

So now that I've confessed to such promiscuity, it's plain I'm not touting an all-blue garden. But friends keep lamenting that good blues nowadays are hard to find, especially perennials. Rubbish! There are blue notes for early spring to late fall, low and high, for major themes in the border, to play a running counterpoint, to serve as punctuating trills or a catchy riff. All provide cool contrast no other color can offer.

Let's start with spring-blooming blues, some already in flower, others soon to come. Phlox *divaricata*, the so-called wild phlox, sings its soft blue song from late April into May. It will take some sun but prefers dappled shade and insists on damp soil, as in its natural woodsy home. Its dainty five-petaled flowers are a true blue and show lavishly above the 12-inch foliage. It spreads nicely, too, putting out new roots in spring from every leaf node. I use it around the early-blooming azalea *mucronulatum*, where it contrasts charmingly—yes, it does—with the magenta-pink blossoms. It's also a nice accompaniment to the delicate apple-green foliage of maidenhair ferns. (Bigger, colony-forming ferns eventually choke it out.)

There's a true-blue phlox *sublata*, too. This is the 2-to-5-inch ubiquitous creeping phlox too often grown in color combinations that are, putting it kindly, disharmonious. Used judiciously, this is a generously spreading creeper that will tumble charmingly over rocks or edge a border and thrive even in poor soil. Full sun, please. New hybrids offered don't get scraggly—although all may need a little summer trimming. I like the sapphire-blue strain coupled with the pure white variety or in contrast to a silvery-needled evergreen, the low-growing silver-mounded artemisia, for example.

Don't spurn myrtle *(Vinca minor)* just because it's a stalwart of ground covers. The beautiful little periwinkle cups are so generously interspersed among the glistening evergreen leaves, they always made me think of Chicken Little lamenting, "The sky is falling, the sky is falling." I have three beds of myrtle, one as underplanting for skinny-legged lilies, another as a green base for pink-cupped perennial tulips, and a third just for itself, around a cluster of big gray rocks that serve as an accent point in the lawn.

Another spring ground cover—earlier to bloom than myrtle—is rock cress *(aubrietia)*, which spreads sheets of rich blue flowers pinpointed with yellow centers. Of graceful trailing habit, it's especially appropriate in the rock garden and couples well with white alyssum or arabis. Long-lasting, it's a prolific bloomer and vigorous—maybe too vigorous. It spreads fast from layered branches but can easily be pruned right after blooming if it gets too rambunctious for your needs.

Forget-me-nots spread another blanket of blue in May, nicely partnering spring-flowering bulbs. They reseed prolifically, even into the lawn. Transplant them so as to create a spreading sky-blue carpet or place them individually as grace notes amongst other flowers.

Among the loveliest blue bloomers of spring are Virginia bluebells, which I have planted among the thousands of daffodils that are a specialty of this Danbury house. Their slim 10-to-14-inch stems, laden with pendulous little azure bells, provide charming contrast in form and color to the yellow daffodil cups. And they reseed generously, popping up in late summer to be left where *they* like, or dug up and replanted where *you* like. We have an annual daffodil party to celebrate this seasonal golden glory and guests always ask, "What are those lovely blue flowers?" Plant them in early fall in full sun or part shade for a pizzicato effect of blue notes next spring.

There's a veritable rhapsody in blue to be had from late-spring and summer-blooming perennials. Among the earliest to flower and continuing intermittently all season is blue flax *(linum)* that wants full sun and good drainage. Open-faced flowers with scalloped edges, some with little white eyes, adorn feathery green leaves on 12-to-18-inch stems. The azure flowers are lovely setting off pink or orange poppies, or, later, separating pink, white or orange lilies, or clumps of pink, white and magenta (!) phlox. This is a nice reseeder so don't deadhead all blooms.

Another lavish reseeder is columbine, which is actually a biennial but sends up so many new plants from seed that you can treat it as a perennial. Put the new plants where you want them in early fall for touches of blue next year. (Wind and birds scatter the seed all over the lot and they root on landing.) The pure blue forms—old and new—are exquisite, their dainty blossoms fluttering over the border like sapphire-winged butterflies.

A friend composed what she called "a blue tone poem" in her garden and played it between drifts of pink-flowering plants. In it, she combined tall blue delphiniums with spiky blue salvia, then blue-penciled the front of the bed with low-growing plumbago. The salvia continued in bloom long after the delphinium blossoms went, overlapping the later flowering time of plumbago. Do give salvia a leading role in your border. There are several varieties, short and tall, with flowers in true-blue tones, whose upright vertical blossom stalks complement the flat or cup-shaped flowers of summer. They will grow into handsome blue groups and can easily be divided for propagation. For several years, I've used tall clusters between clumps of hybrid lilies. The different forms and colors interplay well, enhancing both.

Plumbago is one of the few blue-blooming ground covers of late summer. Brilliant blue flowers come in terminal clusters on 8-to-10-inch stems from August through September, making a wonderful ground hugger. It likes sun or light shade and good drainage, makes a handsome front-of-the border bloomer when a low-growing blue is particularly desirable.

35

Who's the most beautiful blue of all? Delphinium, that's who. But good luck with the Round Table series of the Pacific Coast hybrids acclaimed as the most beautiful delphiniums of all. To 7 feet tall—stake 'em. Their biggest show is in June, with a second blossoming on 3-foot stalks in late July and August. I plant them every year, pamper them, sing to them, love them, *love them*, LOVE THEM—and sometimes, only sometimes, they reciprocate by making a return engagement the following year. But, as the French say, *Ça vaut la peine*—it's worth the trouble. Blue Bird is a medium blue, Summer Skies light blue, Guinevere light blue on her outer petals, lavender on her inner petals. King Arthur, who's not blue but rich royal violet, is so tall, dark and handsome, he gets to me.

Easier to keep coming is the bushy Connecticut Yankee strain developed by the famous photographer Edward Steichen, who lived in West Redding. Plants get 30 inches high, with flowers ranging from sky-blue to cobalt.

For longevity as well as beauty, I enthusiastically recommend species delphiniums. These are easy to grow and get to a dramatic 5 feet in height. *Belladonna* is a pastel blue that will give you flowers all summer if you cut spent blossoms; *bellamosa* manages to be deep blue and bright blue simultaneously. Delphiniums are voracious eaters. Feed them in early spring, again after first bloom.

Veronica is another spiky blue that comes early and repeats not only through the summer but welcomely, year after year. It's an easy perennial that will bloom the first year even from seed, comes sky-blue to violet-blue, grows 18 to 28 inches high. Space clusters of it throughout the perennial border for striking garden harmonics.

Campanula—or cup and saucer bells—is a deservedly popular blue beauty that can be had in lowdown form for edging on the rock garden, in 12-to-15-inch heights for midborder, or 4½ feet high for a striking backdrop. They bloom late June to October; the star-shaped pale blue flowers of the compact creeper, *poscharskyana*, go into November, and the spreading ground cover, *carpatica*, positively blankets itself with blue flowers all summer. As focal points, the taller, large-cupped varieties are showstoppers. The popular medium blue, *lactiflora*, 3 feet in height, will take some shade. Others want full sun. I've got to admit I've lost campanulas, short and tall, to Danbury winters. To be safe, cover with evergreen boughs after the ground freezes. To keep plants vigorous, divide every three or four years.

Adenophora, similar to campanula but not as widely used (although I find it hardier), has drooping bells that grow in most attractive racemes and appear through July and August on 30-inch stems. Color is a wonderful deep blue that is outstanding in the border. Give it rich, not too dry, soil.

For exquisite cornflower-blue bursts, plant *catananche* or Cupid's dart, so named because the ancient Greeks used it in love philters. The blossoms come July through September on 18-inch stems rising from rosettes of foliage. Flowers are good for cutting and will dry handsomely.

Balloon flowers *(platycodon)*, also known as Chinese bellflowers, are pets of mine. In bud they do look like little balloons, then open to four-petaled delicately veined cups. One very floriferous strain never opens up, just keeps sending up balloons. Those that do open include a 3-inch dwarf in lightish blue, which works as a border edging, and a 20-inch, double-flowered strain with unusually deep blue blossoms. Scabiosa or pincushion flower is a delight spring through fall. Blue flowers measure 2½ to 3 inches, even on the 12-inch dwarf variety. They start blossoming late June and go on through summer. The fat cushioned center which gives them their name contains a seductive substance that lures clouds of butterflies.

Another all-summer blue bloomer is stokesia, which looks like an oversize blue aster. If you have a hot, dry spot in the border, plant stokesia there. It can take it, even welcome it. Bushy plants get 20 inches high with silvery-green foliage. Charmingly layered with petals in different shades of blue, flowers cut well for indoor arrangements.

If fall makes you cry the blues, try these cheerer-uppers. Monkshood *(aconitum)* has tall sprays of blue flowers (shaped like miniature monks' hoods) that arch gracefully over other plants in the border, and delphiniumlike deep green foliage. It will take considerable shade. The popular *fischeri* grows to 3 feet and bears its very deep blue flowers September into October. I've seen it used becomingly over a formal bed of mixed chrysanthemums, its curving stems adding both height and soft overhang.

Maybe God has graced you with fall-blooming wild bottled gentian (their blossoms resemble little closed bottles). If so, count your blessings. Only time to transplant them is in the spring—when I can never find them, but maybe you can. (For me, flowers just magically appear every year in early fall.) Transplanting is tricky at best; they tend to languish and die when their roots are disturbed, which is why it's against the law to dig them from the wild.

I've never found bottled gentian in the nurseries but other varieties offered are as pretty—well, almost as pretty. *Septemfida*, which gets to 8 inches tall, has clusters of large, wondrously blue flowers with white throats. A 4-inch dwarf, *angustifolia*, has surprisingly large, 2-inch flowers with very bright blue outer petals and lighter blue centers that grow from apple-green rosettes of lance-shaped leaves. Sunshine or light shade and regular moisture required.

All the above are perennials, but no purist I, so here are two annual beauties I can't be without. One is the Heavenly Blue morning glory, which will climb high and spread wide and give you a daily new bounty of heavenly blue flowers from July to killing cold. Plant seed outside well after frost. The other is annual asters, which provide masses of blue flowers in the garden—and for indoor bouquets. There are tall guys and dwarfs, singles and doubles, powder puffs and one with curled petals called Tiger's Paw. Plant seeds outside after frost or start them indoors six weeks earlier—or buy potted plants at the nursery, like me.

Oh, dear, I forgot the queen of the climbers, clematis, for background accompaniment to your border or for a striking stand-alone statement: Elsa Spath, Ramona and Vyvyan Pennell among the blues. True, they're all tinged with lavender or violet but let's not quibble with beauty. Give them something to climb on—a tree, a trellis, a lamppost, a gate, a house, a garage. They will beautify all, but you'll have to tie stems up, at least to get them started.

Drat. I also forgot (along with other blues, I'm sure) butterfly bush *(buddleia)*. Old-fashioned, yes, but the best all-summer blue-blooming shrub. Long, arching flowered spires bring the butterflies en masse. Given room to spread wide, buddleia makes a gorgeous specimen shrub—musically speaking, a full blue chord.

A word of advice. When you use blue-flowering plants in the border, use several of them in a clump so you get enough blossoms to make a blue statement. Otherwise the warmer flower colors may overwhelm. For subtle harmonies as well as showy tonal contrast, you really want the blues to sing out.

REA LUBAR DUNCAN

SOMETHING WILD
AUGUST 1993

*I*n Lady Bird Johnson's beautiful book, *Wildflowers Across America*, she writes, "I grew up in the country—rather alone—and one of my favorite pastimes was to walk in the woods, exploring, searching for the first wild violets and starry white dogwood blossoms . . . the wild mountain laurel that grew in the pinewoods, its clusters of pale pink flowers freckled with tiny brown spots."

Her co-author is the distinguished horticulturist Carlton B. Lees, now vice president of the National Wildflower Research Center, which Lady Bird founded in 1982, who brings to the book a wealth of botanical knowledge. But Lady Bird gives it its soul.

"When I found myself in the White House, it was natural—and inevitable—for me to turn to the movement we called beautification," she writes. "Because my heart had for so long been in environment, I began to think that I might now have the means to repay something of the debt I owed nature for the enrichment provided from my childhood onward."

The goal of the National Wildflower Research Center is "national and ambitious: to learn as much as we can about wildflower propagation and growth, and to be a clearinghouse to spread that knowledge to developers, park managers, and private citizens everywhere."

My goal in this column is certainly less broad geographically—Connecticut is my turf—and far less ambitious. My purpose is to excite you, dear reader, to the beauty wildflowers can bring to your back yard, big or small—even to your perennial border. Most that I mention are native New Englanders; others, immigrants who, like thee and me, have found Connecticut a congenial place to settle. They recall this part of America as it once was. As Lady Bird puts it, "I like it when the land speaks its own language in its own regional accent."

If perchance this column inspires you to undertake community beautification—to blend a succession of wildflowers into public landscape management, to make room for them in housing developments, malls and school grounds—I'm thrilled. Write to the National Wildflower Research Center, 4801 LaCrosse Ave., Austin, TX 78739. They'll tell you how to go about it locally.

I have a l-o-n-g perennial border—75 feet by 12 feet deep (costly to fill up with purchased plants)—so I welcome wildflowers for budgetary as well as aesthetic and ecological reasons, "reasons of the soul and the pocketbook," as Lady Bird puts it. Blooming in the perennial border right now are some spectacular wildflowers. Butterfly weed, for one, its blazing flat-topped clusters of orange flowers eye-catching above 2-foot stems. If we saw it in the tropics, we'd ooh and aah over its exotic blossoms. Yet it's a New Englander by birth and although it naturally grows in sandy meadow, it will make itself at home in the sunny border. Try it next to blue campanula or white or lavender phlox for color contrast.

And the butterflies it brings! No lepidopterist I, so with so many different kinds of swallowtails sipping from its blossoms, I undertook a little research to identify them. Aha! Turns out that the tiger, spicebush, black and parsnip swallowtails as well as other winged lovelies are devotees of the nectar.

The striking, deep red cardinal flower is also in bloom now in the border, its velvety tube-shaped flowers in long, slim clusters above the erect stalk. Its natural bent is for moist ground, the edge of a brook, even a roadside ditch. I have it in semishade at the south end of the border, which stays moist enough to accommodate it. In the wild, it grows 4 feet—only 2$^{1}/_{2}$ feet here. Nathaniel Hawthorne wrote of it, "The world is made brighter by flowers of such scarlet glory." And the hummingbirds love it. A pair of ruby-throated beauties are so addicted to its nectar they keep imbibing even when I'm working nearby.

Plume-y clusters of the tall wild meadow rue, another wetland lover, have also adapted to this dampish area, its feathery mist of white flowers a welcome cool note in summer. Ten feet tall in the wild, it makes a 5-foot border backdrop. The wind may spread its dusty pollen, so be prepared for it to pop up all over the lot. Pull up unwanted seedlings, or better, transplant them to make a small drift where lawn meets woods, or facing down a thicket of wild brush trees.

In bloom now in my lily garden—a separate bed in which the Asiatics and other pampered lily hybrids I so love are the stars—is a "volunteer" wildling, pearly everlasting, which has sprouted amongst a tumble of gray humped boulders that we set there to give the bed an architectural focus. The spores of wild ferns were first to put down in the narrow crevices between the rocks, and now pearly everlasting has sprouted amongst the ferns, complementing their greenery with clusters of white flowers, which actually are made up of crowded, petal-like white scales around tiny central yellow florets. It's 3 feet tall, with dry places as its natural haunts, but it's tenanting happily in this sunny bed, nicely masking the lilies' skinny stalks with its gray-green woolly foliage.

Are you searching for a summer-blooming border plant with exquisite white lacy blossoms? Just look around Connecticut's highways and byways for Queen Anne's lace, which need not take a back seat to any cultivated prima donna.

A plant of the Old World—Pliny wrote of it—the queen's lace eventually made its way to our eastern shores, obviously loved it here and colonized widely. If you examine a single blossom, you'll see it's made up of several flowers that radiate from the center like a piece of handmade lace. I find its airiness a lovely foil to the more solid blossoms of phlox and other summer cultivars. Let it go to seed—it dries up prettily, curling into a bird's nest shape—and it will multiply, though it's never invasive.

Wild daisies—more properly, oxeye daisies—and black-eyed Susans, both in plentiful splendor in fields and along highways, get a big welcome from me for the profusion of flowers they bring to the border and for in-house bouquets. They will spread, but if they get out of bounds, rip them out. I like alternating them the length of the border, bringing up the rear. If you transplant them in bloom, they'll wilt, but keep them watered and they'll glorify your garden next summer.

All the above are summer bloomers, so let's go backward now to spring's wildflowers, which may not be as splashy but have an exquisitely delicate beauty. Most are not suitable for the perennial border but perhaps you have room for a cluster of them under trees, or in a marshy spot, or in a thicket of bushes, a rocky field or wood.

Hepatica is the first of the wildlings to appear, often blooming from March, when snow is still on the ground, until June. A low-growing plant, it bears delightful, six-petaled pinkish purple, blue or white single flowers, whose stems grow from rosettes of charmingly lobed leaves that stay green all winter. It likes the decaying leaves of a woodland floor, which I've tried to emulate with a moist shady spot under white pines where, for years, pine needles and fallen leaves have enriched the soil. This past March, the snow was still high, but here, where it had started to melt, lo and behold, hepatica! May its tribe increase.

Easier to propagate is the shade-loving bloodroot, which blooms in April or early May. Its brilliant white eight-petaled flowers have golden center anthers, last only a day, but they keep coming. The flowers dry into long pods that contain yellow-brown seeds, which, if you're lucky, will produce progeny. My neighbor has lined a shaded rocky path with it, where it has flourished.

Even easier to cultivate (many nurseries offer plants) is Dutchman's breeches, another lover of rich shade. Above its feathery leaves hang the nodding pantaloonlike flowers that give it its name. It's a charmer.

Violets? Violets! Which suit your terrain? The early blue violet with heart-shaped leaves of rich woods? The common violet and the bird's foot species of dry, sandy places? The lance-leaved violet and sweet white violet of wet meadows and borders of streams? The downy yellow violet of moist thickets? Most transplant easily, many are offered by nurseries. If you have the room, let them grow into a colorful carpet or, at least, an area rug.

Another easy-to-domesticate wildflower—but only in wet ground—is the enchanting marsh marigold, three of which I transplanted from alongside a woodland stream some years ago. They now wind a golden ribbon along the edge of my brook. The bright yellow flowers—they look like oversize buttercups—come in late April.

Given light sun or shade and a humus-y soil, wild phlox *(divaricata)* will spread fairly quickly into drifts of soft blue flowers, each almost an inch around, on 8-inch stems. A June bloomer, it's widely offered in nurseries but started as a wildling. You can plant phlox between the big roots of trees, even maples, provided you feed them spring and fall, and water often.

The trillium's charming common name is wake-robin, although it blooms in May, well after the robins have arrived. It is a native New Englander, with its natural habitat damp woodside. But unbidden, it arrived two years ago amongst the ferns in the hybrid lily bed and has now reseeded into the border and at the edge of the woods that rim our lawn. All parts of the trillium come in threes—the handsome veined big leaves, the silken wide-apart petals and the sepals. The beautiful winy red blossoms are most familiar but there's a white flowering form, too, that was incandescent in the Washington garden of a friend—a generous friend—and now lights up mine.

The cheery bright yellow cupped flowers of celandine poppies obligingly come in abundance mid-May, when the gold of daffodils is over and the iris, poppies and peonies have not yet burst into glory. Their cleft foliage is blue-green on the underside, emerald topside. Don't pick the flowers—they droop immediately and exude an acrid-smelling juice. Better them let it go to seed for more plants next year. They're particularly easy to transplant.

Rivaling any of my hybrid lilies, the May-blooming wild yellow meadow lily, sometimes called fairy caps or witch caps, has exquisite, pendulous, nodding bells, yellow to pale orange, brown-spotted within. En masse, it casts a golden glow over its surroundings. You'll find it in light woods, generally in moist ground. Try to find a home for it at your place. It's one of our most beautiful native wildflowers.

Two other May bloomers that enhance my border are the wild geranium, which grows into a large plant with light purple flowers and delicate, lacy apple-green foliage, and the wild columbine with pink and orange spurred blossoms, as beautiful as the cultivated hybrids. They're both easy to tame and they reseed generously.

Stars among the fall-blooming wildflowers are New England asters (aster means star in Greek), perhaps best known among them the large-leaved aster with broad, heart-shaped leaves and pale lavender or violet-rayed blossoms; the wavy-leaved aster with undulating leaf edges and pale blue flowers; and the smooth or blue aster with sky-blue flower heads. Pliny wrote that a brew of asters was good for snakebite and that an amulet made of the plants would cure sciatica. You don't have these problems? Plant them anyway, for their beauty and bounty of blossoms.

I've left out many, many other New England wildlings that will adapt to a home setting. Regal blue flag or blue iris, tinted with yellow or white, that likes the damp. Goldenrod—white and yellow varieties—that gilds the fields in late summer and fall. Tall blue bellflowers, forerunners of cultivated campanula. Tufted silky pussyfoot. Some nurseries specialize in them, offering protected species *not* to be disturbed in the wild, lady's slipper and trailing arbutus among them. But many can be had for the digging. Just look around—and carry a pail and shovel.

TO LIFE
SEPTEMBER 1994

Afraid, now that the failing sap
has stained the leaves, I set a trap
for April, baited with bulbs, squills,
tulips, daffodils.
I plant them as amulets to sustain
me through winter, for they contain
the thrusting stem, the fisted bloom
that will burst alive from the frozen tomb.
I set them in circlets, each magic ring,
my grasp upon another spring.

I wrote that poem more than 30 years ago when I was young enough, or so it would seem, not to have worried about a lifeline to another spring. I titled it "Amulets," invoking a little magic against what is so fittingly called "the dead of winter." Yes, as Bliss Carman wrote, "The scarlet of the maples/tears me like a cry/of bugles going by." Nonetheless, fall has always been a downer for me, dark with intimations of mortality.

Nor am I alone in that, my psychiatrist friends tell me. Indeed, a friend who was severely depressed after a series of tragedies last autumn was advised by her psychiatrist to plant some daffodils. *"Daffodils?"* she repeated incredulously. So I gave her a dozen King Alfreds, those big-cupped golden oldies that are the embodiment of spring renascence, and dumped them in her hands. No gardener, she stared at the brown, lifeless-looking lumps and finally asked, "What am I supposed to do with these!" "Just dig a hole and stick 'em in," I said. She did, all the while muttering in disbelief, "These are going to bloom in spring? I'd like to be around to see it." Aha—that was the idea. And she was.

There are more practical reasons—though none more important—for fall planting. A selfish reason, for your sake (and mine), is to free up time in spring, when garden chores are at their heaviest. An unselfish reason, for the plants' sake, is to give them a head start on next year's growth. Most plants benefit mightily from a couple of autumn months to put down roots and settle in. Sure, you can buy phlox, daylilies and other perennials all potted up in spring, but they'll be puny the first season. I'm not saying you'll have a great clump if you plant them now, but they'll be more substantial and will have had time to recover from the shock of moving to a new home.

Certain plants *must* be set in in fall, the sooner the better. Iris, for example, could well have been planted—

42

or divided—in August, but can still go in through September. To divide, lift out the whole clump of rhizomes, cut away pieces that are hole-y or dried up, and make good-size new plants—two or three rhizomes each. Cut the bladelike foliage down to 3 or 4 inches in a pretty fan shape. Set them—divisions or new material—so the stems are close together and the rhizomes facing outward. That way, you'll get a denser cluster of flowers. Feed with bone meal or another organic fertilizer. Plant shallowly in full sun, at least three of one kind in a group so as to make a color statement.

Do try some iris other than the bearded giants, gorgeous though they are. Iris *tectorum*, famed for growing in the thatched roofs of Japanese houses, bloom earlier than the bearded varieties and form a charming rosette of foliage, rather like, if you'll pardon the analogy, a round crown roast of pork. Blossoms come in a circle. They're smaller, but daintier, than those of the big guys, and more numerous.

Another variety, the dwarf bearded iris, are particularly welcome in the early garden because they bloom just after the daffodils, filling the flowerless gap before the peonies and poppies explode. Use them at the front of the border. Their height is dwarf—6 inches or so—but the blossoms—singing yellow, pure white, rich blue, garnet—are good-size.

Try iris *cristata*, too. It's a very low grower that blooms in April and early May and prefers deep shade. Blossoms are blue or white. I grow them under peonies and have made a whole edging simply by breaking off rhizomes and transplanting them.

Oriental poppies, too, could have been planted in August. Not too late in September, however. Make sure to plant them deep so that their longtap root is covered full length in the earth. Failure with poppies is generally from too shallow planting. Also, think carefully about location. I move things around so much I've been advised to plant on wheels. Poppies, however, do not welcome moving. Give them a permanent home and you'll have great clumps in years to come—30 to 40 huge satin cups on each plant in June. Spectacular.

Peonies, too, must be planted, transplanted or divided in fall. If you're dividing a clump, wait till foliage has pretty much withered, then cut off dead stalks, lift the whole plant from the ground, and with a sharp knife, cut into several good-size divisions of three or four tubers so you won't have a spindly new plant. Make sure you have "eyes" on every tuber. Mix half a pound of bone meal in the soil and set the plants so they're covered with earth right up to where the stems start. Peonies are easy to grow and will give you armloads of bloom in late May and June. And they're long-lived. So make your hole spacious.

Do, *do* plant a tree peony or two along with the more popular herbaceous types. They get the same planting treatment but may need winter protection the first year. A simple way is to invert a basket over each plant, weight it with a rock. Tree peonies are just as easy as the shrubby types and are dazzlers in bloom. Blossoms are dinner-plate-size and as lustrous as the finest porcelain. Each "tree" will have 50 to 75 blossoms in two or three years, so leave room for middle-age spread. Don't, *don't* cut the stalks as you would on herbaceous peonies. These are *trees*. The stalks are woody branches.

Bulbs, of course, must be planted in the fall, most of them—daffodils, tulips, crocus, hyacinth, grape hyacinth and lilies—through October, even into November. But there are certain less common species which I recommend that should be planted straightaway. Winter aconites, for example, whose little buttercuplike blossoms with frilled collars come even before the first crocus, sometimes as the snow melts. Unlike most other bulbs, they are happy in shade, even the deep shade under big evergreen trees. They're not expensive so plant a lot together, at least two dozen, 50 if you can. You'll have a golden carpet in early April—and they really do increase into what the catalogs call a "colony."

Get to know species tulips if you haven't already. These are the little fellows—most get only about 6 inches tall—that bloom early and don't "run out" like the dazzling Darwin and Triumph hybrids, but keep coming for many years. Most come from Asia Minor, where summers are hot and dry and winters are cold, so they do fine here. Just give them lots of sun and let the foliage brown off.

Most species tulips show two colors. Heart's Delight, a Kaufmanniana type, has a bright red exterior, opens in the sun to pale pink. Corsage, a Greigii variety, is a warm rose outside, paler rose feathered golden yellow inside. A favorite of mine is Tarda (Daystemon), which has clusters of yellow star-shaped flowers flushed white. I've had them in our foundation planting fronting azaleas and evergreen shrubs for some 10 years now and always, in early May, they lighten and brighten the greenery with little bunches of white gold.

All tulips are as caviar to deer, so when you set the bulbs in, spray them with a deer repellent, a *systemic* repellent. But just to make sure, spray again when the first leaves come in the spring.

Except for the Madonna lily, which must be planted in September, lily bulbs can be set in through late fall, even winter. Nurserymen can't dig up the big beauties—Asiatic and Oriental hybrids—till they've bloomed and ripened off, so they ship late. Truth is, I've gotten chilblains from chopping frozen earth in December so as to get lilies in. A smart thing to do is to dig your holes at least 6 inches deep when the ground is still soft (lily bulbs are big), fill them with leaves, pile dirt on the side, and cover this with leaves to protect from freezing. When the bulbs come, even in December, take leaves out of holes, tuck in the bulbs and cover with the pile of earth. Yes, you can plant bulbs in the spring or buy them potted up. But plants will be a third smaller, flowers a third fewer.

Lilies, like tulips, make a gourmet meal for deer, so *don't fail to spray bulbs with a systemic repellent and, more important, spray spring growth.* I was ill last spring and didn't spray. The two dozen new tiger lilies I planted came up vigorously—but only two bloomed. The rest were "et." I don't know if my deer left those two out of kindness (so I could see how gorgeous the recurved blossoms are) or out of spite (so I could mourn what might have been).

Virtually all perennial plants will do better planted, transplanted and divided in fall. This includes phlox, daylilies (do divide those costly varieties this fall for nice clumps in spring), coneflowers, boltonia, astilbe, perennial geraniums, Shasta daisies, coreopsis, gaillardia, salvia, baptisia—all, in fact, except the late summer and autumn-blooming varieties such as perennial aster, snakeroot, monkshood and chrysanthemums.

I have my work cut out for me this fall. To be divided for new plants are: astilbe that have expanded to 4 feet in width, phlox, coneflowers that have reseeded everywhere, iris *tectorum* that can be split easily to grace the length of the front of border, bearded iris that can now be divided into accent points where needed, and peonies that have grown into such great masses that I can make more. The withered foliage of the tall plants should be cut down to a few inches. Plants should then be lifted out and, with a sharp knife, cut into substantial divisions. Any unhealthy-looking roots or stalks should be removed.

Among the flowering shrubs that will get a head start by fall planting are azaleas, mountain laurel, rhododendron (mulch heavily with pine needles or buckwheat hulls the first year), lilacs and viburnum (mulch but not with oak leaves—they're too acid for these sweet-toothed types). By bitter experience, I've found, however, that dogwoods and hemlocks do better planted in spring. I've also had better luck planting roses in the spring.

About fall fertilizing, in a phrase, *do it*. Fertilize your lawn *now* so the fall rains will wash in the nourishing stuff. Fertilize plants, shrubs and trees *after* the ground has frozen. Use Holly-tone on the acid-loving types—evergreens, laurel, rhododendrons, dogwood trees; use an organic fertilizer such as bone meal on perennials, lilacs, clematis. (Don't fertilize roses till spring. You don't want them to make a false start.)

All evergreen shrubs will benefit from a spritz of an antiperspirant such as Wilt-Pruf that coats the leaves and needles against excessive moisture loss from winter's drying winds. I find it also sheaths heaths and heathers from the wintry blast. *Spray after the ground is frozen.*

Last year's murderous winter killed stalwarts I had thought immortal: a beloved 10-year-old Gruss an Aachen shrub rose, an enormous deutzia bush and two fringe trees. And we had no bloom on our forsythia except low to the ground, where branches were blanketed by snow, nor on our weeping Japanese cherry, nor on our heretofore never-fail Sargent's crab apple.

So I'll do it all this fall, feed and spray and mound and mulch. But for good measure, I'm going to add a heavy dose of prayer. And plant daffodils.

THEMES &
VARIATIONS

REA LUBAR DUNCAN

GROUND COVERS

APRIL 1984

*I*f I seem to care more about ground covers than most gardeners do, it's because they've been a highly necessary part of my life since 1973, when we bought 13 acres of land in Danbury enfolding a 3-acre pond. What isn't water is almost all up-and-down woodland. So, to build four houses (one at a time over 11 years, each on 3-plus acres), we had to scoop, slice and dig out a ton of soil, leaving raw earth behind that demanded covering.

By now I have pretty tough requirements for ground covers. First, they have to look pretty—in form, leaf and flower. Second, if they're touted as evergreen, they have to stay evergreen—not yellow-green or brown-green but green-green. Third, they have to be superhardy, not only surviving 20 degrees below zero, but

47

bouncing back bigger and better when spring comes. And fourth, they have to cover ground. Fast.

I confess I make exceptions but only for exceptional performance. That applies to two ground covers that go everywhere with me, even though they don't stand up on all four counts. One is epimedium, called "the aristocrat of ground covers." Elegant in form, its heart-shaped leaves start out ruby-tinged green, then turn emerald. In May and June come delicate spurred flowers in red, yellow or white, reminiscent of columbine. Epimedium makes large shapely clumps but it does not spread fast and is unlikely to spread at all unless you surround it with a foot of peat 2 or 3 inches deep into which it likes to expand. Still, even a small cluster is so beautiful, it's worth planting.

And second, forget-me-nots. You hadn't thought of them as a ground cover? Try them. The clumps get bigger every year and they reseed all over the place. Dig up the seedlings in early spring and add them to your carpeted area. True, they look a bit scraggly when left unsheared to go to seed, but their intense gentian-blue little flowers start in May, last through June and are like a patch of blue sky on the earth.

But let's start at the beginning with House No. 1, where we lived the first six years. Here, a sloping bank of earth about 5 feet deep and 30 feet long had been left naked by the bulldozer. It was my very first cover job and I used myrtle *(Vinca minor)*—or tried to. One of the two most popular ground covers (pachysandra is the other), myrtle stays glossy evergreen all winter and is superhardy. But it remains one of my "exceptions" because it's such a slow grower. You really need a lot of plants set 4 to 6 inches apart to get even a thin cover in two years. I naively started with a hundred plants, bought a hundred more, finally got up to 400. And still, it was four springs before cover was dense.

But there are those glorious periwinkle-blue blossoms (periwinkle is a common name for myrtle), delicately cup-shaped and plentiful. The sight of that blue-blooming bank from my kitchen window every May and June made the whole backbreaking exercise worthwhile.

To go in the dense shade of big pines bordering the gravel road we put down at the first house, I needed another ground cover. Pachysandra would have done it, but although it's evergreen and very hardy, it's too formal for my kind of landscaping. In all fairness, it can look very beautiful, especially a new silvery-edged variety that shows up handsomely edging a green velvety lawn—which I don't have.

My nurseryman suggested lamium. Never heard of it? Well, it's become my favorite ground cover for shady places. (Don't try it in bright sun. It will wilt and ultimately die.) From the nettle family of weeds (not stinging nettle), lamium does, indeed, spread like a weed. But the resemblance ends there. Its variegated leaves are charmingly splotched green and white and are edged in tiny scalloping. In April and May, yellow-sprigged flowers stand upright and bloom long and heavily. Totally hardy, lamium spreads so fast that bare-root plants can be set a foot apart (well-rooted clumps 2 feet apart), for thick coverage the first year. It's not supposed to be evergreen, but it's almost. In late February, it goes yellow, but by mid-April, it's lush and green again.

On to House No. 2, where we lived four years and where I finally planted what has become my favorite ground cover for sunny places, *Waldsteinia ternata* (sorry, no common name). Brightly evergreen, it has strawberrylike leaves and in April and May lots of perky yellow flowers like miniature snapdragons. While not as fast-growing as lamium—except for poison ivy, is anything?—it makes good-sized clumps in one season and spreads by fast runner. It will give you thick, curly cover by the second spring and plenty of plants to divide by the third. I edged a 50-foot terrace with it and my only complaint is that it covered too much. Had I not snipped and trimmed, it would have blanketed the terrace.

Before striking pay dirt with lamium, I had edged the terrace with English ivy. No good, at least not in that open location. It stayed rich green through summer, fall and early winter. Then, ouch, the late February and early March winds burned it yellow-green, then brown-green. Next season I covered it with hay, which did keep it green. But since the terrace is just outside the sliding glass doors of the living room, our winter view was not of a green carpet but of a dreary hayfield. Out it came.

But to the south of House 2, with the protection of an overhang and some big trees to fend off wind, it stays glossy green all winter long. Its leaves intertwine above and below, creating a lovely and interesting dimensional effect. And it covers ground. Fast.

In front of House 2, a gentle bank slopes from a natural rock outcropping to the graveled pathway leading to the house. It's hot, dry and very sunny here so, on advice, I planted creeping juniper. Perfection. Its angular branching complements the big gray boulders for a contemporary, even Japanese look. Creeping juniper comes in blue-needled and green-needled varieties. I covered about 30 running feet with it and, to avoid a too-uniform expanse, I alternated a band of blue, a band of green, another band of blue. The striated shading is subtly exciting. As the light changes, different colors seem to move over the needles.

On the far side of the rocks, I bordered the entire length of the driveway—a couple of hundred feet—with a plant not commonly thought of as a ground cover. Daylilies. Yes, daylilies. Hardly a low carpet, they form fountains of narrow arching leaves with flower stalks 12 to 40 inches high. I planted the 12-inch varieties up front, taller ones climbing the bank behind them. Planted on 16-inch centers, daylilies will almost touch in a year, fully cover in two, and keep weeds from coming up in three. And, of course, there's the bonus of gorgeous yellow, peach, flame, red and pink blooms from May to September. Just feed them all heavily in early spring.

We always knew that someday we would end up in House No. 3. (Someone else bought the fourth site and built his own house.) My husband started site planning the day we bought the property, I think. Using the boulders scattered on the land, he designed a 30-foot horizontal S-shape of rocks on the flat, grassy area behind the house. At far left, I set in two dozen tiny plants of an interesting ground cover called *Alchemilla vulgaris*. They were big in a year, about 16 inches high, with apple-green scalloped leaves. Evergreen, *alchemilla* spreads nicely, if a bit blowsily, and creates a soft touch next to the stark rocks.

At far right, I planted some creeping blue spruce that is extraordinarily beautiful—and extraordinarily slow-growing. A miniature evergreen, it looks like a decorative arrangement of blue spruce branches laid flat on the ground. But to keep it flat, you have to snip off upright leaders, and to cover any amount of ground, you have to be a millionaire. I saw a dazzling carpet of it at White Flower Farm in Litchfield, 16 feet in diameter—but 12 years old. Still, it so inspired me that I set out four little plants ($25 each) and interplanted them with lily bulbs. Some day it will look as I dreamed it, the pendant lily blossoms nodding above a solid-needled blue carpet. But right now I'm still waiting for the time the catalog prophesied, when "no weeds will come up between its lovely needles."

House 3 is really a story unto itself. It's built across a brook, a bridge spanning the water, glass-sided north and south for magical views up and down the stream. Like a bridge, it's built on piers high enough above possible flood level so that you can see both banks of the stream under the house.

I need a ground cover to fill in between the giant rocks with which my husband studded the banks, something that will survive being submerged during periods of high water and look beautiful when the water recedes.

Any ideas?

REA LUBAR DUNCAN

WEEPERS

JUNE 1985

$\mathcal{O}$n a talk show some years ago, Paul Newman was asked to critique his wife Joanne Woodward's performance in a new film. "I'm afraid I can't be objective," he said. "You see, she gets to me."

Well, neither can I be objective about weepers. They get to me. It's that arching, pendant form I love—whether in the perfect symmetry of a Japanese weeping cherry whose blossoms hang like pink-jeweled lavalieres, or in a skewed, single-branched weeping pine, or in a drooping little weeper spruce.

But—and it's a big BUT—weepers have to be artfully placed for graceful effect, especially the oddly shaped evergreens. I've learned this the hard way. Truth is, I've moved some so many times that my garden helper, David Weidt, suggests I plant them on wheels. In the right location, however, the interplay of their rounded overhang with the flat plane of the earth can create an asymmetrical design of unique beauty. Spilling fluidly over rocks, they gentle the hard surface. Pendulous above water, they enhance a still surface or a rushing stream. And the shimmering reflection is a watercolor to remember.

Last fall, when a concerned friend asked, "What's the matter with that bush? It looks like it needs a cane," I got the message that my little weeping spruce might be better situated. Poor tyke, it had already been moved three times (from House No. 1 to House No. 2 to House No. 3). Although I rarely take any plants with me, this spruce was such a hunched little fellow, I feared the new owners might not be as appreciative as I.

So, OK, the spruce was moved one more time, to what seems a permanent and happy home. Only 3 feet high, it used to have only one puny bough drooping from its standard, which now, eight years later, is luxuriant and full-needled, with lesser side sprays curving from it. Set between a rounded boulder and a cluster of flattish rocks, it has enough space surrounding it to set off its continuously bending lines. It looks like a small green waterfall. Last October, I underplanted it with the little soft red botanical tulip Fritz Kreisler, and, beginning the last week in March and through the first week in April, the whole pink-and-green scheme worked as I dreamed it. At last.

Evergreen weepers—spruces, pines and hemlocks—give you a special winter bonus, brightening the bleak landscape with close-to-the-earth green forms that also stand out vividly against snow. My 6-foot weeping white pine flings forward a great feathery branch that curves upward, then groundward, like Baryshnikov caught in midair in a jeté. Strikingly beautiful all year, it shadows the snow with a rich green canopy.

Do remember that weeping white pines are not true dwarfs and may have to be pruned to fit your landscape needs. But if you have the space, let 'em grow. Last July, I saw a 12-foot weeping pine placed to the front and side of a much taller *kousa* dogwood. The combination of the massed upright white dogwood blossoms and the downward plumes of green-needled boughs was breathtaking.

Weeping hemlocks come in a variety of shapes, all glorious. Expensive and slow-growing, they're worth both the price and the wait for their thickly branched, overhanging spread. The most gorgeous weeping hemlock I've ever seen is at Richter Park in Danbury, an estate given to the city by the Richter family, now a public golf course and cultural center. Bordering the driveway is an ancient weeping hemlock—15 feet tall and just as wide—that has been sculptured into a cave big enough to crawl inside. (I have.) The family gardener who now works for the park keeps the inside branches pruned, leaving a mysterious domed enclosure about 8 feet high and perhaps 12 feet wide.

I planted my first weeping hemlock about 12 years ago against the white stucco wall of House 1. It was then about 2 1/2 feet high with only one branch on its standard. Now 4 feet high, thick and bushy, it was moved by my neighbor when it got too big and crowded the wall. She placed it in a superb location, at the very top of a sloping lawn so its branches arch over the grass. Last spring I planted a shrubbier weeping hemlock between two garden lights about 12 feet apart on the lawn at House 3. My dream is that it will someday reach out to dapple their glow. That won't be tomorrow, but it's already grown more than a foot in width, so I figure there's hope.

A word of care for weeping evergreens. Since they've either been grafted onto standards or have slender trunks supporting a great weight, try not to let heavy masses of snow or ice sit on them. They can snap in the middle. Ach.

Our best-known deciduous weeper is, of course, the weeping willow, so common that we tend to take it for granted. But in the parklike estates of England's great houses, it's treasured as a centerpiece on the lawn or as a backdrop for a border or as a giant green parasol at water's edge.

If you have a wet area—a big wet area—a willow will transform it from a hummocky bog or near-marsh into a green-mansioned site. Yes, it will make a mess in spring when the capsule seed pods burst and litter the ground, so plant it away from the house or terrace. But its pluses more than compensate. Like a giant green geyser, a 40-foot willow stands at the head of our 3-acre pond, its branches dripping emerald green above the water. It's the first tree to leaf out in spring, with pale yellow foliage starting end of March, and the last to lose its leaves in fall. And it can hold a bank that's in danger of erosion from floods.

But keep in mind, weeping willows get big. Fast. To 70 feet in height with a spread of 20 to 30 feet. So leave room.

When the weeping Japanese flowering cherry is good, it's very, very good. But when it's bad, it's heartbreaking. You've waited a year—and no blossoms. That's apt to happen, especially to young trees, if there's a late spring frost or if our Connecticut winter has been deadly cold. Still, I wouldn't be without one. Even when not in bloom, its form is lovely, the slender branches climbing gracefully skyward, then falling into delicate pendant sprays. At House 2, we planted one in front of the brook so we could glimpse the tumbling water as through a pink-beaded curtain. At House 3, we've planted a skinny sapling, to the fron and side of the house— it bloomed bounteously despite its youth—that, hopefully, will double in height, quadruple in width, to soften the linear contemporary architecture.

The only weeper I've loved that hasn't reciprocated my affection is the crab apple Red Jade. About it, as the old pop tune goes, "They're singing songs of love, but not for me." It's supposed to be a mass of white blossoms in spring and of red fruits in fall. Ha! I bought a tall slender one about six years ago, and it hasn't gained an ounce or an inch since. Yes, it gets a few pretty pink blossoms that turn to white every *other* year—they don't tell you that in the catalogs—and a few red berries in autumn. But it also gets every blight apple trees are prone to.

I take full blame for the situation. There's something I'm not doing—or doing wrong. So at House 3, I planted a midget Red Jade whip bought by mail order three years ago. It's grown a smidgen, but nary a blossom yet. Hope springs eternal in this gardener's breast.

I've saved the best for last—the two weepers framing a 30-foot-long outcropping of big gray rocks that we looked out on from our living room at House 2. Far left is a tree I'd never seen before—a weeping dogwood. Upright, on a 3-foot standard, it has one main branch that arches forward about 4 feet. I confess, there are those who think it more odd than beautiful. Not I. I love looking *down* on the blossoms that open flat, like circlets of fine lace, first pale green, then snow-white. We thought of moving it with us to House 3, but it was rooted between giant boulders and we feared it wouldn't survive being dug up. I want another, but I haven't found a nursery that carries a weeping dogwood. Maybe you have?

Far right in the rock outcropping is my favorite weeper of all, a weeping birch that is a thing of beauty from early spring, when it trails a full skirt of trembling golden tassels, through summer's shimmering fountain of green leaves, to winter's crown of pendulous white branches. Late every summer, I'd have to crawl under its full petticoat to thin the dense, dangling branches. To keep it about 5 feet high, I also cut off the branches trying to grow from the top. But if you have room, it makes a magnificent specimen when left to grow tall. What a tree! In full leaf tip to toe, it seems poised *à pointe*, like a ballerina in a long, gauzy green tutu.

Oh, yes, there are other weepers I could love—if only I could afford to. Have you seen those color-catalog pictures of the weeping Japanese red maple Crimson Queen? A ball of flame, it has fern-shaped leaves that cascade solidly to the ground. And there's a purple weeping beech—it's like a shaft of amethyst—that I covet. In a decent size, each one costs a small fortune. I'm saving up. You see, they get to me.

CLIMBERS

JULY 1986

A violent hurricane tore through southern Connecticut and northern Westchester on Sept. 7, 1979—the very day that we moved from House No. 1 to House No. 2.

Toppled by the high winds, a tree fell across the railroad tracks at Mt. Kisco so that Carrie Burt, our housekeeper of 25 years who was coming from New York to help us move, waited on the blocked train two hours while Ken waited for her at the Brewster station. Finally they connected. Then, just as they arrived at our property, a giant swamp maple crashed across the driveway, missing them, thank God, but making it impossible for the movers or us to carry things from house to house except by hand and foot. What's more, the dishwasher exploded and then the electricity went off. We couldn't find candles so, in darkness, unable even to make a cup of coffee, irritable and tired, we gave up unpacking and went to bed.

I was awakened about 3 a.m. by the brilliant light of a full moon pouring through the glass doors into our bedroom. House 2 looks down on a big grassy area shadowed by tall, twisted maples to a wide curve in a brook, which was then rushing with molten silver. All was flooded with moonlight like a glade in a Greek myth, so I would not have blinked an eye had dryads emerged from the gnarled tree trunks.

I woke Ken and Carrie and the three of us stood on the terrace letting the scene work its magic. "It's the kind of night you could see a unicorn," I said.

"Only virgins see unicorns," Ken answered dryly, "and the only virgin around here is Shiki." Shiki, our blue point Siamese cat, had been spayed before she could savor the joys of nubility.

All of which is a long-winded preamble to saying that you don't have to be a virgin to enjoy the beauty of that great climber, clematis *paniculata*, more romantically called Virgin's Bower. Oh, dear. It now has a new and difficult name: clematis *maximowicziana*. (*Mein Gott*, why didn't they leave well enough alone?) No matter. By any name, it ascends rampantly and can reach 14 feet in a season, 30 thereafter. It blooms late, in August and September (sometimes it's also called Sweet Autumn clematis), with masses of intertwining pure white small flowers. Planted to mask the gaping space below a deck at House 1, it did the job in one year, mounting to the roof by the next. To create the full bower effect, plant several 2 or 3 feet apart.

Large-flowered clematis have more spectacular individual blooms, but are not as spirited climbers. Perhaps the most popular is Jackmanii, with big, four-petaled, flat-out blossoms in deepest plum-purple in June. Henryii is a white Jackmanii with the extra merit of glistening bronze early foliage. Crimson King is a rich velvety-red type with 5-inch flowers and contrasting pale yellow anthers.

A particular pet of mine is the old reliable and still very beautiful hybrid, Nellie Moser, with 9-inch blossoms that are delicate pink striped with deep rose down the center of each petal. It can climb to 12 feet.

Clematis have certain demands, not hard but specific. They like their roots in shade, their leaves in sun. Cover the roots with annuals or shallow-rooted perennials rather than with dried leaves, peat or such, which might harbor the wilt virus to which clematis are susceptible. (Spray with a fungicide if yours are afflicted.) Also, clematis insist on lime so mix a trowelful into the soil when you plant them and scratch in a little every spring thereafter if your soil, like most in Connecticut, is acidic.

Pruning varies from species to species, but for all clematis, prune the stems to 18 inches in early spring the year *after* planting to encourage strong root growth. The Jackmanii hybrids bloom on new shoots so be sure to prune very clearly before new growth starts. This is necessary only every other year. The *lanuginosa* varieties produce flowers from the previous season's stems, so prune lightly *after* flowering. I haven't yet grown any *lanuginosas* but cannot resist ordering one called Silver Moon, with palest mauve petals, almost the color of mother-of-pearl. It's said to bloom even in shade.

Hydrangea *petiolaris*, the climbing hydrangea, has much more refined foliage and flowers than those of the popular shrubs. Its leaves are smooth and its blossoms, in May and June, are like exquisite, finely hand-crocheted antimacassars. In point of fact, each bloom is made up of sterile white sepals that show together with small, fertile white flowers. The combination is big and lacy.

Slow to get started in a new place, hydrangea *petiolaris* will climb to 40 feet once it gets going. Peg it against a wall—after a while it will cling by itself—so its graceful, wide, lateral branching will show off. Plants like a well-drained loamy soil and will take full sun or a little shade. Plant spring or fall. My neighbor at House 1 circled three around a telephone pole at the entrance to our driveway. What they do for that ugly pole deserves a month's free phone service, at least.

The wisteria bloomed in the third year of our nine-year residency on East 83rd Street in New York. Our landlady had planted it three years before we came, in a right-angled corner formed by the front wall of our house and the side wall of the next. Facing the generous southern sun, it had climbed the four floors of the house (60 feet!) by the time we arrived. Its leaves were lush and its stems thick enough to support a resident house finch's nest. But no bloom.

And then, one June evening, rushing home from work, I was stopped in my tracks by a miracle. Lo and behold, the whole ornery thing was hung with lavender-blue flower racemes from the roof to the ground. Had it been leaf-pruned? Root-pruned? Fed some delicacy? Nothing, said our landlady. It has bloomed every year since. Although we moved away 10 years ago, like the poet A.E. Housman, who wrote, "About the woodlands I will go/To see the cherry hung with snow," I make an annual June pilgrimage to 83rd Street to see the wisteria hung with amethyst.

It's curious that the purple and white wisteria trees that are really unnatural forms of the vine, grafted onto standards, should have bloomed bountifully in Danbury every year since we planted them. Yet the pink wisteria vines I set out three years ago to drape the carport trellis have still not produced a blossom. The numerous articles I've read on how to get balky wisteria to bloom advise full sun, no nitrogenous fertilizers (they produce leaves instead of flowers) and, if all else fails, root pruning. That means cutting the roots with a sharp knife in a deep circle about a foot-and-a-half out from the vine.

But in White Plains where I grew up, a very old lady named Mrs. Crandall lived in an even older house. You couldn't see the porch, for the solid curtain of wisteria that draped it in dense shade. She never fed it anything, nitrogenous or otherwise, and certainly never root-pruned it.

You can plant wisteria in the spring or fall. If in fall, set a bushel basket weighted with a rock upside down over the plant the first winte.. The Chinese form (*sinesis*) is the best known, with fragrant, long-blooming, lilac-blue flowers in pendant racemes. The double floribunda clones come in pink, white or blue-purple. The blue is said to flower young. Good luck.

The most beautiful wisteria I've ever seen is at the Brooklyn Botanic Garden, where, in the Japanese gardens outside, vines have been planted at the top edge of a massive, natural rock wall about 20 feet high and equally wide. Instead of climbing up, the vines hang down. In June bloom, they cascade into a fountain of purple. On one visit, by chance, I saw the gardener at work and asked him what is needed to spur such glorious bloom. "Patience," he said. "Patience."

Native bittersweet (*Celastrus scandens*) is a wildly spreading climber that wants full sun—and watching. Like wild grape, it will enwrap even the topmost boughs of nearby trees. But in late summer and fall, the tawny red and yellow berries hang from the boughs like garlands of gemstones, and the sprays make colorful dried arrangements all winter long. I especially love them trailing over gourds and pumpkins as a Thanksgiving table centerpiece.

Forget the fertilizer. Native bittersweet fends for itself. But you must have a male and female plant for fruiting, and full sun. A cultivated variety, however, called *loeseneri*, is said to bear berries even in shade, to be self-fruiting and less invasive. It's worth tracking down.

NICHOLAS JACOBS

FLOWERING TREES
APRIL 1987

*H*ard frost predicted tonight. Cover the magnolia with blankets right away." It was David Weidt, my garden helper, urgently telephoning one Saturday night, four Aprils ago. Even as he spoke, snow was beginning to fall. So my husband Ken and I, much to the amusement of our dinner guests, clambered up—and slid down—the big boulders surrounding our 8-foot magnolia, trying to cover it with a moth-eaten old blue blanket (our cats' security blanket) without knocking off all the buds.

We did it! Next week, bloom was gorgeous. "Just those few degrees make the difference between blossoms and blasted buds," David said approvingly. But twice in seven years (not a bad record), we've departed Danbury for New York at dawn Monday morning, leaving a tree massed with buds, only to return Friday night

56

to find shriveled brown packets of petals that looked like dead little birds—heartbreaking.

Which brings up a problem all we Connecticut gardeners face, even in the southerly part of the state: Our spring just isn't as predictable as we'd like it to be. I've looked through all the catalogs for flowering trees that are said to be hardy in our weather zones, and found many of them borderline at best, and at worst, well, they simply won't bloom—or may not even survive—after a February like this past one.

The beautiful *Stewartia pseudo camellua*, for example, with white blossoms in July and handsome ornamental bark, really needs a very sheltered spot and lots of protection—and even then may not make it. Ditto the appealing little silver bell tree (*Halesia*) that has showers of white flowers in spring—but only when spring is right on time.

So in this column I have recommended only plant materials that have survived and thrived for me in Danbury or at a friend's home nearby. My dream is to have a succession of bloom from flowering trees early spring through summer. I've barely made a start at it, but here's a beginner's list. You can plant flowering trees spring or fall. I prefer early fall, even August, for a head start on strong growth next year.

The first tree to flower for us, in April when its leaves are half out, is the native *amelanchier* or shadblow, so-called because it blooms when shad run in the rivers. Like a low, fleecy white cloud among bare gray branches, its airy blossoms show before most other trees have leafed out. It likes woodsy soil and will take shade part of the day. Try one. You'll like it. Shadblows make spring come sooner.

Our magnolia blooms next (when it does). Wayside Gardens in Hodges, S.C., now offers some new magnolia varieties that "bloom about a week later than other cultivars, thus avoiding frost damage." I may try one this fall. But even the old varieties are more than worth the gamble for their shapely twisted branches and leathery green foliage. The slim, tapered buds are uniquely beautiful and mysterious, sheathing the flowers within in furry gray leaves. The big waxy blossoms are pink- to purple-stained outside, ivory-white within.

Half a mile from us, a magnificent avenue of some 20 magnolias blooms spectacularly year in, year out. Yours can, too, as long as they are planted facing south (out of cold winds). Save an old blanket for emergencies, just in case.

Next comes our small wonder, the never-fail Sargent's crab apple, which sports pink bud on May Day, white bloom on Mother's Day, red berry in August. The berries last through the winter till new leaves and buds crowd them off. Yellow-stamened flowers cover every inch of old branch and new twig, even masking the pale green leaf shoots. Sargent's crab apples get only 8 to 10 feet high and their graceful fanlike form makes them perfect ornamentals for the lawn. *Full sun, please*, and a balanced fertilizer scratched into the soil in early spring—and a little gentle pruning, for shapeliness, after bloom.

Next, in mid-May, come the American dogwoods, which, sadly, have been dying off in parts of Connecticut and Westchester County. The agricultural extension services now speculate that the blight may not have had a single cause such as "the virus" that was commonly blamed but, in fact, never identified. Rather, a combination of very cold winters, wet springs and summers and then drought may have "distressed" the trees and made them vulnerable to a virus that in a healthier state they could have resisted.

That's just a theory, but if you have dogwoods, keep them healthy by watering well through summer—they have shallow roots that can dry out—and feeding them heavily in early spring with Holly-tone. The best way is to circle the tree about 2 feet out from the trunk with 1-foot-deep holes set about 2 feet apart, then packing the holes with Holly-tone.

My neighbor does all this—and sprays her trees with a fungicide. There's no proof that it works, but it can't hurt. And all her dogwoods, old and new, pink and white, are thriving.

Thank goodness for the Chinese *kousa* variety, for it would be a terrible loss to be without dogwoods. Like the American dogwoods, *kousas* are trees for all seasons, with pale green lacy buds, masses of white flowers, red berries and winy fall foliage. More upright than the American varieties, with narrower leaves, they bloom a full month later than native types, so they're a wonderful addition as well as a substitute. Care for them as above.

Two wisteria trees I bought 13 years ago have unfailingly produced their exquisite, blue-purple racemes every June since. Remember, they're vines grafted onto a standard and they never give up trying to revert to their natural state. So prune the climbing tendrils mercilessly—*after they bloom*—and keep it up whenever they get out of bounds. A perfectly cultured wisteria tree will be pleasingly plump, round and heavy, with long, pendant panicles of flowers, in pink, white or blue-purple.

When you plant wisteria trees, set a strong, 8-foot-tall metal stake a good foot into the ground and about a foot out from the trunk. Then tie trunk and stake together firmly with strong twine. This will help the trunk to grow straight. *Don't fertilize.* It makes for leaves, not flowers.

The native viburnum *(tomentosum)* comes into bloom as the dogwoods finish, with round lacelike blossoms that lie like snow on its branches. Fan-shaped, it shows its blossoms to best advantage when they're seen from above. We look down on ours from our deck, so we get a perfect view of the individual blossoms and the whole shapely tree. Prune it to keep it shapely—after it blooms—and give it sunshine. In return, it will give you three weeks of beauty.

Even though a fierce Connecticut winter can kill flowering Japanese cherries, I wouldn't be without one. In bloom, they veil themselves in pale pink blossoms from head to toe. In leaf—and even bare—their branches climb gracefully skyward, then arch down, to enhance the landscape year-round. Plant them where the southern sun warms them, out of high winds. They can be glorious.

Laburnum vossii, the golden chain tree, and *Chionanthus virginicus*, the fringe tree, are rarely seen in Connecticut gardens. I can't imagine why. Both are hardy free-blooming, lovely in leaf, flower and form. With its 10-inch-long yellow racemes that look like yellow wisteria blooms, the golden chain tree is a late June dazzler. Although it doesn't get very wide, it likes space around it, perhaps to show off the eye-stopping flowers that hang from every branch. Ultimate height, about 20 feet. Give it a little afternoon shade.

Like silken fringe, the white blossoms of the fringe tree flutter in the slightest breeze in late June and early July. Because of its diminutive size and delicate form (it grows to only about 12 feet), you probably can accommodate two. I've paired a single-trunked tree with one that's shorter and multibranched—it's a good match. Some catalogs say fringe trees are dioecious (have male and female flowers on separate plants), so you need both to produce the purple grapelike fruit. But all the nurserymen to whom I've spoken assure me of full blossoming from just one tree. A word of warning: Fringe trees are among the last to leaf out in spring—don't give them up for dead. Also, they are heavy drinkers.

I'm experimenting with two other flowering trees, starting with little ones. One, viburnum *plicata*, has wide-spreading, horizontally tabulated branches that tier a mature tree with white blossoms in May. The other is a variety of hawthorn called *toba*, said to have double pink flowers, then red berries that lure grosbeaks and grouse. Planted in fall '85, the little viburnum produced some blossoms even its first spring. As for the hawthorn, which started as a mail-order skinny whip, it's filled out beautifully and this past May, after three years, produced, as promised, a thousand (!) blossoms and berries. But not a grouse or grosbeak yet. Still looking.

REA LUBAR DUNCAN

FLOWERING SHRUBS
AUGUST 1989

*A*bout 15 years ago, I read in James Underwood Crockett's book, *Evergreens*, that the best way to keep deer from dining on trees and shrubs is to spread lion manure around them. (Doesn't matter that Connecticut deer have never met a lion—the warning instinct embedded in their genes sounds off.) So when we were on safari in Kenya a few years ago, I had the bright idea of bagging some of the smelly stuff—it was plentiful—and smuggling it home.

"Lug that stuff? Are you nuts?" my husband roared.

I was. Even if I could have deceived the U.S. Customs Service by claiming it was dirty laundry—very dirty, indeed, from the high aroma—what a terrible disservice I'd be doing the land I love, maybe bringing in tsetse

59

flies or cholera bugs or mange or God knows what else. In the end, reason and patriotism prevailed.

If you, too, don't have any lion manure on hand, the next best deer deterrent is fencing in individual shrubs over your entire property, or, easier, spraying plants with deer repellent. A commercial product called Ro-Pel has worked well for me but not, I hasten to add, for my immediate neighbor, who shares the very same six-member deer family and whose garden was decimated. So I can't make an unqualified recommendation. Yet except for a few perennial tulips that I didn't spray in time last April, none of my plants or shrubs has been eaten.

Except for deer, flowering shrubs have few enemies, and those they do have can generally be controlled by keeping plants healthy through feeding and watering and, in cases of dire emergency, spraying with an insecticide or fungicide. (I use as few poisons as possible, strongly preferring to lose a plant over a deer, raccoon or my cats.) These ornamentals give you such lavish bloom from earliest spring to late fall that friends of ours with second homes in Vermont and Rhode Island rely on them as their only source of flowers all season long. "We can't get away every weekend to tend a garden. But whenever we arrive, there's always something lovely in bloom," the Vermonter reports.

The first shrub to bloom for me, in mid-April, is the delicately flowered deciduous rhododendron *mucronulatum*, which resembles an azalea in leaf and blossom. Hardy to minus 25 degrees, it bears masses of tubular blossoms centered with wispy anthers that bloom when gloomy gray is the prevailing landscape color. *Mucronulatum* traditionally has lavender flowers, but several nurseries now offer some pink-flowered seedlings. Knowing I'm a pink freak, a neighbor presented me with one for my birthday a year ago March. It stands about 3 feet high now, will eventually get to 8 feet. Like azaleas, it likes sun or light shade—very light—and a peaty, acid soil. Feed it with an acidic fertilizer spring and/or fall. (I do both.)

You can also find a dwarf form of *mucronulatum* in an intense shade of lavender that ultimately grows into a 3-foot mound. In a rock garden, it makes a very early and welcome splash of color.

Next to bloom at our place is one of those plants often disdained as "common"—forsythia. This point of view always makes me think of travelers who scorn visiting some of the wonders of the world in season because they "seethe with tourists," as one self-proclaimed sophisticate recently described such sights as Michelangelo's *David* in Florence and the Sphinx in Egypt. Ridiculous. Better to be crowded among tourists who, like me, can't get away in the off-season, than not to see the wonder at all.

So it is with certain shrubs. Gardens "seethe" with them because they're plain wonderful. What would spring be without the golden glory of forsythia? I have lots of kinds, one very "common" variety that was planted on the property some 40 years ago, and six of a relative newcomer called Meadowlark offered by Wayside Gardens in Hodges, S.C. The buds of the old variety are sometimes blasted by a late spring frost—ergo, no blooms—but not the new ones. En masse, forsythia are a dazzling sight. About 20 feet of our driveway is lined with huge old bushes, and what a glad hand they give us as we drive in on a rainy April day.

Don't, *don't* manicure forsythia. Let the branches grow tall as a beanstalk. They will eventually arch over into luxurious sprays of gold in bloom. Do your pruning from within the bush, cutting out only old wood. The only other pruning I do is to cut branches for forcing in water in February or early March. Make sure to take only budded boughs, which become lovely yellow-blossomed bouquets in two to three weeks.

Coming into bloom not long after the forsythia, in mid- to late May, are the Pinkshell azaleas *(vaseyi)*, native to the mountains of western North Carolina. Their 1½-inch pale pink petals seem to dance on the bushes, reminding me of the wings of a great night moth. They want acid soil and a fall dose of acidic fertilizer. I have four spaced out on the sloping bank edging our brook, set among ferns, wild phlox and Jack-in-the-pulpit to suit their woodland heritage. But they could certainly grace a perennial border or stand alone as specimen shrubs.

In France in late May, the yellow pealike blossoms of broom *(Cytisus leguminosae)* solidly line the roadsides from Brittany to Provence, gilding even the garbage dumps. In Connecticut, only two varieties of this lovely evergreen shrub are hardy, the creamy yellow-flowered *praecox*, and an extraordinary color break, which White Flower Farm discovered in Woodbury and propagated. Named Lucky, it has blossoms flushed deep pink at their base and standards. Both types grow into 6-foot rounded shrubs with thin, pendant branches. They insist on good drainage and plenty of sunshine.

Well before the large-leaved evergreen rhododendrons do their gorgeous stuff, between the first and second week in May, the smaller-leaved varieties come into exquisite bloom. Less widely used, these types range from low ground covers to 6-foot shrubs and are more delicate in leaf and flower. I use the variety Pioneer Silvery Pink that grows to 4 feet in a foundation planting that hides the empty space below our entrance deck. In bloom they make a spectacular showing and their evergreen foliage looks good year-round.

No need to extoll the virtues of large-leaved rhododendrons. Connecticut gardens "seethe" with them. And rightly so. But the *yakusimanum* hybrids, "yaks," as they are affectionately termed, are only now coming into supply at nurseries and are superb in the border or for landscaping. Originally developed by the late Tony Shammarello in Euclid, Ohio, they are hybrids of species found on the cold mountaintops of Yaku Shima, an island in the South China Sea, so they take our cold weather without a wilt. Plants are compact, reaching an ultimate height of 4 feet, with rich green leaves distinguished by velvety indumentum on the undersides and heavenly camellialike large blossoms in shades from apple-blossom pink to white. Carlson's Gardens in South Salem, N.Y., has the largest supply, but White Flower Farm in Litchfield and Claire's Garden Center in Patterson, N.Y., stock some. Mist Maiden and Pink Princess are my favorites, but they're all great. Buy whatever's available. Blooming time is early to mid-June.

Other June bloomers include the so-called "old-fashioned" shrubs beautybush *(Kolkwitzia)* and weigela. Why old-fashioned? Because they've been used so much by gardeners, I guess. They sure look in fashion to me. Beautybush is a small-leaved shrub whose branches, each loaded with pink blossoms, curve to the ground. In bloom, it's truly a fountain of pink. Mine is about 4 feet tall, but they grow to 6 feet or more. If you cut off old stems, they won't get leggy. A new variety from England offered by Wayside Gardens grows to 10 feet and is appropriately called Pink Cloud.

As for weigela, another old-timer, it's a fast-growing, never-fail, spreading pink marvel. Little tunnel-shaped pink blossoms smother the branches in June. Two years ago in Innsbruck, Austria, I nearly fell off an Alp, jamming on the brakes to look at what seemed a weigela with variegated leaves. It was. Happily, I found one last summer at White Flower Farm. It's a little fellow, but it bloomed heavily this year, the white-shaded pink blossoms set off strikingly by the green-and-white leaves.

On to July and, surprise, more azaleas, some of which bloom even into August. Native species, these deciduous shrubs include the Plumleaf azalea *(prunifolium)* with 1½-to-2-inch flowers, usually orange-red but also in clear orange and yellow. Its threadlike anthers are like butterfly antennae. Bushes get tall, although mine is holding at about 3½ feet. The Sweet azalea *(arborescens)* has tubular white flowers that bloom late June into July, with a heavenly scent much like heliotrope. It grows 6 to 10 feet and is hardy to minus 20 degrees. The Hammocksweet azalea *(serrulatum),* with slender white flowers occasionally tinged pale violet, blooms in July and August. Since it hails from the mild Southern coastal plain, a late spring frost can sometimes blast the buds. But try it anyway. It's clove-scented and a beaut.

This next tree stays so small and shapely—generally only about 6 to 8 feet—that I think of it as a shrub. It's the fringe tree *(Chionanthus virginicus)* whose tasselled white blossoms adorn the branches like silken trim from the end of June well into July. Be sure to give fringe trees plenty of water in times of drought (last summer's dry spell almost did my pair in) and don't think they're dead when they don't leaf out with other shrubs. Sometimes it's mid-June before there's a sign of life. Place them on a slight incline so you can best see the fringe shimmy and shake with the slightest breeze.

Smoke tree *(Rhus cotinus)* is a fascinating shrub of old gardens—and new—that in time will grow to 12 feet or more. It has a billowy effect as soon as its panicles of oblong seedpods form. Later, when they become full-blown, the bush is covered with whorls of filmy "smoke" in a soft mauve-purple color. Later still, the smoke turns gray and the leaves take on vivid fall colors—flame and scarlet. As an all-season accent point, it's a star. And mixed with green-leaved bushes, it provides pleasant contrast. But be patient. Young trees do not smoke.

For late summer and fall bloom—and dried flowers on the bush all winter long—the oak-leaf hydrangea *(quercifolia)* is unsurpassed. Its huge conical blossoms start out pure white, gradually turning pinkish as they mature in late August and September. The handsome oak-leaf-shaped foliage turns red-purple in fall. A fine variety is Snow Queen, which has the extra attraction of textural exfoliating bark. The long-planted shrubs you see all over New England reach majestic heights—to 15 feet. Snow Queen gets to only about 6 feet. Nice thing is that these hydrangeas do well in sun or shade. Give them space to grow and show off.

I think of fothergilla as a fall standout even though it bears pretty 1-inch, honey-scented white blossoms in early spring. But what gives it stardom is its spectacular display of color in the fall, when its deep green leaves turn to blazing orange, red and yellow. A petite type, fothergilla grows only to 2 to 3 feet. One of the best sources of color from mid-September through hard frost, it adds brilliant interest to a grouping of azaleas and rhodies and is also a striking addition to the perennial border. Acid soil required and full sun demanded for full color.

FAMILY PLANNING

AZALEA PETITES
SEPTEMBER 1984

"Jack," said Jill, "That dear Mrs. Hill
Has planted North Tisbury azaleas.
Now when we fall down,
You won't break your crown
'Cause Polly's azaleas are traileas."

The verse writer is Bob Carlson of Carlson's Gardens in South Salem, N.Y., where he and his wife, Jan, specialize in special azaleas and rhododendrons.

The lady of the limerick is Mrs. Polly Hill of North Tisbury, Mass., who's been raising her now-famous breed of azaleas on Martha's Vineyard for more than 20 years, from seeds sent from Japan. They're evergreen, hardy, low-growing, spreading and heavily blooming. Perfect ground-cover material? Absolutely. But there's more good news. Mostly pink and red, their blossoms start coming in May and, depending on variety, last into August. Yes, August. Late Love, which may be the latest-blooming, starts giving out its pink, big-as-petunia blooms at the end of June and continues well into late summer. Seeing is believing. I saw them.

Other North Tisburys that lie low but spread wide include Michael Hill, with 2½-inch shrimp-pink flowers starting in June, and Jeff Hill, with sparkling, slightly ruffled flowers in a warm pink with delicate purplish blotch. It gets about 15 inches high, blooms all through June. Pink Pancake, which I planted last September, covered itself for me with wavy bright pink blossoms from early June till mid-July. It never got over 10 inches high but it's already spread at least a foot.

If Polly Hill is the queen of ground-cover azaleas, Robert Gartrell of Wycoff, N.J., is the king. In 50 years of hybridizing, he has introduced more than 200 Robin Hill azaleas, as he calls the breed, which are, like the North Tisburys, evergreen, low-growing, spreading, hardy and floriferous. Blossoms run a mite bigger than the North Tisburys. Plants are generally taller and slower in spreading. But why quibble? Robin Hills reach 16 to 18 inches in height, spread to 36 inches in 10 years. (Most Polly Hill babies grow only to about 12 to 15 inches, fatten to 40. Hardly a difference to fret over.)

Blossoms of the Robin Hills are open and flaring with softly luminous petals, mostly in muted pastel pinks or white. Plants flower late May through June. Some look remarkably like camellias. Mrs. Emil Hager, for instance, has flowers layered like a camellia, though smaller, of course. Mrs. H is a hotter pink than most Robin Hills, but not loud.

Other exciting, low-growing azalea varieties that are not part of either Polly Hill's or Robert Gartrell's royal

65

families can, nonetheless, be princes or princesses in your garden. An enchanting pink called Kozan lies almost prostrate on the ground, spreading widely. Put it by itself center stage so its pearly seashell color can get the attention it merits. *Balsaminaeflorum* is also a ground-hugging trailer, with vivid salmon-pink double blooms. I saw it in a rock garden creeping lushly above, below, over and around a weathered gray stone.

Flat Out is a delightfully vigorous low fellow with satiny white blossoms that open—how else?—flat out. Gunrei is a charmingly frilled white with delicate petal markings like pink snowflakes which, like Flat Out, blooms late May through late June. Gunbi is another knockout with frilled white blossoms, flecked with red in a most painterly manner.

These are all hardy types I've singled out. Besides being a waste of money, it's heartbreaking to have fragile kinds that live only one season and leave you with dead plants and dead space. Robin Hills are probably hardier than North Tisburys, which are, remember, bred in Martha's Vineyard, where temperatures are gentled by the sea, rarely dropping much below zero or rising above 90 degrees Fahrenheit. Danbury, where I garden, gets hotter and colder. So does South Salem, N.Y. But Polly Hill is known for dumping any varieties that don't weather her weather—and worse. She reports that a blanket of snow, which God provides, helps. So does a mulch, which you and I can provide.

Last September I planted 20 of these dwarf azaleas to mask a 2-foot-high open space between a deck and the ground in a 30-foot-long foundation planting. The width of the bed curves from 6 to 8 feet. Striving for a clean, low look in keeping with the lines of the house, I alternated five Pink Pancake, five Flat Out, five more Pink Pancake, five more Flat Out. For an accent point between the two groups of 10, I planted two small-leaved rhododendrons called Pioneer Silvery Pink, which grow only to about 3 feet.

The azaleas have, indeed, been "traileas." By now some of their branches have reached out to touch neighboring plants a foot-and-a-half away. I admit they're well planted. The holes I dug were more than twice the size of the plant, as the catalogs advise. Also as recommended, the soil is half good topsoil, half peat moss. I mulched the plants with several inches of pine needles, of which I have a God-given supply. Bob Carlson advises mulching with several layers of newspaper covered with pine needles, pine bark, wood chips or oak leaves. In any case, make your mulch at least 3 inches thick so it will last through the summer and winter or longer. Don't use peat moss as a mulch. It becomes virtually water-resistant when dry and can remain a soggy blanket when wet.

September is a great time for planting these petites—and any other azaleas—although you can, with care, set plants in from May through early fall. You can order them by mail from Carlson's Gardens. There are one or two other sources but they're far away and I figure if plants will live and thrive in South Salem, they're apt to do the same in Connecticut.

Whenever you plant, feed only in early spring, before June. Use a heaping tablespoon of cottonseed meal for each plant or a half trowelful of Holly-tone.

You can use these azalea petites not only as a ground cover but also as an edging to the perennial border, trailing over a stone wall, in a rock garden or in front of tall azaleas or rhodies. (I've just planted four Gunrei in front of bigger-growing relatives. I'll let you know how they do.) To get all the blooms these plants are capable of giving, plant them in plenty of sun. Half the day is a must; more is better. In the shade you'll have lovely green ground cover all year. But what a blooming waste of talent.

REA LUBAR DUNCAN

LAURELS
SEPTEMBER 1985

*A*lthough it was only in 1907 that the General Assembly of Connecticut designated mountain laurel our state flower, the beauty of this shrub has delighted travelers since the earliest days of our colonization. John Smith mentioned laurel in 1624 in his *General History*. (Maybe he wooed Pocahontas with a bouquet.) In 1750, a Swedish explorer named Peter Kalm sent some specimens of it to Linnaeus, the renowned Swedish botanist, who returned the favor by naming the plant *Kalmia* (in Mr. Kalm's honor) *latifolia* (wide-leaved).

Surely for centuries before, the Indians must have enjoyed laurel's year-round shiny green and its June wash of colored blossoms over the woodsides and hills.

Pale pink, those blossoms, always pink, until 1961, when along came young Richard Jaynes, fresh out of

67

Yale with a master's degree and Ph.D. in botany, who started fooling around with the color at the Connecticut Agricultural Experiment Station in New Haven. And he hasn't stopped since.

"For heaven's sake, why?" I bluntly asked Mr. Jaynes, who, after more than 20 years, has retired from the station but continues his genetic tampering at Broken Arrow Nursery in Hamden, which he owns. "Isn't it like gilding the lily?"

"No," he replied with equal bluntness. "Now we have a much wider choice of plants. Not only a variety of colors, but better-shaped, denser bushes—you know how bare-legged older native laurel can get—plus miniature plants that fit in smaller gardens, even borders. Besides," he added, looking me straight in the eye, "all laurel isn't pure pink."

So much for this dirt gardener.

Seems there's a wild laurel *(Kalmia latifolia fuscata)* that's banded with brownish purple or cinnamon within the pink cup-shaped little flower (corolla). Sometimes the bands are so broad, the pink hardly shows.

Then there's a native laurel called *myrtifolia*, a miniature with myrtlelike glossy leaves. It's rare in the wild but Dick Jaynes found some. And then there's a native laurel with bright red or vivid pink blossoms, as opposed to the common whitish pink. Ah, so.

So, after experimenting unsuccessfully with many other varieties, Jaynes settled down to hybridizing with these three types. By 1980, through his efforts, the Agricultural Experiment Station was able to announce eight new hybrids and make them available to the nursery trade. That's a remarkable achievement. Consider that it takes five years from the first hybrid seed to a blossoming plant that may well be—often is—a dud.

Deriving from the banded *fuscata* type are the hybrids: Freckles, with 10 charming purple-brown freckles circling the rim inside the pink flower, as appealing as its name; Goodrich, an off-white with a cinnamon-brown band broken with white; and Carousel, with intricate banding of bright brown-purple.

Hybridized from the miniature *myrtifolia* is the diminutive Elf, with light pink buds and nearly white blossoms. Although the bush is about a third the size of standard laurel, its blossoms are almost full-size. Ah, an enchantment.

The brightest colored hybrids include Sarah, Dick Jaynes' favorite—he named it for his wife—with brilliant red buds that open pink. When buds and blossoms show together on the plant—which they do—it's a knockout. Ostbo Red has iridescent red buds that open white, *then* turn pink. But it's hardy only to zone 6, south of and slightly warmer than zone 5. The others mentioned here make it in 5, unless otherwise stated.

Silver Dollar bears flowers the size of its name, about 1$\frac{1}{2}$ inches across, which is twice the size of the species. Its blooms are light pink with a rose-colored ring at the base of each corolla, and are rosy-spotted. Pink Surprise is a deep pink with handsome dark green foliage that makes vigorous growth. Prune it after it blooms to keep its nice full shape.

The feathery-petaled kind became a parent of the new hybrid, Shooting Star, blooming white to light pink with unusual delicate flowers that have reflexed petals. It's a bit less hardy than the other new cultivars, only safe to zone 6. But since it comes originally from Danbury, N.C., I'm going to give it food and shelter in Danbury, Conn. Maybe it will feel at home.

So last year, Dick Jaynes "retired" from the Agricultural Experiment Station. Well, it's hardly retirement. He's hybridizing like mad in his own greenhouses both with laurel (he gave me a short lecture on artificial insemination of laurel) and rhododendron. He also consults with professional and amateur garden groups all over the country—and raises Christmas trees. Acres of them.

I bought three new laurel cultivars from him: the little one, Elf, the red-budded pink-blossoming Sarah and Silver Dollar. I also bought one plain-old pale pink Connecticut Yankee. Couldn't resist. Mr. Jaynes smiled approvingly. "It's beautiful," he said. "But mind, it will get leggy in five or six years." I'll risk it.

All laurel, the new kind and the old, insist on acid soil. If yours isn't, add aluminum sulfate, ferrous sulfate or plain sulfur. Sulfur is the cheapest but takes six to nine weeks to work. The first two do the trick in two to three weeks. Watch out if you're creating a foundation planting near the foundation of your house. The soil there is apt to be more alkaline because of construction debris from plaster or cement. Make it acid.

When you plant, use half peat moss, half good topsoil. If you have some leaf mold, mix it in. Mulch after planting with at least 3 inches of wood chips, pine bark or pine needles (all acid). Keep that level of mulch over the years. Laurel doesn't like open soil that freezes deep in winter or dries out in summer. Every spring, carefully push a little of the mulch away and fertilize with cottonseed meal or Holly-tone. Just scratch it lightly, water, and spread the mulch back in place.

Laurel will take some shade, but for a mass of blossoms, provide sun. Redder kinds *demand* full sun for full color.

Dr. Jaynes didn't say so, but speaking from experience, I find that while laurel blooms every June, it goes bananas every three or four years and lavishes blossoms like Lady Bountiful, en masse. Those are the very good years. (Lilacs and dogwood and apple trees have them, too.) But year in, year out, spring, summer, fall and winter, it's a handsome shrub. Some experts rank it above rhododendron, another broad-leaved evergreen, because its leaves do not curl up nearly as much when temperatures drop below 30 degrees.

REA LUBAR DUNCAN

HYBRID LILIES
NOVEMBER 1985

70

Once, high in the Himalayas in the Vale of Kashmir, we were on the deck of our houseboat-hotel on Lake Dal when one of the many lake-plying vendors approached us in his gondolalike boat, jam-packed with everything from saris and sculpture to toothpaste and toilet tissue. His sun-creased dusky face beaming, he gestured proudly to his piles of treasure and sang out in Brooklyn-ese the only English words he knew. "Gawgeous! Mahvelous! Fantestic!"

That's how my lilies were from mid-June through September. But the credit goes to the great hybridizers of the Pacific Northwest, not to me. Starting with native Asiatic and Oriental species, they have developed clones, strains and hybrids that are strong and hardy, highly disease-resistant, and absolutely "Gawgeous!

Mahvelous! Fantestic!" All I did was provide a well-drained site (if your ground is wet, add builder's sand), decent soil lightened with peat moss, a half trowelful of bone meal at planting time or a half trowelful of Plant-tone in early spring when the first shoots show, and water in long dry spells.

Horticulturally speaking, a clone is a named variety each bulb of which produces identical flowers, as opposed to a strain or hybrid grown from seeds, scales or bulblets bearing flowers that are very similar but not necessarily identical. Speaking as a dirt gardener, I group lilies by shape into five general categories, with variations and overlapping among them. First, those with pendant, recurved blossoms, some up to 10 inches, others diminutive. Second, exotic funnel-shaped trumpets up to 6 inches long. Third, types with bowl-shaped, outward-facing blooms, some enormous, others petite. Fourth, flat-outs, some petaled like stars, others ruffled or twisted. And fifth, sunburst types rather like flaring cups of color.

Colors? *Colors!* Pure white to ivory to candlelight. Pink to fuchsia to plum. Cream to buttercup-yellow. Rose to neon-red. Peach to flame to rust. All these, spotted or spotless; clear or shaded; starred, margined or brush-stroked.

Height? From a foot-and-a-half to 7 feet.

Blooming season? From May through frost. Hardiness? Total. Culture? Easy as daffodils. What else can a gardener want? Miracles? Well, you get those, too. The most exotic and spectacular blossoms that can be grown outdoors, except in tropical rain forests, where orchids make their steamy home.

But don't believe me. Send for a good lily catalog—with lots of color pictures—and see for yourself. White Flower Farm in Litchfield also carries top-quality bulbs. In fact, the very first lilies I ever bought, a dozen Jamborees that hooked me on growing lilies, came from White Flower.

I have a whole bed devoted to lilies. With a group of gray boulders as a centerpiece, it's roughly diamond-shaped, about 12 feet long and up to 6 feet deep. But in a mixed border, a lily cluster of three or more of one kind will give blossoms that form living bouquets front, middle and rear. Or try a clump in front of shrubs or evergreen trees for a striking color burst. Or group a few together on either side to herald the start of a path. In brief, plant them wherever you have room and make room if you don't.

Twilight started the lily season for me in mid-June, with outward-facing, lilac-pink blossoms in great profusion. It's one of my favorites for its unusual and lovely color and also for its bushy 2-to-3-foot growth. I've just ordered an even earlier-blooming clone called Debutante; it's only 2 feet tall but described as having 7-to-8-inch, raspberry-pink, star-shaped blossoms in late May. Can't wait.

While Twilight was in bloom, two little charmers opened up: Citronella hybrids with dozens—dozens!—of small, tightly reflexed pendant blossoms in luminous buttercup-yellow, spotted brown, that hovered like butterflies over the garden; and Avalon, a dainty, upright white with purple freckles, also a heavy bloomer. Avalon grows to about 2¹/₂ feet. The Citronellas got to 3 feet their first year, 4 feet their second.

Beginning in late June and blooming a full month was upward-facing Sunray, as bright and shining as its name. On July Fourth, it set off golden fireworks. I've never grown Jan de Graaff's great nasturtium-colored clone, Enchantment, said to be the most heavily blooming lily (and the fastest-spreading), but Sunray must come close. Secondary buds open all the way down its 2¹/₂-foot stems to prolong blooming.

A 2-foot clone called Barber that also bloomed in late June rather surprised me by turning out salmon-pink instead of the catalog's "lilac pink." But it was such an unusual bicolor, with stunning dark and light rings, I have no complaints.

I also got a surprise from Pink Perfection, one of the great trumpet hybrids, with 6-inch-long, funnel-shaped blooms shaded pink to fuchsia as if from an artist's palette. Its first year, it grew to only 4 feet, but this past summer it towered at 6 feet. Of course, it was misplaced, in the middle rather than the back of the border. I'll transplant the bulbs late this month. Lilies are never dormant but are least active in growth from October through the winter, which is the best time to move them.

The real showstoppers, the Oriental hybrids, took center stage in late July and August. Everest came first, not as tall as those to follow, only about 4 feet, with exquisite, snowy white flowers, sometimes lightly sprinkled with purple, and very special for its gracefully twisted, curling petals. I get six or seven 6-inch blossoms on a stem. (The catalogs say more and bigger, but I'm happy.) Pink Gold also gets to about 4 feet, too, but has 8-inch fragrant, pink-to-gold flowers. It's an outward-facer, with slightly curved-back petals. Just one alone in a bud vase is breathtaking. Incidentally, as cut flowers, lilies last a week, and look exotic.

The first lily I grew, Jamboree, is still my favorite. Its 7-to-10-inch recurved blossoms are warm pink rimmed with white, heavily sprinkled all over with maroon. A relatively new clone, Red Jamboree, is intensely red with white-margined petals. A major hybridizing achievement, it's as easy to grow as the other Jamborees. All bloom so generously that their 4-to-6-foot stems need staking to support the flowers. Do this when they're in bud (the same applies to staking all lilies), tying the stems at several points to sturdy green stakes with twist ties or twine.

A resplendent imperial procession starts in August: Imperial Pink, Imperial Gold and Imperial Silver. There are other Imperials, but I've grown only these three. Dazzlers all, with bowl-shaped blooms up to 12 inches wide, they can have a dozen or more flowers on each plant. Imperial Gold is white with an iridescent gold stripe down the center of each petal; Imperial Silver, white with maroon spots; Imperial Pink, gloriously pink with a green star at its heart. Stake them and plant them where they get a little afternoon shade as protection against the hottest sun.

Last to bloom for me is the clone of *Speciosum rubrum* called Journey's End, which has been called the crowning achievement of distinguished Melford hybridizers. Its petals are an amazing rich lavender-crimson barely edged with white and wondrously recurved, as are all speciosums. It grows to 6 feet, is very vigorous and lasts well into September. *Speciosum album* is a bit earlier and shorter. Its snowy, twisted petals, feathered as if with down, are one of those blooming miracles lilies pull off.

There are dozens of varieties to choose from, but these all bloomed in my weekend Danbury garden this past summer (that's some kind of miracle, too). I learned a lot from them—for example, that they like their roots cool. That means mulching or underplanting. Underplanting is prettier because it provides much-needed foliage to soften the skinny lily stalks. And it gives nice color contrast. I tried to achieve an underpinning of all blue-purple from both annuals and perennials: early forget-me-nots, columbine, Chinese delphiniums, summer-blooming annual forget-me-nots, and a late-blooming annual called eustoma with little tulip-shaped blossoms. Monkshood's deep blue, pealike blooms arch over the rocks from behind.

Lilies are shipped late in fall and sometimes, because of weather problems, in early spring. I prefer fall planting for a good head start. Most bulbs should be planted at a depth twice the depth of the bulb itself, except for the humongous Oriental hybrids, which should go down to three times their depth. Bargains don't merit your effort. Buy big bulbs for big blooms.

As a weekend gardener, I can't always plant when the bulbs come, so sometimes I've been out there in bitter December, chopping away at frozen ground, risking frostbite and chilblains and aggravating my arthritis.

It's been worth it.

REA LUBAR DUNCAN

IRIS
MAY 1986

*W*hat if the stars came out only one night a year, Emerson speculated in an essay. What a wonder it would be! How we would look and marvel and stage all-night celebrations!

Well, that's how I feel about iris. Just suppose that the bearded iris we take so for granted in Northeastern gardens bloomed but a single day in early June. Ah, what a spectacle! How closely we'd watch the slim, sheathed bud so as not to miss a moment of the grand opening. And we'd have iris-watching parties the whole day long. Slow-motion cameras would record the first of the standards (the top three petals) unfurling from the bud, then the second, then the third. Then the falls (the bottom three petals) curving downward, sometimes one at a time, sometimes all at once. Not to mention the exquisite beards on each fall. Or the colors!

73

Iris was the Greek goddess of the rainbow and it is for her the flowers are named. They do her proud.

Today's gorgeous bearded iris (they used to be called German iris) are all tetraploids (hybrids with four chromosome cells instead of one) that have been developed since about 1920. There are "selfs"—all one color; "bicolors"—standards one shade, falls another; and "plicatas"—generally stippled with a darker color on a white ground. Beards may be a contrasting hue or of the same color family as the falls. Blossoms, coming forth from mid-May to mid-June, are huge. They're satiny or crepe-finished, veined, shaded or picotéed, ruffled, flaring or lacy.

These tall bearded types insist on well-drained—even dry—soil and full sunlight. Plant them in shallow earth August to September. If the tubers hump above the earth, that's OK. Keep the roots covered, of course. Don't plant fewer than three of one kind in a group—four to six is even more striking. And for rhythmic effect, repeat the same variety at least once in the border.

For stupendous blossoms—and lots of them—sprinkle each clump in early spring with a *little* superphosphate, no more than a tablespoonful or blooms will be so big that they'll fall over from their own weight. (The superphosphate trick is good with rhododendron, too, but do the sprinkling after they have bloomed so they'll set more buds.)

A few of my favorite bearded iris—a very few—are Merry Christmas (snow-white with a red beard), Henry Shaw (ruffled all-over white), Crystal Blue (blue even to its beard), Esther Fay (pure pink with a bright red beard), Peach Taffeta (delicate peach with a vivid tangerine beard), and any yellow at all from palest lemon to brilliant gold. There are also rich wines, black-purples, vibrant bronzes, lavenders and mauves.

Besides the big bearded wonders, other iris varieties will add beauty to your garden and lengthen the blooming season from the end of April to late July. The dwarf bearded varieties, for example, come into blossom two to three weeks ahead of the biggies. Little charmers only 8 inches high, they are a delight in the front of the border, planted right in amongst your ground-cover edging. Mine pop up amidst dense *Waldsteinia ternata*. Plant them any time, spring to fall. They come in cherry-red, light and dark blue, lavender, white, yellow, apricot. Some are even scented. Like the big fellows, they show up best planted in groups of one variety.

A little used but absolutely delightful low-growing iris variety, *cristata*, takes light shade and forms fat clumps. In fact, it spreads so fast that it works as a ground cover in front of leggy plants. I have about a dozen of them in alternating groups of white and blue in front of a low row of herbaceous peonies. In spring before the peony foliage is full, they cover the naked ground. Later they snuggle under the peony leaves, enjoying the shade. And they're hardy. Plant them in early spring to get May blossoms or throughout the summer and fall. Their clean, green spearlike leaves grow to only about 6 inches high.

Iris *tectorum* or Japanese roof iris (although they're native to China) began as a living binding to thatched roofs. Occasionally, you still see them used that way. There once was a house in Rye that we would drive past in early spring just to see the iris sprouting on the roof. But for most of us they're easier on the ground, where they make lush plants about 12 to 16 inches high with a wealth of open-petaled 6-inch blossoms in late May. I know them in two colorations: a clear lilac with crinkled falls veined a darker purple and sparkling white crests on the standards, and a satiny white with cheery yellow crests. Plant them from August to September in good rich soil. If you keep them well mulched, they may be evergreen. (I didn't and they weren't.)

Japanese Higo iris, if they bloomed but one day a year, would certainly rivet attention as a miracle of nature. They do anyhow. Called "the orchid of iris," their exotic, 6-to-9-inch flat-out blossoms have silky crepe-finished petals, some heavily veined or marbled, others pure and clear, in blue, purple, mauve, pink and white, and in both single and double varieties. They bloom from late June to the end of July—but only if they get lots of water, particularly when they're coming into bud and bloom. I know from sad experience that if you don't give them water, they won't give you flowers. They do very well, of course, at water's edge (they like wet feet but dry ankles). If you have a soggy spot, plant a big clump. They'll be happy. Acid soil is a must.

Siberian iris grow into massive clumps and can last a lifetime. They have tall, grassy foliage and come today in a large variety of blues and whites, with wide-petaled flowers that generally are feathered with charming little yellow tufts on the standards. Siberians like acid soil and lots of water, too. They'll not only give their all next to a stream, but also make beautiful informal specimen plantings. Just water well. Their roots go way down (good for holding a steep bank), so dig the soil deep before planting. You'll have a 2-foot clump in one season.

The glorious fleur-de-lis that was the royal crest for the kings of France is said to have been taken from iris *pseudacorus*, another variety that rarely graces Connecticut plantings but should, especially near or even in water. I've planted them in shallow spots in our brook as well as at brookside, and I've seen huge masses of them growing right in the water in shallow lakes and ponds. They will also do well for you in a swampy spot. But watch out. In a few years, they spread into humongous drifts. Don't fret—they divide easily and you'll have lots for friends who will, I promise, ask for them.

Large yellow blossoms come from May to mid-July in both single and double varieties. Shimmering in sunlight, they make a luminous display against rippling water. Foliage is handsome, too, and grows to about 3 feet. Plant them August through September. They're easy and hardy. Two years ago when we had flooding spring rains and our brook looked like Niagara, I surely thought they'd drown. Not at all. The very first weekend in June—voilà, there were our fleurs-de-lis. Ooh-la-la.

Most iris varieties need dividing every three or four years. Do this in August, using a sharp knife to cut each rhizome into two or three pieces. Don't divide all your plants at once or next spring's bloom will be sparse.

REA LUBAR DUNCAN

DAFFODILS
OCTOBER 1986

*W*hen my daughter was a 3-year-old mite, our dear friend "Aunt" Dottie sat next to her at dinner and asked her (since she was unusually quiet), "Are you feeling all right, Laurie?" First came a long, world-weary sigh, and then the Camille-toned reply, "No, I have the *krasmus*." That's phonetic spelling because neither Webster's nor any medical encyclopedia lists this ailment. Nonetheless, the *krasmus* has been an affliction in our family ever since, describing the "blahs" or not being "in the pink" or similar maladies. It generally strikes most forcibly at the end of March and beginning of April—when winter has long overstayed, and body and soul sag under cold leaden skies that seem never-ending.

Although not a permanent cure, daffodils can provide six weeks of golden relief. Yes, all spring-blooming bulbs—in fact, all perennials—signify renascence. But to me, daffodils are the very embodiment of life renewed. Perhaps it's because they're indomitable, triumphing over winter and thrusting up from the frozen earth year after year. Or perhaps it's because they multiply so amazingly. Or because they burst upon us when trees and shrubs are still bare. Or because they take their color from the life-giving sun itself. Whatever the reason, I plant them as amulets every fall and shamelessly invoke their magical powers to link me to yet one more spring.

Over the past four years, I've set out some 2,000 daffodil bulbs that give bloom from early April through mid-May. They are at their height from about May 3 to May 10, so I try to hold my annual daffodil party (everyone has to wear yellow) on the Sunday that falls during that time. One year was a near disaster. The party got pushed up to May 10. The week before, the temperature hit 90 degrees and almost did the daffs in. But last year, on May 8, nature smiled and some 8,000 blossoms sashed and studded the grounds with gold.

Horticulturally speaking, daffodils are called *narcissi* and are classified into so many ever-changing categories that White Flower Farm, way back in '62, called the system a "hopeless jumble of numbers and symbols" and gave up trying to catalog them all in its garden book. In Rockwell and Grayson's reference, *The Complete Book of Bulbs* (my well-worn copy dates back to '53), the authors have boiled down the categories to 11, but even these are really for *narcissi* professionals. *Trumpet narcissi,* for example, are described as having a "trumpet (or corona) as long or longer than the perianth (outer petal) segments." *Large-cupped narcissi* have cups "more than one-third but less than equal to, the length of the perianth segments." *Small cups* are "not more than one-third the length of the perianth segment," and so on.

As the authors point out, the one merit of this gobbledygook is to bring gardeners up to date on the remarkable range in size and form of today's daffodils. But other than that, isn't it enough to know that there are trumpets, flatcups, small cups, singles, doubles, multiflowered types and miniatures in a glorious array of solid colors, monochromes, bicolors and even tricolors that now lengthen the blooming season to six weeks?

Recently, Jean-Louis Dumas-Hermès, the chairman of the famous Paris-based fashion house of Hermès, revealed to a group of fashion editors that the company can spend a year choosing a print for its fabled scarves. Then, laughing, he confessed, "But women don't buy the print. They buy the colors. Just this morning," he continued, "a woman told me she has had an Hermès scarf for 20 years that was given to her by her mother, who had it for 20 years before. I was thrilled and asked what print it was. She had absolutely no idea. 'It's a lovely soft pink and gray,' she said."

Well, that's how I buy daffodils: first and foremost by color and only then by form, shape, height and time of bloom. Among today's utterly delectable colors are pure whites and creams; solid yellows ranging from pale lemon to brilliant gold; bicolors of yellow with white, orange, apricot and lettuce-green; more bicolors of white with pink, peach, gold, flame and chartreuse; tricolors of yellow, orange and bright red; white, apricot and terra-cotta—and more.

Shapes? Upright and pendant; flat-out, overlapping and "split" petals; fat and skinny long-cupped trumpets—ruffled, flaring or crinkled; dainty minitrumpets; 2-inch flatcups to tiny "pheasant's eyes"; single and clustered blooms; heights from 3 inches to a foot-and-a-half.

Miraculously, *they all look good together.* Truth is, daffodils are the only plants I'll buy by the "mix." Despite the catalogs' fevered urging, I won't order their mixes of daylilies, tulips, iris or roses. For better or worse, I want to do it myself, to create my own color contrasts or fashion a great swath in just one color. (Funny, White Flower Farm, which so enthusiastically pushes on customers its daylily mix, has a 20-year-old bed of solely yellow daylilies in its own landscape design.) But daffs make beautiful music together. They sing in sweet, close harmony with not one striking a discordant note. Even so, certain kinds should be singled out for solo performances. The delicately hued pink cups, for example, should be set off so as not to be drowned out by bolder colors. The new "split" or "collared" types (actually, they're the old "broken" varieties, rediscovered) are such standouts they should stand alone. And of course, the dainty miniatures mustn't be dwarfed by big fellows.

As landscaping material, daffodils work in countless design treatments. On the great English estates, they're naturalized in the fields—acres and acres of them. (If you plant them this way, just remember you can't mow till the foliage browns off.) But daffs will shine even on us peasants who don't have grand estates. At the far edge of my lawn, just where it meets the woods, they serve as a golden border. (Big, bright yellow ones show up best at this distance from the house.) At waterside, they meander along our brook and don't even mind being temporarily submerged by flooding spring and fall rains. They solidly encircle the massive trunk of a towering tulip tree and delicately ring a graceful clump of birches. They face down evergreen trees and shrubs, stud the rock garden and soften the base of the bird feeder.

But it's in the perennial border that I have the most daffodils. If "border" suggests to you a nice, neat, flat, cultivated plot of earth, you have the wrong border. My perennials are set in and around the tumbled-down rocks of an old stone wall. Fifty feet wide and 6 to 8 feet deep, it's planted with more than a thousand daffodil bulbs along with a couple hundred other perennials.

Everything thrives. Before the perennials come up, the daffodils entirely fill the space. Later the perennials hide their yellowing foliage. Of course, everything gets well fed and a heavy mulch of wood chips keeps out weeds.

Daffodils are best planted in October—the sooner the better so they have time to put out strong root growth before the ground freezes. When they're planted late, spring growth is sparse. Buy top-size bulbs. Bargains give few blooms and are not worth the labor. To plant, dig a hole deep enough to cover the "shoulders" of the bulbs with 6 inches of soil and put a trowelful of bone meal or a big spoonful of sewage sludge at the bottom of each hole. Daffs are not fussy about soil except for heavy wet clay, which can keep them down forever. (Add sand, peat and good topsoil to correct the condition.) Mice won't bother them, nor moles nor bugs.

I've always scattered bone meal heavily over them just *after* they've bloomed. But on rereading *The Complete Book of Bulbs,* I learned that they need the most nourishment in August and September, when growth is heaviest. This year I've done it that way. It takes almost 50 pounds of bone meal for me to do the job thoroughly. At today's prices, that ain't cheap. But it's a lifetime investment. Bulbs spread, increase and give gorgeous flowers.

Not to mention chasing off the *krasmus.*

LILACS

MAY 1987

Go down to Kew in lilac-time, in lilac-time, in lilac-time;
Go down to Kew in lilac-time (it isn't far from London!)
And you shall wander hand in hand with love in summer's wonderland;
Go down to Kew in lilac-time (it isn't far from London!)

So chants the British poet Alfred Noyes in his lilting poem, "The Barrel-Organ." But you don't have to go that far. Just travel any Connecticut highway or byway this month and you'll see them. Tall hedges lavishly panicled with purple-blue blossoms. Great clumps giving their flowering all next to tumbledown deserted houses. Spreading bushes in full bloom above a ground cover of poison ivy.

They're *Syringa vulgaris*, the common lilac. But to me there's nothing vulgar or common about them. When my children were little, we visited The Cloisters, the great museum of medieval art high above Riverside Drive in upper Manhattan. After a bit, the kids got rambunctious, so I took them outside to let off steam, and quite by chance, we came upon a wondrous sight: a long walkway sloping all the way down to the drive, solidly lined on both sides with lilacs so tall their heavy blooms touched above our heads, enveloping us in beauty and fragrance. If they're good enough for The Cloisters, a branch of the Metropolitan Museum of Art, they're certainly good enough for me.

These lilacs, in purple or white, were the only kind I knew until I went to Europe for the first time. (I was in my 30s, not like today's lucky kids who go in their teens.) It was in May, and the whole city of Zurich was in bloom with towering white-flowered horse chestnut trees and tall lilac bushes massed with huge sprays of deepest blue-purple. The splendor of it has never left me. And then, one night, I heard my first nightingale singing his heart out from a lilac bush in the hotel gardens. *Wunderbar!*

A hybrid variety of lilac from Wayside Gardens, called Andenken an Ludwig Spaeth, approximates that blue-purple most closely. Its single blooms are rich and dark and come into flower about a week later than our common lilacs, which nicely extends the flowering season. Called French hybrids because the French led in developing them, they're offspring of *Syringa vulgaris* but come in a wondrous assortment of colors—white to cream, lavender to purple, light blue to periwinkle, seashell-pink to claret to dark wine, even bright red. An unusual hybrid called Sensation is just that: a sensation. Blossoms are deep wine-red with white picotéed edges. They come in tall clusters, glint silvery in sunlight and are ultrafragrant. President Lincoln is another standout hybrid with true almost Wedgwood-blue flowers—rare in lilacs—in pyramidal clusters of florets that open out very wide.

White lilacs should be used *en masse*, three or more bushes together, for an eye-stopping burst of white against dark green leaves. The common white remains a winner, fragrant and free-blooming. A particularly good hybrid white, Miss Ellen Wilmott, is intensely sweet-smelling and very generous with its rather late-blooming trusses.

The tall hybrids can reach 12 feet in height with a 6-foot spread on top. I find them not as thickly branched as the common type and a bit spindly-legged. Put them where you see their crowns rather than their skinny shanks. Or try the dwarf hybrid Congo in front. Its striking single red blossoms come midseason. For a formal effect, use the dwarf tree lilac, trained to a single trunk, to mark the entrance to the garden or the start of a path or drive. Called *velutina*, it's of Korean origin and has upright pink-tinted panicles in mid-June long after most other lilacs have come and gone. And it's a heavy bloomer.

Another Korean variety, a favorite of mine, is *Palibiniana* (named after the Russian botanist, Palibin), which makes a stunning specimen shrub that spreads out thickly. Leaves are small and very dark green; flower panicles, about 6 inches long. In bud, they're very dark but open a lavender-lilac. The scent is heavy and heavenly. I bought a baby from White Flower Farm about 11 years ago that has had to be transplanted three times to accommodate its growth. Obviously, it likes its Danbury home because it's now 8 feet wide and a good 7 feet tall. The books say it won't top 8 feet. Wanna bet?

Plainly, you can stretch the lovely lilac-blooming season to a good six weeks if you choose appropriate varieties. Imagine having lilacs the very beginning of May, even the end of April if we get an early spring. You can, with *oblata*, which has palest lavender blossoms that create a misty effect. Then, starting about May 8 in my Danbury garden, come our common lovelies, with great boughs of bloom in lavender or white that scent the air with their delicious fragrance. For indoor bouquets, clip off some leaf sprigs so the flower panicles aren't hidden behind all that foliage. It's a florists' trick.

A week or so later, the Persian lilacs *(persica)*, bloom. I'm pleased with these. They have very small, dainty leaves, stay under 6 feet, with rather loose form and lilac or white flowers. A cluster of two or three makes a beautiful landscape focal point. Chinese hybrids *(chinensis)* bloom mid-May, lilac to a pale purple—and tall.

Depending on the French hybrids you choose, you can get bloom from May 1 through mid-June. And the Rock Garden or Daphne lilac (it looks a little like the shrub, daphne) is said to bloom twice, in mid-June and again in mid-August. Seldom over 7 feet tall, it has mahogany-red buds that open to soft pink. Another variety that also blooms in June is the Japanese tree lilac *(amonesis,* variety *japonica)*. Very tall, with creamy white flowers, it makes a handsome specimen for a show-off spot.

All lilacs must have full sun to bloom. I had three bushes planted in sun a good half of the day that never gave me a blossom, although they grew handsomely. A year ago I dug them up and moved them into all-day sun. I'm happy to report they're loaded with buds right now.

Lilacs prefer a neutral to limy soil, so scratch a little lime, a trowelful, into the top of the earth early every spring. Don't mix it into the soil when you're planting new bushes, since it can burn the roots. Fertilize with bone meal very early in the spring although, heaven knows, the roadside types do very well without any.

Pruning? New bushes don't need it except for shaping. Use the clippers *after* plants have bloomed, while you're cutting off spent blossoms. Our common lilacs can grow to 20 feet, so if you want to keep them low enough to reach the blossoms, snip off top growth. Prune twiggy old bushes from the base, way inside the shrub, if need be. Clip off suckers.

If you want to see a glory of lilacs, visit the Arnold Arboretum in Boston in May or the city parks in Rochester, N.Y. You'll be dazzled at the different colors, contours, foliage.

REA LUBAR DUNCAN

PEONIES

JUNE 1987

$\mathcal{O}$n my first trip to England some 20 years ago, I made a pilgrimage to Sissinghurst Castle in Kent, where Vita Sackville-West and her husband, Harold Nicolson, created their fabled gardens. I went with two friends, one of whom had lived in England many years. Still, we got lost and arrived at Sissinghurst, all right, but another Sissinghurst. This was a smallish estate with emerald lawns (all that English rain does it) rimmed by a deep border in the shade of towering ancient deciduous trees solidly underplanted with camellias. Hundreds of camellias all in blossom—it was the very end of April—from white-tinged pink to deep carmine. I'd never seen anything like it before, nor have I since, even in botanical-garden displays.

"You go get directions. I'll stay here," I told my friends.

The grounds seemed deserted so I wandered around, following the undulating border until I came into the sunshine and onto a terrible sight, a long mansion house whose roof had been devoured by fire. Charred wood, dangling rafters and ugly holes told the tragic story. In front of the house to the left was a perennial border and there, sitting on the wet earth, was a woman in handsome but, not surprisingly, very muddy tweeds, her face almost invisible under a tweed pork-pie hat, except for a cigarette dangling from her lips. Not only was she an apparition but so was the peony she was cultivating with her trowel.

"It's a yellow peony," I breathed, "a yellow double herbaceous peony. I've never seen one before."

"Not many around," she said in clipped British upper-class cadence, and I knew at once that this was not the gardener. Here was the lady of the house.

I introduced myself and apologized for intruding. "We got lost looking for Sissinghurst and I stayed to admire the camellias. We can't grow them outside where I come from in the States."

"Howdyoudo, I'm Lady Drummond," she said, the cigarette still in her mouth. "This is Sissinghurst, but not the one you're looking for. This house has been in my husband's family for generations, and we lived here till last winter, when the roof caught fire. Old rotten wood. Now that the weather is decent, we'll rebuild it. Three years ago, a friend of mine sent me some yellow peony seeds from China," she went on without a break, "and I've managed to get a few plants to grow. Most have bloomed already—this is the last—and I've taken seeds. Would you like some?"

Would I like some? Would I! But I'm bitterly ashamed to say that instead of giving those seeds to a nursery or a fine plantsman, I attempted to grow them myself. I didn't—still don't—have proper seed-raising facilities. They sprouted, but, without constant care, wilted and died. How stupid and wasteful of me even to have tried.

But back to Sissinghurst. I squatted down next to Lady Drummond—she hadn't stopped digging—and we joyously talked gardens for about half an hour. "Would you like tea?" she asked. I longed to accept, but just then my two friends returned, and I felt like the girl who stands at the roadside alone thumbing a ride, and when a car stops, brings out a hidden clutch of pals from the bushes.

My friends and I did go to the famous Sissinghurst, and it was—is—indeed a garden miracle. But that brief moment in the "wrong" Sissinghurst remains a special event in my life. I wrote thanking Lady Drummond for the seeds and we exchanged Christmas cards for several years—and then, silence. She was in her late 50s when we met and one wonders.

To this day, despite the intense efforts of hybridizers, there are no true yellow peonies available commercially. A Japanese herbaceous variety gets about as close as they've come. Called Gold Standard, it has white petals tinted yellow and a cushion of yellow staminodes in the center. But it's not a real double. At the "wrong Sissinghurst," I was looking at a pure yellow, heavily double, ball-shaped, honest-to-God double herbaceous peony.

Yellow may be a breeder's dream, but for us gardeners, it almost doesn't matter, so many other exquisite colors are available, from vivid scarlets and hot pinks to misted and luminous pastels. Best known and most used in American gardens is the double herbaceous variety, so intensely double that as the bloom opens, a center never shows, just in-curling layers of petals. One understands perfectly why these are so loved. They're utterly beautiful plants, apt to outlive thee and me, requiring little or no care. My mother and father were very talented people, she an opera singer and a licensed dentist, he a doctor. But gardeners they weren't—knew nothing, cared less. Yet at our house in White Plains, a long row of great peony plants bloomed lavishly every June, untended, unweeded, unwatered except by God's sweet rain.

They were there when my parents bought the house before World War II and they're there today. Last June, en route to Danbury, I took a short detour off the Hutchinson River Parkway just to see the old homestead. There they were in full glory, 20-odd blossoms to each bush. The variety is Festiva Maxima, introduced in 1851, still not only a favorite but also a standard against which new varieties are measured. Thickly double, it has white petals flecked blood-red at the heart.

Other beautiful doubles—there are many—are blush-pink Nick Shaylor, which is slightly fragrant (I seek out fragrance) with occasional deep red markings on its center petals; Elsa Sass, a very fragrant pink that ages to white; Best Man, a late-blooming, tall deep red; Jean Bockstocie, an early-flowering burgundy-red; Bowl of Cream, with huge, bowl-shaped creamy white flowers that come midseason. Plainly, you can get a succession of bloom from early to late June if you plan it so. If you have room, group three of one kind together for mass color effect. Foliage stays green and decorative all summer.

Lesser known and rarely used in the States are Japanese single and double peony varieties. Why? Although the flowers do not curve into petaled balls, they have a delicate beauty and are spectacular in form. Like a feathered pincushion, the center of each flower is a round pillow of staminodes surrounded by layered or single petals. Picture Largo, a single-petaled pink with white center staminodes tipped yellow. Or Postillion, a semidouble, brilliant cherry-red with yellow staminodes. Or Karen Gray, a new hybrid with fuchsia petals and yellow center. Or Gay Paree, with unusual curly pink petals surrounding its domed pink center.

All are just as hardy and long-lived as our familiar herbaceous doubles. Of course, a cluster of three is a knockout.

Tree peonies, which also are rarely used in American gardens, have a fascinating history that is briefly documented in *White Flower Farm The Garden Book* as follows: "They were discovered about 1,600 years ago in the bamboo groves of the Chinese Imperial Palace Gardens. But Westerners, who saw drawings of the huge, flat, fairylike blossoms on silk and pottery, simply did not believe that such a flower existed until plants were brought to England from Canton by Sir Joseph Banks, the creator of Kew Gardens. The English sought Chinese 'moutans' passionately during the early 1800s . . . the new blooms spread to France between the wars. Today there are fine American varieties."

Do remember that tree peonies are trees and you must not cut them back in the fall as you do other peonies, whose dead stems should be clipped off. These tree types want to grow big. They'll get to 4 or 5 feet and almost as wide in a few years and are said to give 75 blooms when fully mature. Mine have never given me more than 10 but they're still young. So don't be discouraged if plants don't give their all the first two years. Even the two or three huge blooms you get their very first June will be the wonder of the neighborhood.

Tree peonies come single and double in lovely shades of pink, red, white and wisteria-purple. Champion of Flowers is a cherry-blossom pink. Hesperus is a radiant rose-pink single with gold undertones. Taiyo is a demidouble with crimson flowers, satin-finished. Companion of Serenity has white ruffled petals flared violet-red. Kamata Fuji, which means Wisteria of Kamata, is another beauty, with double wisteria-colored blossoms.

All peonies like slightly alkaline soil, although left to their own devices, they grow uncomplainingly in Connecticut's naturally acid earth. Still, they'll do better with a little limestone scratched in around them in early spring and an inch or two of wood ashes from your fireplace as a winter cover. New plants should get a shot of a fungicide, Benomyl or Captan, the first spring. If branches wilt or leaves blacken, cut them off and burn them.

Now is a good time to case the nurseries, where potted peonies are in bloom, to see which varieties you like. You can set out these potted plants now but you must plant tubers in the fall. For the herbaceous doubles and single and double Japanese varieties, set the eyes of the tubers—the little fleshy white sprouts—exactly an inch-and-a-half below ground level in rich topsoil enriched even more with a good half pound of bone meal. Remember, they're going to be there forever so give them a good start.

Tree peonies want the same rich soil but require a different planting technique. They're trees, so plant them deep with the tree peony scion—you can't miss it, the joining point where the tree peony has been grafted to the herbaceous root—6 to 7 inches below the soil's surface. Roots should be spread out first, buried and muddied-in with water. Cover the plant the first winter with an inverted bushel basket weighted with a stone. After that, it needs no shelter. Give it a pound—yes, a pound—of bone meal its second spring. Don't be stingy. Generous feeding will result in generous bloom, each flower big as a salad plate with crinkled, crepe-textured or satin-finished petals.

DELPHINIUMS

MAY 1988

*T*here's an old gardeners' saying, "If you want to grow beautiful roses, move to England." The same goes for delphiniums, those devils. They really do prefer the gentled clime of England— no blistering sieges of 95-degree dog days, no onslaughts of subzero cold, no attacks from killing winter winds. Lots of intermittent, soft, lovely rain, and England's sweet alkaline soil as home ground. At Heale House Garden in Wiltshire last June, clumps of deep blue dels standing 10 feet or higher towered above me, without stakes for support. Hundreds of big, perfectly formed individual flowers crowded the length of each spire, 8 to 10 spires to each plant.

The name "delphinium" comes from the Greek *delphis*, which means dolphin, supposedly for the resemblance between the spur of the bud and a dolphin's tail. Well, at Heale House Garden the buds were sufficiently big and so perfectly formed that I could glimpse—or imagine—a likeness. Back home, getting even one year of bloom from those gorgeous hybrid dels is a considerable achievement.

Even the late William Harris, founder of White Flower Farm—and under his pen name, Amos Pettingill, creator and author of its witty and informative catalogs—warned of delphiniums' idiosyncrasies. In his *White Flower Farm The Garden Book* published by Knopf in 1971 (an expanded version of the catalogs, and still a treasure), he begins his section on delphiniums by calling them "the queen of the perennial garden," but adds, two pages later, "Treat dels as annuals, then one that lives over winter is a bonus. You will always find that some live several years."

Some, but not many, although I shouldn't complain. I've had lavish bloom from even the demanding Pacific hybrids for three years running, and longer from the less difficult varieties. You just have to accede to dels' finicky demands. They will thrive only if you plant them in very fertile soil, then enrich them at frequent intervals most of the spring and summer.

More persnickety traits. Delphiniums want to be planted in full sun—but prolonged blazing sunshine can scorch them. Under a cozy blanket of snow, they can withstand Connecticut cold—but they'll shrivel if bared to freezes and thaws and to New England's blustering winds. Moisture? They can't live without it, but God forbid they should stand in water for any length of time. They're susceptible to black spot on the leaves, which generally can be cured by spraying with Captan or Benomyl, and to crown rot, which can be cured only by prayer. And the tall ones will topple at the drop of a hat—literally.

Even visiting the great gardens of the Northeast, or looking at pictures of them, one notices that stands of delphiniums are sparse compared to other late-June and July-blooming perennials. At the handsome Abby Aldrich Rockefeller Garden in Seal Harbor, Maine, for example, pictured in *The American Woman's Garden* (Little Brown, 1984), the famous "cool border" (soft grays, blues, lilacs, pale pinks) has lots of campanulas, early phlox, penstemon and anchusa in bloom in early July, but just a couple of clumps of delphiniums (the state of my own border exactly).

So if they're so much trouble, why bother with delphiniums at all? Because they're glorious, that's why, and when well-grown, truly the queen of the perennial garden. Some varieties—not the spectacular Pacific hybrids, which are never easy—are easier in Connecticut than others, however.

Let's start with the easiest and first to bloom, the little Chinese delphiniums, which have brilliant deep blue flowers as eye-catching and delightful as the color of gentians that surprise you in the fall woods. They're said to get 2 feet high—mine have never made it above a foot-and-a-half, at most—and are touted as "bushy." How bushy? Mine produce three or four nice stalks—no complaints. Each is loaded with intricately spurred blossoms from late June into early July and will keep blooming if spent flowers and stems are cut off.

Treat Chinese dels as biennials, the catalogs say. And I do, partly, letting some of the blossoms go to seed to take sprout for next year, but snipping off the rest. Whether it's the new seedlings or the old plants I can't say for sure, but the end result is that these little Chinese fellows work as regular perennials for me. Plant them in front of the border, where they can be seen. Interspersed with poppies or other round-blossoming plants, the spires provide charming contrast in form. They're especially nice in my lily garden, helping to mask the bare bottom stalks of the lilies and painting a pretty deep blue base for the brightly colored lily blooms. They come in light blue as well, but it's the deep gentian-blue that's the beauty of the family.

Native species delphinium also will grow easily, while many of the hybrids display temperament. Their first spires can reach 5 feet—not as tall as the Pacific hybrids but not short either. They start to bloom beginning of July, and if you cut faded flowers and stems, will bloom most of the summer—but shorter. *Belladonna* is a long-lasting light blue that gets to 5 feet; *bellamosa*, a deep blue that's a bit shorter; and Casablanca is the pure white form of *belladonna* that also reaches 5 feet. If you have a pure white border, or you want a clump of white to serve as a buffer between bright-colored blooms, Casablanca is a cool knockout. It's also an especially vigorous grower.

Some catalogs tell you that these species types are so bushy they will support each other without staking. Don't believe it. A heavy rain will topple that first tall-blooming spire sure as shootin'. Stake 'em.

The earliest hybrids to bloom are the exquisite British strain of Blackmore and Langdon hybrids. One of the hardiest of the tall columnar—as opposed to bushy—delphinium, one can reach 7 feet. Colors are marvelous, from deep to light blue, rich purple to lilac (also white). Most nurseries don't sell them by individual color—you get a mix—but that's all right. They're heavenly together. And for heaven's sake, stake them. Neither all the king's horses nor all the king's men can put a fallen delphinium back together again.

There's a less spectacular but very pleasant hybrid variety that was developed here in Connecticut by the great photographer, Edward Steichen. Called Connecticut Yankee, this del resembles the bushy species more than the columnar hybrids, is quite strongly branched and gets to only about 30 inches in height. Its blossoms make a beautiful blue splash in the border, and the fine foliage is a bonus.

Now on to the gorgeous Pacific Coast hybrids, the famous Round Table Series, which are perhaps the most beautiful dels. Their marvelous spires get to 10 feet and *must be staked* because the flowers are so heavy that the slightest wind—even a heavy dew—can knock them flat. I worry even about the weight of the bumblebees that cleverly probe beneath the two-petaled blossom roof to where honey is stored at the heart of the spur. (In a charming book titled *The Romance of Garden Flowers* printed by the University of Glasgow Press in the late 1940s, author Hilda M. Coley writes, "Only the most intelligent insects can push in past the ripe anthers to do their job of pollinating; and I have actually seen the great but fragile blossom shafts bend from their weight.")

These glorious hybrids come into bloom in July, but again, you can get a shorter growth of flowering spikes, perhaps 3 feet high, in later summer and early fall. (All delphiniums—species and hybrids—need to be fed with organic fertilizer and heavily watered in order to give a second period of bloom.) Colors of the Pacific hybrids are all wonderful, but some are even more wonderful than others. It's the splotch or "bee" at the blossom's center that makes them so striking. My favorite, King Arthur, is a giant, very dark royal-purple with a flashing white bee; Guinevere is light blue with lavender inner petals and a white bee; Black Knight looks solid black but is actually darkest violet with a black bee, Astolat is violet-pink with a black or gold bee. Galahad, which blooms a week later than the others, is, as might be expected, pure white throughout—no bee.

Having recounted the delights of delphiniums, let me tell you the dirty work they entail. First of all, you gotta dig a deep bed for them, at least 2 feet down, get rid of all the subsoil you've dug out and fill the hole with top soil—whew. Now, spread well-ripened manure over the whole bed, 2 inches of the stuff, and dig into the soil. Then add 5-10-5 organic fertilizer over the same place (a half pound for 50 square feet) and dig that in. Then put 2 more inches of humus or well-ripened manure over all and dig that in. Now water it all in *heavily*. Should you use peat moss instead of humus (you can, but it's not as good), water even more heavily to make sure the peat is fully soaked.

These instructions are for starting a new bed. If you're planting in an established border, you needn't dig as deep nor feed as much, but it's better if you do. Delphiniums are greedy. In fact, they should be fed three times between the time the first shoots appear and the time they bloom in late June—once, when you see the first pale green sprouts, later when they're half their final growth, and then again just as the first color shows.

The catalogs don't all say so, but I recommend adding a scant trowelful of lime to the bed in early spring (sweetens the soil so plants will think they're in England). Late April and May are the best time for planting. Most mail-order nurseries offer one-year-old plants, and that's fine. But you'll do better if you can scout around locally for bigger plants, generally in 6-inch pots. The bigger the better to get these babies off to a good start. Avoid mail-order "bare root" plants.

Set the big types 2 to 2½ feet apart; the medium size, a foot-and-a-half apart; the small Chinese types, perhaps just a foot apart. I confess crowding these little ones a bit in order to get a more intense blue showing.

As for staking, all dels need it, even the little Chinese types for which I use branched twigs set between them as leaning posts. For the big dels, three strong stakes 5 to 6 feet high should be set as closely around the crown of the plant as possible without damaging it. For firmness of support, twist twine or coated metal stripping around the stakes, winding it around each stake separately before going on to the next. Those gorgeous blooms you're going to get—*yes, you are*—can now be sure of support to hold up their lovely heads. They deserve it, and after all that work, so do you.

PHLOX

JUNE 1988

The waves and eddies of creeping phlox that swirl through every other Connecticut garden—or so it seems—vividly bring to mind a man who lived more than 200 years ago but whom I feel I know well, John Bartram. America's first botanist, Bartram discovered the species phlox *subulata*, in the wild. In fact, if you ever hear me complaining about the trials and tribulations of being a weekend gardener—of working from sunup to sundown every Saturday and Sunday, of going back to New York with aching back and stiffened hands (not to mention fingernails that won't come clean even after a soaking in bleach)—cut me short. All you have to do is mention the early plant hunters like John Bartram, those horticultural pioneers who lived—and often died—finding and bringing back plants from around the world that we now take for granted in our gardens. That will bring home the blunt truth: The hardest work you and I do—or can envision doing—is a piece of cake compared to their labors.

Bartram was a farmer who lived on the Schuylkill River near Philadelphia. The father of 11, he got into botany to augment his income (after all, he had to feed all those kids) by collecting seeds and sending them by the boxload to England, where they were sold for five guineas *apiece*, maybe a thousand times more than he was paid for them. Totally self-taught, he introduced more than 200 species of American plants to cultivation over 30 years of arduous exploration in the Allegheny and Blue Ridge mountains, in the Catskills, in Georgia and Florida. Most of his discoveries, sadly, were originally credited not to him but to the botanists and horticulturists to whom he sent his findings.

Not a skilled writer, he published only one book—one that his friend, the great Swedish botanist Peter Kalm, said did him more harm than good, because he did not put into it "a thousandth part of the great knowledge" he had acquired. Bartram did, however, pour out his heart and his findings in his letters, and after he died (after repeated bouts of malaria), the letters were made public and won him such acclaim that by now "his every footstep has been traced by assiduous American scholars" (*The Plant Hunters,* by Alice M. Coates, McGraw Hill, 1969).

Although many, many of the seeds and plants Bartram collected have become Connecticut regulars (snakeroot, rhododendron *maximum*, ostrich fern, iris *cristata*, climbing Dutchman's Pipe, *Leucothoe racemosa*, several native lilies and, his most famous tree find, the beautiful *Franklinia alatamaha*, which he named after one of his heroes, Benjamin Franklin), it's phlox *subulata*, otherwise known as creeping phlox, mossy phlox and moss pink, that we're inescapably aware of this season. In fact, with all due respect to the late Mr. Bartram, I could do without much of it—namely, the torrid color combinations of magenta, crimson and purple that surely must make him turn over in his grave.

Used tastefully, however, creeping phlox is wonderful as carpeting or an area rug in the early-summer garden. It also makes a charming tumbled edging for the border, or a spreading runner in the rock garden. Tucked into a cranny of a stone wall, it takes hold easily and spills down prettily. My favorite varieties are a dainty apple-blossom pink, a soft blue that gives a bonus of especially rich green foliage, and a pure white that is so clean and shining, it even makes bright red or magenta look good in contrast. There's also a pretty warm pink and a muted lavender. All will blossom in full sun only, and demand heavy shearing after bloom to keep from becoming a scraggly mat.

We're also indebted to Bartram for another delightful phlox species, phlox *divaricata*. That blooms very early, in April and the beginning of May. I've read that it makes a charming companion to species tulips. Maybe so, but not for me. My species tulips start even earlier—the light red Fritz Kreisler was in bloom March 30 and the multiflowered yellow Tarda by mid-April. They not only beat out phlox *divaricata* but also require full sun, whereas my phlox *divaricata* like light to heavy shade. I wish I could put them together—the lavender-blue of the phlox would make a lovely foil for the tulips. Best I can do at this point is to have them nearby.

Divaricata gets about 15 inches tall, has small broad leaves and masses of airy flowers. It naturalizes easily and will spread into graceful drifts. The leaves virtually disappear a couple of weeks after bloom, so you can plant other things nearby. Ferns are especially nice and in keeping with the natural feeling of *divaricata*. A white *divaricata* form (available at some nurseries) is very pretty, too, but has not been as fast a spreader for me as the blue. In a wildflower garden or a woodland of deciduous trees—or an informal border—*divaricata* is a charmer. Thank you, John Bartram.

Last June at the spectacular Winterthur Gardens in Delaware, I saw a pure pink phlox that looked remarkably like *divaricata* but was taller and had florets twice the size. I found it described in the catalog as "Ozark Phlox (*Phlox pilosa var. ozarkana*)"—propagated by Winterthur Gardens and oh, so beautiful. It's said to be evergreen, to spread by underground stems and thus to make a good ground cover. Delaware is warmer than Danbury, but since this hybrid is supposed to be hardy in zone 5, I'm giving it a try. Full sun and good drainage are required—plus, in Danbury, it will need heavy winter protection, I'd say.

What can I tell you about phlox that you don't already know? That they stand from 20 to 40 inches high, with great panicles of flowers, each a cluster of exquisite individual pips, come in glorious colors, some solid, others with an engaging center "eye" in a contrasting shade, that their decorative foliage ranges from gray-green to emerald, that their fragrance is delicious—in brief, that they are the glory of the midsummer garden. And some brighten the fall garden, too. At least two varieties, World Peace, a pure white, and Fall Days, a warm rose, start to bloom in late August or early September and continue to do so till hard frost.

It's in mid-July that phlox make the biggest splash of color. But some begin blossoming earlier. Starfire, a brilliant red, starts bloom in late June. So does Fairy's Petticoat, a delicate pink with a darker pink eye—altogether an enchantress, even to having an unusually long period of bloom. Other lovelies include Fairest One, a pale salmon-pink variety with a red eye surrounded by a heavenly white halo (rather dwarf for me and handy for the front of the border), Blue Lagoon with giant heads of lavender-blue, also very long-lasting, and Dodo Hanbury Forbes, a veritable marvel with huge flower heads 16 inches across, in clear, singing pink.

For rhythmic effect, I repeat the same colors several times in the border: a group of three pale pink, then, 4 feet along, a group of deeper pink, then 4 feet or so later, a lavender-blue, then a cluster of white, and then the whole shooting match all over again. You're safe alternating colors, for almost all phlox go well together. But you can heighten the overall effect by leaving space between them to set them off.

Now for my very favorite phlox. I know I have many favorites, but this lady really is special. Miss Lingard is her name and she's been around for some 80 years. The species is phlox *carolina* and it blooms earlier than the better-known phlox *decussata* or *paniculata*, all through June and July, and will bloom again if dead-headed, though not as tall the second time around. The giant, loose flower heads are somewhat tubular in shape and shining, luminous white in color. The plants grow into huge clumps—in three years you'll have a 6-foot mass from just three plants. Interspersed with clumps of yellow evening primrose, let's say, or blue delphiniums, it will give you a gorgeous garden picture. And—a welcome trait—Miss Lingard doesn't get mildew as readily as her *paniculata* relations.

"It is a sad moment when the first phlox appears," Vita Sackville-West wrote about phlox *paniculata* in one of her famous columns in the British *Observer*. "It is the amber light indicating the end of the great burst of early summer and suggesting that we must now start looking forward to autumn. . . . The herbaceous phlox will do much to comfort us in the late summer and early autumn months. It does give a sumptuous glowing show, especially if you can plant it in a half-shady bed where its colors will curiously change with the sinking sun and will deepen with twilight into colors you never thought it possessed. . . . I feel sure this is the way to grow phlox: in a cool, north-aspect border, all to themselves, not mixed up with other things in a hot sunny border."

Vita Sackville-West was, of course, the creator of one of the world's greatest and most beautiful gardens— at Sissinghurst in Kent—and a weekly columnist in the *Observer* for 14 years. Her gardening columns were witty and wise, poetic and practical. She never talked down to amateurs—she started as one—so her words are both an inspiration and a comfort to trial-and-error dirt gardeners like thee and me.

Still, I'm not in complete accord with her observations on phlox *paniculata*. These remarks were made in a column she wrote in July, and maybe the light already does bespeak fall in England. But it doesn't happen for me till one of those crisp crystal days in mid-August, when autumn stretches out a chill warning finger. Also, I'm not as sure as she that phlox should *always* be grown alone, although a big clump, by itself, is as striking as a flowering shrub and makes a fine specimen grouping—provided you use three of the same color. But they're also beautiful in the mixed border, superb in combination with coneflowers, *Malva fastigiata*, blue balloon flowers, lilies, even daylilies.

Although I fear taking exception to my revered Sackville-West, I find myself disagreeing on another point. My best phlox bloom comes in full sun, *not* light shade. Your choice, but either way, the single most important planting tip I can give you about phlox is not to crowd them. Plant them a good 2 feet apart to improve both their looks and health. They're far less likely to get mildew if there's good air circulation around them, although a prolonged spell of damp, warm weather is bound to cause mold to coat the leaves a thick, sick gray. No permanent damage—it just looks awful.

I've always dusted with sulfur or sprayed with Benomyl to counteract mildew, but I've just learned that the fungicide, Funginex, is supposed to be a sure cure. It's been around for several years, long enough for that great gardener, Glenn Waruch at Claire's Garden Center in Patterson, N.Y., to recommend it. I've used it for other things—spraying dogwoods, for example—but never as a cure for mildew on phlox. I'll try it on lilac, too, and will report to you.

Other care and feeding tips? Phlox want lots of water but *never from overhead*. Wetting the leaves can cause mildew. Give the earth below a good soaking instead. They also want a rich soil and fertilizer in early spring. I prefer bone meal or an organic plant food. Although it seems paradoxical, you'll get thicker growth by heavily thinning old plants—pinching out even half the new shoots will not be too drastic. Last summer I hadn't the heart to thin Blue Lagoon, a pastel lavender-blue, as I knew I should. It was a knockout, big and fat, until it fell over flat on its lovely heads. The roots simply couldn't support such a heavy load.

So even if you're buying new plants from the nursery to set out this month, don't be afraid to cut out some shoots. Three or four stalks are plenty to grow into a great bushy plant that will stay upright as it should. If you snip dead flower heads, you'll get repeat bloom from side shoots, though not quite so tall as the first. Also, you will keep the plant strong by preventing the formation of seeds, and the small forest of ugly magenta volunteer seedlings that sprout from them and ultimately crowd out the mother plant.

REA LUBAR DUNCAN

POPPIES

JUNE 1989

*A*ccording to Greek mythology, poppies symbolize "eternal sleep and oblivion"—a state not unlike that sought by habitual users of opium, the drug derived from the milky latex of the opium poppy *Papaver somniferum* (which means sleep-inducing). An annual, it bears wide blue-purple or white flowers, with lobed or toothed silver-green leaves. No one knows who first experimented with the plant, but early Assyrian herb lists and medical texts, as translated from cuneiform writings, include both the *Papaver somniferum* and opium. Apparently they didn't know about growing poppies for opium in China until the seventh or eighth century, and opium smoking, a fad that was outlawed by the emperor in 1729, didn't begin until after the discovery of America, where pipe smoking originated.

Nowadays, of course, opium poppies are illegal to cultivate, but you do see them in late-spring gardens, the descendants of a few seeds that came in with a grain shipment 100 years ago. I found instructions for making opium in an old botany book but, honest, fellas, it's not worth the time or effort—or going to jail. Besides, you need a fieldful of flowers to get a pipeful.

So let's stick to ornamental poppies—a clan that includes annuals, biennials and perennials, with my far-and-away favorite, the perennial Oriental poppy (*Papaver orientale*). Although it originated in Mediterranean climes, it is, in fact, one of the loveliest and easiest of perennials for Connecticut gardens, blooming gorgeously—and lavishly—year in, year out, in late May and June. One plant will grow into a clump 2 feet in diameter by the third season, with dozens of cup-shaped blossoms 4 to 6 inches across. The satiny petals partially overlay one another in the singles, and are heavily layered in the doubles. All have a charming black knob at their heart housing stamens and seeds.

A Frenchman, Joseph Pitton de Tournefort, is credited with discovering this exotic beauty in Erzerum, Turkey, in 1701, and successfully introducing it into Europe. "This fine species of poppy is mightily pleased with the king's garden, nay, and with Holland, too, where we have communicated it to our friends," he wrote in his book, *A Voyage Into the Levant*, published in 1718.

I have a soft spot in my heart for de Tournefort—first, because, although he always yearned to be a botanist, he studied for the clergy as his father wanted him to, and waited, like a good son, until after his father died to turn from the church to a career as plant hunter (he became one of the greatest as well as the head of Les Jardins des Roses in Paris); and second, because he wisely chose as compatriots on his very first voyage not only a doctor—those were rough trips full of accidents and illness—but also a young artist to record his finds.

The artist was none other than Claude Aubriet, whose drawings and paintings of plants and flowers can be seen in museums around the world today. They're extraordinary not only for their scientific accuracy but for their beauty and grace. Among Aubriet's loveliest drawings is one of the Oriental poppy de Tournefort found in Turkey, which pictures it in marvelous cloaked bud within its mysterious calyx, and in bloom after the calyx has split open, freeing the jewel of a flower within.

The poppy the Frenchman brought back, *Papaver orientale*, was a separate and distinct form from one found in Siberia in the early 19th century called *Papaver bracteatum*, named for the bracts from which the flowers emerge. The two forms remained quite distinct until about 90 years ago, when the great English nurseryman Amos Perry, of the Hardy Plant Farm at Enfield, began experimenting with combining them and developing colors other than fire-engine red. His first prize-winning flower was Miss Marsh, a scarlet and white, which won an Award of Merit from the Royal Horticultural Society. Then he moved into pinks—thank you, Mr. Perry, I'm a pink addict—and produced Mrs. Perry, an apricot-pink, which is still listed in the catalogs. Then in 1912 he made history with his first all-white flowered variety, Silver Queen, which was soon to abdicate her throne to a seedling raised from a Mrs. Perry by a customer. It was a satin-white with a conspicuous eye. "Mr. Perry went to see the plant, bought it and put it on the market in 1914 as Perry's White." (This bit of history from *How We Got Our Flowers*, Dover Publishing, 1950.) It still ranks as one of the best white-flowered Oriental poppies.

Today, thanks to hybridizers, Oriental poppies come in glorious colors, most of them with knockout contrasting splotches (although my favorite, Helen Elizabeth, is a pure pink). All have a signature central heart of black stamens that makes them a thing apart. The brilliant orange is perhaps best-known and most widely raised. At Giverny, Claude Monet's fabled gardens outside Paris, they light up the plantings with bursts of flame. If you favor hot yellows, orange and scarlet massed together, these fiery blooms are for you.

Although I can't resist one or two of these dazzlers, the subtler colors work best in my border—the pure pink Helen Elizabeth; a deep rose-pink called Curlilocks that has deeply laciniated petals; Maiden's Blush, with white petals banded in pink; Show Girl, a crinkled and ruffled bicolor, white in the center, pink all around; Watermelon, which is—what else?—watermelon-pink; Pinnacle, white shaded from light pink to salmon-orange; and the pristine whites—extra large Marshall von der Glotz and others.

The transformation from bud to bloom is one of the wonders of the late May garden. First comes the long, slim, sheathed bud that gradually fattens to a round shape, still totally enclosed within a calyx but starting to burst at the seams. Then, presto!—the calyx splits in half—and there you have it, lustrously petaled, the Oriental poppy.

These flowers are so showy, they're best spaced out in the border so that each clump enjoys solo stardom. All bloom from the end of May into June. Do visit your local nursery early to see shapes and colors. Most have them planted up in pots. Yes, you can set out the plants in your garden, but please take care. Disturbing the roots just a little can keep them from blooming. I now put the pots in the ground till after they bloom, then set the plants in the earth. The best planting time, however, is late August and early fall. That's when the roots take least offense at being disarranged. Plant them deep—the crowns should go 3 inches below the ground—in good loam and full sun. Feed them with bone meal.

"In Flanders fields the poppies blow/ Among the crosses row on row. . . ." goes John McCrae's haunting poem immortalizing the nameless dead of World War I. These are the little scarlet corn poppies that are our Memorial Day poppies in America and that grow wild through the fields of Europe. Some 10 years ago in May, we drove from Lisbon south to the Algarve in Portugal, and were compelled to stop the car again and again at the crest of a gentle hill to revel in the view of fields below that were solidly blanketed with scarlet poppies.

The cultivated form of these airy annual lovelies is the Shirley poppy, named for the small English village in Surrey where they were bred by the Rev. W. Wilkes from a single plant he found in 1880—a flower whose petals were margined in white instead of being solid red. The good reverend marked the plant and saved the seeds so that the next season he had several hundred seedlings, only a few of which showed any variation. But he persevered, year by year, selecting all desirable seedlings so that in time he developed a strain that comes true from seed.

Today Shirley poppies have not only the loose, informal grace of wildflowers—they do, indeed, seem to "blow"—but also come in a wide range of colors from crimson and orange-scarlet through rose-pink, even smoky blue. Seed of the scarlet Flanders form, with a single black blotch, is still available in a variety appropriately called Lady Bird for our first lady of the wildflowers. I was happy to see that the Rev. Wilkes himself has not been forgotten. In their catalog, Thompson and Morgan in Jackson, N.J., offer "Rev. Wilkes mixed, very lovely semidouble and single poppies, simplicity to grow, colours include picotées, bicolours, pinks, carmine, rose, scarlet and so on." If you plant the Shirleys in early spring when the temperature hits 55, you'll have blossoms from June through summer.

Another annual variety with a wild ancestry, the California poppy, also comes in a wide range of colors and has deeply cut, fernlike foliage in the soft gray-green coloring typical of all poppies. In the bud, petals are exquisitely fluted and swathed to fit into their tiny enveloping calyx so as to emerge uncrushed when the calyx falls away to the ground. Unlike other poppy varieties whose calyx splits in half, the calyx of the Californians gets pushed off in one piece by the growing corolla within. Because it has the shape of a little dunce cap as it lies on the ground, the French have prettily named the breed *bonnet tombant*, falling bonnet.

I've scattered seeds of these in the border in late fall—once, in winter—and had them come up the following spring, and the next. (They reseed when they're happy.) They come in yellow, orange and pink and are particularly pretty among blue flowers.

The Iceland poppy is a charming biennial whose seeds should be sown directly in the border in early summer and moved to where you want them in early fall for bloom the following year. One variety, however, Sparkling Bubbles (also offered in the Thompson and Morgan catalog), will bloom in late summer if you get the seeds in early March. Like the rest of the poppy breed, Icelanders put down long, thonglike roots that don't take easily to transplanting, so I have taken to sowing the seeds in their final destination, eliminating the need for moving them. Although the variety comes from the cold climes of Iceland, northernmost Canada and Siberia, and the poppies are sometimes said to be perennial, they ain't for me. In fact, I treat them like annuals and plant more every summer for bloom the next year.

They're worth the trouble. Dance-y things in the garden, growing 12 to 15 inches high, they have silken-petaled double and single blooms that keep coming for a full three months in lovely shades of pink from pastel to rose, as well as white, flame and red. The poppy's family crest—the black mound at the heart—is hidden within the blossoms in the morning, then shows up dramatically when the sun opens the flowers wide. Petals are often blotched with black in charming helter-skelter fashion. And unlike other poppies, Icelanders do well as cut flowers. Pick them early in the day before blossoms open, and singe the bottoms of the stems with a flame to seal in the juices. It works—well, most of the time.

Nothing's perfect—not even Oriental poppies. The lovely hairy foliage amongst which the flower bouquets appear dies to the ground by July, leaving you with big patches of bare earth (leaving me with *very* big patches because I clump two or three plants together). To hide them, interplant your poppies with perennials that are relatively small in spring and early summer, then get big so that their foliage covers the naked places. Blue or white balloon flower *(platycodon)* or the pincushion flower *(scabiosa)*, also blue or white, will fill in prettily. So will the taller (2 to 3 feet) pink *Malva fastigiata*. You don't want a really rampant grower whose heavy foliage will shade the poppies because they make new growth in August and need sunshine to grow on.

Or set annuals among the poppies, but again choose varieties that don't become huge bushes. Most zinnias and marigolds get too leafy, I think, but snapdragons are nice, and so is eustoma, sometimes called lisianthus, which is the cultivated form of the wild prairie gentian, found originally in Nebraska. It comes in a subtle shade of mauve-pink and a beautiful periwinkle-blue and can be bought potted up at many nurseries ready to set in the ground right now.

REA LUBAR DUNCAN

CLEMATIS
APRIL 1990

*N*ot so long ago, I came across the 1986 catalog of Fisk's Clematis Nursery—one of the world's greatest—"Westleton Nr. Saxmundham, Suffolk 1P173AJ England" (you can't get much more British than that for an address). I've saved it not only for its straight talk about raising clematis and its beautiful photographs, but also for its humor. Here's a notable example from a reprinted article by a noted British gardener, Ted Phillips.

"Suppose, in one of those crash quizzes, someone were to stop me and inquire, 'As a God-fearing gardener and qualified factotum, what do you consider the most spectacular, cussed, fascinating, frustrating, delightful, mutinous, enigmatic and pig-headed garden plant?' I would look my inquisitor straight between the ears and say, 'Clematis!'"

Yes, clematis is all of that, and yet—and yet—I have two of the Sweet Autumn clematis Virgin's Bower (*maximowicziana*, formerly and more pronounceably known as *paniculata*) that have, with little help from me, merrily climbed about 10 feet in two years to drape the trunk of a giant tulip tree in late August and September with thousands—*thousands*—of little white star-shaped flowers with threadlike golden stamens at their heart. My clematis merit only two of Mr. Phillips' adjectives: spectacular and delightful, particularly against the gray-brown tree bark.

They don't cling without support, however (though some varieties do), so what I've done is to spiral green twine around the trunk to give them a leg up. If you decide to do the same, make sure that you affix the twine securely. Growth is heavy and can bring down the whole works. Ditto for a high wind. Just ask me.

Incidentally, I once saw *maximowicziana* let loose on the ground in a Roxbury garden. It had been trained to follow the path of a stream and it was a knockout in bloom, like a trail of stars in the grass. One of these days I'm going to try it on the sunny side of my brook. Since it's a rampant grower, two plants should cover 30 feet or so in a season—if you treat them right.

There are many other small-flowered clematis that Connecticut gardeners too often pass up for the huge blooms of the more flamboyant members of the family. Understandable, but why not both? In fact, why not both together? Clematis is one of the few vines that doesn't strangle a host tree or another vine. I'll suggest combinations as we go along, but first let me tell you of some other enchanting small-flowered types that thrive here and have a long period of spectacular—Mr. Phillips' word again—bloom.

Actually, the flowers of small-flowered clematis are not always so small. Some are $3^1/_2$ inches across. But their most remarkable feature is the enormous number of blooms they produce. Plus the decorative seed heads that follow. Yet another bonus: They almost never contract clematis wilt, a scourge of the large-flowered hybrids. Among the most beautiful small-flowered types is Duchess of Albany, which is generally available at nurseries now, although it is a cultivar of a species that is rather rare in the States, *texensis*. This duchess is a royal beauty with extraordinary blossoms in rich pink, shaped like lily-flowered tulips. She blooms in abundance July through September. A rampant climber, the duchess can put on as much as 9 feet a year. She has a 6-foot spread, so give her room. But get out the ladder. Not a strong clinger, she needs a little support. She's well worth the trouble, however, and will be a show-stopper in your garden.

The duchess' seed heads, incidentally, are not only charming on the vine but also make gleaming holiday decorations. The delicate stamens look as if they were spun of gold. You may have seen them in Christmas wreaths and not known they were part of the Duchess' finery. If you want to try your hand at decorating with them, cut them while they're fresh and spray them with hair spray to keep them shiny, then twist them into bayberry or other evergreen branches for holiday glitter.

Another hybrid family, *viticella*, numbers several other small-flowered clematis that are beautiful by themselves or planted in combination with large-flowered types or other flowering shrubs. Etoile Violette has masses of deep purple velvety-petaled flowers centered with white stamens. Like all dark-flowered clematis, it's striking in combination with lighter plants, such as the big white Marie Boisselet clematis, a bright yellow honeysuckle or a pink or white shrub rose. Its blooming season is long: July through September if kept well fed.

One of the most beautiful *viticella* hybrids, and one of the easiest to grow, is Mme. Julia Correvon, which rises only 6 or 8 feet and is covered from mid-June through September with clear red flowers that start as long slender buds and then open to exquisite, slightly recurved blooms. Stamens are golden. She's perfect for the small garden or for growing in a pot (as are many other clematis), and couples happily with large-flowered blue or white clematis or white roses.

95

For a very different look, another small-flowered species, clematis *tangutica*, is a standout on two counts. First, its graceful buttercup-yellow flowers hang like bells from mid-July through September. Second, the seed heads are magnificent, forming a silken mass of white mop heads. Because of the long blooming season, seed heads and blossoms often come together and are a glory to behold.

Another lovely small-flowered variety comes in white and pink, *Montana alba* and *Montana rubens*. Early bloomers—May and June—they're very vigorous and send out a wealth of new shoots every year. Flowers are star-shaped with yellow stamens. Now that I've learned you can pair clematis with another climber without fear of strangulation, I'm going to plant the white *montana* alongside some pink wisteria plants that have never bloomed for me. Well, that's not quite true. I did get two panicles last spring, but hardly the pink bower I dreamed of. The wisteria have climbed up the posts of our carport and drape themselves gracefully over the roof, so I do have a leafy bower. Maybe with the clematis I'll have flowers, too. And should the wisteria take it into their heads to bloom, the pink-and-white combination should be lovely.

Now for the large-flowered hybrids with blossoms that are sensational not just for size—up to 9 inches across—but for color and shape as well. Rather like eight-pointed stars, the blossoms open flat, with long, pointy sepals (petals) around a center pillow of silky stamens. Just look through the catalogs and you'll be hooked. One of the older and most popular varieties is Nellie Moser, to which I personally give four stars. In a crummy little garden we had at a summer cottage in Brewster, N.Y., Nellie climbed a dead wild cherry tree and lavished us in May and June with pink blossoms, each petal striped darker pink, with a little cushion of yellow-and-brown stamens at center. The catalogs promise repeat bloom in September; we never had any. Nellie will do well in partial shade, while most clematis want lots of sun.

Another very popular variety is the deep purple Jackmanii, which is supposed to bloom June through September but for me gives forth only in June and July. I planted it at the base of a giant ash at our first house in Danbury 12 years ago. My neighbor who lives there now has added more plants and together they've climbed 15 feet up the tree. Although Jackmanii does regally cloak its support in a mantle of purple, I prefer more intense color. You really have to set Jackmanii against a light background for the color to show up. On our old ash, the blossoms virtually disappear against the dark tree trunk. Bluebird, which is a dark, clear blue, shows up better. So does the lavender-blue Mrs. Cholmondeley (Chumley).

So what color large-flowered clematis do you want and when do you want bloom? Niobe is bright red with a tiny cushion of white stamens and is said to blossom June through September. Among varieties with the same period of bloom, Henryii is a gorgeous white with long pointed petals accented by a deep cream midrib stripe and dark stamens; Duchess of Edinburgh is a pure white double highlighted with noticeable yellow stamens, an old variety but still the best white double (gets 10 feet high); Ville de Lyon grows to 12 feet and has charming rounded flowers of orange-red that shade to deep crimson at the edges.

Among the early (May and June) bloomers, Dawn opens a shimmering pearly pink and gradually matures to white. Stamens are purple for contrast and the foliage is special—leaves are heart-shaped, margined in purple. It gets tall, 8 to 12 feet, and is fussy about a moisture-retentive soil. Dr. Ruppel is a spectacular climber with 6-to-8-inch flowers of bright strawberry-pink with a deep carmine central bar on each sepal. A particularly good late bloomer is the very vigorous and free-flowering Lady Betty Balfour in bright violet-blue. This lady insists on full sun and hard pruning.

Which leads us to the whole scary subject of pruning. I confess I almost never prune. I'm afraid to. I simply let the vines climb and after they green up, snip out dead brown wood. Jackmanii, Lady Betty Balfour, Ville de Lyon and other strong growers, however, like to be cut back to within 2 feet of ground level in March before new growth appears. I suggest you peruse the catalogs carefully to find which want to be pruned and which don't. White Flower Farm in Litchfield offers some small-flowered varieties and lots of large-flowered types. Wayside Gardens in Hodges, S.C., offers a remarkable selection of both.

On the care of clematis, I can't resist quoting Mr. Phillips again. "When planting," he writes, "I don't recommend the antics of folk who play music to get them going. You might take in roses or dahlias with such nonsense, but you won't fool clematis. But an alternative is to mention within the plant's hearing that you'll *try* it here. The spot doesn't look too good, but it will just have to lump it and take its chances. You then adopt classic planting procedures. Nice big hole to commiserate with its existing roots, plenty of good compost, touch of bone meal, roots spread out, main stem planted deep, all the time stressing aloud that the thing might possibly hold the fort until you can get your hands on a *decent* climber. This gets it keen. You try it and see. It will shin up its support and start to wave about before you get a chance to tie it in."

A bit more specifically, dig a deep hole a foot-and-a-half square in good, moisture-retentive soil, but not a swamp. Add 6 inches of well-rotted manure or compost. Fill in with enough topsoil to cover the manure. If the plants are dry, soak for an hour in a bucket before planting. Place the root ball well down in the hole so that a few inches of stem are below the soil level. Roots will form on this buried stem and the buds will send up shoots should the stem above ground become damaged (which happened to me when an overzealous helper mowed down the plant). Fill in the rest of the soil, mix in a trowelful of lime and tread down firmly. Keep a supporting cane in place so the plant will have support as it grows.

Clematis want shade for their roots but full sun for strong growth and lots of flowers. To shade the roots, try pebbles around the plant over the soil. (I use gravel from our driveway.) Summer and winter mulch is helpful provided it doesn't mat and prevent drainage. (No peat moss, please.) A good way to keep roots moist is to sink a pot with a hole in its bottom in front of the plant. Fill it with water two or three times a week, if possible. This is also a good way to apply liquid fertilizer.

Clematis are heavy feeders. Work in two or three handfuls of bone meal every autumn, and give a good soaking with a liquid fertilizer once a week, spring through summer. Sure, clematis will bloom without all this bother, but flowers will get smaller every year.

As for training, clematis can be grown on walls, fences, trellises, over trees and shrubs, even on the ground as bedding plants. They climb by twining their leafstalks around whatever support is handy, like tendrils on pea vines. Some are clingier than others. In all cases, plastic-coated wire gives the best support (uncoated wire would burn the stalks). If you plant next to trees, keep a safe distance from the trunk so as not to interfere with roots, and plant on the north side so plants will reach toward the light.

I'm going to try some this summer in tubs against the railing of my deck, supported with a wire frame. Pots must be 18 inches deep with a hole in the bottom. Roots need to be shaded with gravel, and I'll have to be extra generous with liquid fertilizer and water. Pots dry out fast.

If your plant is in full bud and suddenly, heartbreakingly, collapses, this is probably the notorious clematis wilt at work. All is not lost, however. The roots are likely to still be healthy, so cut the plant to ground level, burn the sick parts, and feed the roots once a week with liquid fertilizer. Fisk's recommends spraying with a fungicide in spring and fall and several times during the summer, drenching the bottom 2 to 3 feet of the plant.

So is clematis worth the trouble? To quote Mr. Phillips yet again, "Ah, yes. She is indeed the Queen of Climbers."

DAYLILIES
MAY 1990

*B*ack in 1985, in a CONNECTICUT column on cultivating wildflowers for the home garden, I recommended cutting—with a scissors, not tearing—bouquets of the prolific orange daylilies that brighten the highways and byways of New England in late June and July. Well! Some anonymous person wrote a letter to the magazine that opened, "For Shame!" and went on to vilify me for desecrating the landscape; the irate reader ended by threatening to shoot me if I appeared on his—or her—property. (Since no name was given—for shame!—the sex of the writer was shrouded in mystery.)

The incident has rankled ever since, because cutting flowers actually helps daylily plants to grow. I'm not advising shearing the plant. Some green stems must be left to fade off so chlorophyll will be ingested. But c'mon. With the thousands upon thousands of daylilies that bloom wild everywhere in Connecticut—especially in vacant lots and garbage dumps, which are where I find the best pickings—murder seems a rather harsh punishment for picking a couple of bouquets. At personal peril, I'm going to risk it again.

These lovely daylilies of the roadsides (*Hemerocallis fulva*)—in both single and double forms—are all descendants of a common Oriental ancestor, probably Japanese, which has made itself totally at home in the Occident, and especially so in the temperate United States. They're so prolific that one otherwise buttoned-down gardening tome describes them as having "gone wild." Good. Like the seasons of lilacs, daffodils and peonies, the season of daylilies is one of the wonders of living in the Northeast, all the more precious because it is not year-round. (Oh, how I'd miss the change of seasons if I had to live where it's warm all the time.)

The wild orange *(fulva)* daylily's double form, beautifully frilled and ruffled, is not as common as the single variety. But I'm blessed with some, pondside, which I am carefully propagating.

Another wild daylily, *flava*, with delicate lemon-yellow blossoms (ergo its common name, lemon lily), is no longer prevalent. (Note to my would-be murderer: I *never* pick those.) I remember seeing lots of them some 35 years ago—we ourselves had several clumps lakeside in Brewster, N.Y.—but they seem to have disappeared. Well, the good news is that White Flower Farm in Litchfield is offering them. Needless to say, I've ordered some. They bloom early and lavishly—in late May, which is about a month before any of the other varieties do.

The word *Hemerocallis* is from the Greek, *hemera* meaning day and *kallos*, beauty, referring to the large blossoms, each of which is beautiful for a day, then fades. But the blossoms come in such profusion, 20 or 30 a day on one plant, with new buds opening over a six-week period, that bloom seems to be constant. Even when the lilies are cut, buds open every morning so that you have a long-lasting bouquet. Just pick off spent flowers for tidiness.

In some parts of the world, daylilies are valued for more than their beauty. In China some daylily buds are eaten raw (golden cabbage), dried and powdered (gum tsoy), and in England leaves have been used for cattle fodder. I once tried drying spent flowers and frying them in butter. Forget it. For my money, daylilies are better in the garden than on the menu, especially since they may well be the easiest of all perennials to grow, and give the most return in beauty for the least amount of work.

Daylilies don't have the long recorded history of some of our flowers. (Poppies, lilies and daffodils were written about even in ancient days.) Although they were introduced to England from Asia and central Europe in the 16th century, it was not until the 19th century that hybridization was attempted. The pioneer was George Yeld, an English schoolteacher and amateur gardener who began his work in 1877 and continued for almost half a century. His first publicized hybrid, which he named Apricot, was recorded in 1892. Then the famous plantsman, Amos Perry of England, and others in Italy, France, Holland and Germany, took up the work.

In the United States, which is far and away the leader in hybridization, the first recorded hybrid, Florham by name, was raised in New Jersey in 1899 by one Arthur Herrington. Since then, American breeders have introduced literally thousands of new varieties—and the end is nowhere in sight. (Just look at the spring catalogs if you don't believe me.) In 1921, the distinguished geneticist and plant breeder, Dr. A.B. Stout, began assembling at the New York Botanical Gardens in the Bronx all the daylily varieties he could find from around the world. For 30 years he kept on breeding and promoting daylilies, laying the groundwork for today's hybridizers and for the glorious diversity of colors, shapes and sizes that now grace our gardens.

Among the newest daylily innovations are the tetraploids (four chromosomes instead of two, as in diploids), some of which are giant-size and exquisite, others merely giant-size. Work on tetraploids started in the late '40s, but it wasn't till the '60s that the greatest strides were made. More than 80 tetraploid varieties already have been registered with the American Hemerocallis Society, which itself was founded only in 1946. The new tetraploids are generally pricey—$17 and $18 a plant, or more. But do evaluate them carefully and don't mistake new for better. Hyperion, which was introduced in 1925, still ranks among the best yellows—prolific, long-lived, fragrant—and remains the standard by which new yellows are judged.

Although the best planting times are spring and fall, daylilies can be planted *anytime* except in the dead of winter. If you spot a hole in your July border that cries out for greenery and flowers, plant—or transplant—a daylily. If it's a scorcher of a day, be kind and give it plenty of water, maybe even a newspaper parasol. But you don't have to worry about established plants. They can cope even with prolonged drought. Feed your plants generously in early spring for fast growth and plentiful flowers—bone meal or other organic fertilizers, or low-nitrogen chemical fertilizer (5-10-10) is fine. (Too much nitrogen is said to muddy the reds and weaken the leaves.) Just dig the fertilizer in under the leaves around the plant, and water it in. A small plant with three or four rhizomes will be a big one in one season. In three years, plants grouped together will form a clump dense enough to keep out weeds. And daylilies are easy to divide. Early spring or fall is best. Just make sure to take husky divisions with good roots so you have a decent-sized new plant.

After the lemon lilies in May, you can have daylilies in constant bloom from late June through late September. You can stagger them in height from 12 inches to 7 feet, and in size of blossom from 2 to 6 inches—maybe even bigger. As for color, ah! From creamy yellow (hybridizers are still striving for pure white) to burnished gold, pale peach to flame, shell-pink to deep burgundy, muted terra-cotta to fiery brick, mauve to rich purple, even some near pure reds. Additionally, there are knock-your-socks-off bicolors in bold color contrasts, and in delicate pastel blends. Petals often appear to be dusted with diamonds. Some blossoms have exquisite green hearts. Even the shapes vary. Although the classic daylily form is funnel- to bell-shaped, blossoms today come frilled, ruffled, crimped, curved, recurved, and even lacy.

Moving from the front of the border to the rear, I'm going to start with some of my favorite dwarfs and other low-growing varieties and then build up to the tall types. A true dwarf, Eenie Weenie is only 12 inches high when in bloom, a lovely light yellow with petals that curve back slightly. It blooms early to midsummer, its flowers last well into the evening, and it thrives in hot, dry places. If you're creating a whole bed of daylilies, this is the ideal plant for the front edging. And, of course, it works up front in a mixed border, too.

The most popular daylily in the world today, and deservedly so, is Stella de Oro, which is not a true dwarf but reaches only 15 to 20 inches in bloom. What makes it such a winner? Well, it starts blooming mid-June and continues flowering into midsummer, which, according to White Flower Farm, makes it the all-time blooming champion among daylilies. Blossoms are a rich golden yellow with petals crimped around the edges. In brief, it's a charmer.

I had an unhappy experience with it, not because of the plant but because of the purveyor, but it has had a happy ending. I bought three plants by mail order—they were costly—last spring from a nursery that shall remain nameless, and was sent two puny plants with a couple of threads for roots. I never thought they'd live, let alone blossom, but my stars, they did both. Only one or two flowers, of course, but by fall they'd fattened up, and this year they should be better.

Three other low-growers—Little Much, a ruffled lemon-yellow, Bonanza, a yellow-and-bronze bicolor, and Small Ways, a lemon-yellow brushed peach—get to about 20 to 24 inches, which is short for daylilies. (Most rise from 28 to 40 inches.) The first two start to blossom in July, the last from Aug. 1 to Sept. 1, so they're nice for continuing bloom from the front to the middle of the border.

So many exquisite daylilies bloom from July on, it's terribly—no, wonderfully—hard to pick and choose. Do look through the catalogs. White Flower Farm, Wayside Gardens in Hodges, S.C., and Van Bourgondien in Babylon, N.Y., are among the mail-order houses that offer extensive collections. Better still, check your local nurseries and see what you like. Try, *try* to get to the New York Botanical Gardens in July. Dr. Stout's collection has been marvelously augmented and the spectacle is dazzling.

The varieties listed below are mostly my personal favorites, tried and true in my garden or those of a gardener friend. Sure, there are a few I haven't tried—they're beyond my budget—but we can dream, can't we? Blooming dates generally are from mid-July into late August. If a variety differs in timing, I'll mention it. Starting with cream-to-yellow tones, that old standby, Hyperion, has very large canary-yellow flowers and is still one of the best summer performers. Ten years ago, I circled a large outcropping of boulders with it. The foliage today has grown into dense green fountains and the plants have provided many subdivisions for transplants and gifts for neighbors. A very light yellow, Lexington, is heavily ruffled and wonderfully fragrant. Winning Ways is an unusually large flower shaded green to yellow. The ruffled blooms open wide and flat and last into the evening.

There are many more charming yellows, some chartreuse-tinted, others rich as butter, others creamy pale. Try mixing several yellows. Although new colors come and go, an all-yellow daylily garden ranging from pale to bright is still an enchantment, particularly when set near deep green trees and shrubbery.

Among the best gold and orange-blooming varieties, Heirloom Lace has very large, frilled blossoms in deep gold with a soft green throat. Flowers stay open in the evenings. Repeat bloom comes in September—a nice bonus. Also deep gold, Evergold blooms from the end of July into the first week of September, with large, ruffled flowers that come in profusion. With 40-inch flower scapes (stems and flowers), it is a very strong grower, and will spread handsomely into a tall ground cover. Mary Hamilton, a tetraploid, has huge 6-inch blossoms in a painterly blend of pale cream, apricot and several yellows. It's exquisite.

Outstanding pinks, peach-pinks and orchid-pinks include the tetraploid Tree Swallow, with 6$\frac{1}{2}$-inch flowers of orchid-pink suffused with tan. Midribs are soft cream and petals are veined in deeper orchid-pink. This is one of the famous Song and Garden Bird series developed by the noted hybridizer, Dr. Robert Grieshbach. Another tetraploid, Chicago Petticoats, created by the late great hybridizer James Marsh, is a beautifully formed, ruffled peach flower with rose colors splashed on the fringes. A lovely blush-pink that's *not* a tetraploid, Catherine Woodbury has crinkled 5$\frac{1}{2}$-inch flowers with a yellow-green throat.

Among the socko bright reds, the tetraploid Ruby Throat is a standout. Its 6-inch blooms are highlighted with a green throat. Another red, which James Marsh considered his finest breeding achievement—it's named for him—is bright scarlet. Its petals are like shimmering satin-finished crepe, and it's expensive.

I've saved for last the *altissima* strain of daylilies because they are not only the tallest, but also the very last to bloom. Scapes grow to 6 feet, yet are graceful and sturdy. In my border, the Autumn Minaret, with 4-inch golden flowers lightly dusted with bronze, starts to bloom in August and keeps on going into *October*. I have a group of them massed behind lower-growing daylilies, and what a splendid backdrop they make. Be patient, though. It takes a year until they reach full height.

As landscaping material, daylilies can be used in many, many ways. They make a fine grouping in a perennial border, serve strikingly as accent points when clustered together, hold banks in place when planted close together, face down trees, soften foundation plantings, edge pathways, ribbon a stream, mark off lawns and more. In my opinion, they're best massed together in groups of a *single color family*. Not for me the mixed-color collections the catalogs try to sell. I find each color story too special for that. A friend planted a thousand of the wild orange *fulva* along a quarter mile of river bank in Roxbury. (She advertised for them in the local paper and a farmer brought her a fieldful.) What a show all that orange makes! Another friend, in Armonk, N.Y., beautified a lumpy, bumpy meadow with varied shades of yellow daylilies. The plants totally mask the uneven earth and dazzle with their yellow blooms. In Danbury I've circled daylilies—by color—around big rocks, each tumble of granite softened and brightened by one surrounding color, one in peach tones, one in orange, another in yellows, yet another bright golds.

I've also used daylilies in a giant circle so that they solidly ring a thick-trunked tulip tree. The circle is big enough for me to have used several colors, but always with groupings of at least three plants of the same kind. The circle shades from yellow to pink to gold, and back to yellow again with those tall *altissimas*.

There's one more daylily I yearn for—but not till the price comes down—a diploid called Prairie Blue Eyes. Its flowers are pure lavender-blue highlighted by a clear yellow throat. Ah, someday.

HEATHS AND HEATHERS

MAY 1991

*I*t was in black and white, of course, but in my mind's eye it's glorious Technicolor, forever soft blue-purple—the heather-covered moor, that is, in *Wuthering Heights*, where Cathy and Heathcliff played as children, then loved and lost as grown-ups. Driving from the West Highlands to Glasgow last August, I saw the real thing, the great Rannoch moor—famed not only as the trysting place in *Wuthering Heights* but as the hideout in Robert Louis Stevenson's *Kidnapped*—with its textured coverlet of rich blue-purple heather stretching for miles and softening the barren land.

In ancient Greek times, heathers and heaths were one botanical family, *ericaceae* from the Greek *ereike*, but because there were so many species in cultivation, they were divided into *ericas* (heaths) and *callunas* (heathers) in 1802. Out of necessity, they have been used for thousands of years by highland and moorland dwellers for building material, brooms, beds, and even drinks. (There was a famous brew of heather ale but the recipe was lost about the time of the Picts, back in the ninth century.)

They also have been grown as fodder for sheep, deer and grouse. Talk about male chauvinism—*calluna*, which was considered far superior as food, was known as "he-heath," and the inferior *ericas* as "she-heath." Both, however, were considered so important to agriculture that there have been laws governing their burning since 1401.

In England, early botanists recorded a white *Calluna vulgaris*, still a beauty in the garden, in 1597, and by the 1800s growing heaths and heathers was the "in" thing in the mother country, where they were used in edgings, formal beds, pot plants and greenhouses. Then they fell out of favor, but since World War II they've been on the upswing again.

Why? Why not? Some 50 varieties of each, suitable for growing in the Northeast, are on the market today. They will bloom in Connecticut from early spring to late fall. (In the south of England, where the Gulf Stream gentles the winter, they bloom through the year.) Colors of blossoms are wondrously varied—not only the best-known purply-blue heather that dries into lasting bouquets, but lovely whites and shades of orange, pink and red. Foliage has an even wider range of colors; thus, even when plants are out of bloom, they put on an eye-catching show. Additionally, heights range from ground-huggers to 4-footers, so they work for many landscape purposes. And forms range from vase-shaped spreading spires to slim columns and globular mounds. Some are even fragrant. And they're evergreen.

Plainly, you can build a garden of many colors and contours just out of heaths and heathers. In fact, I did. When we built our first house in Danbury, back in '73, we had a steep slope from deck to lawn, some 15 feet high and 20 feet wide, which I planted entirely with them—the tall guys at the back, the low-down types up front. This was "builder's land," as I call it, so we gave it the full treatment, putting in top soil, peat, sand and leaf mold to make it friable. To add a bit of drama and dimensional interest, we placed rocks of different sizes and shapes here and there—sometimes a big boulder singly, in other spots a cluster of smaller ones. Then I planted about 100 heaths and heathers ordered from a nursery specializing in them. (Sadly, it's since gone out of business.)

The plants were thumb-size when I set them in—I have an old snapshot that shows large expanses of brown earth in between—but they grew beautifully even the first year, so that very soon they looked a proper rock garden.

For three or four more years, they were glorious, the whole garden a showpiece. And then, disaster. Came a winter when temperatures dropped to 20 below zero and they all died or were so stricken they weren't worth saving. Except one—*erica* Springwood Pink, which survived and bloomed and flourishes still for my neighbor, who now lives in that house. It's a charming ground cover that gets 6 to 12 inches high, spreads fast and has masses of clear rose-pink flowers in early spring. (The catalogs say it will bloom in January and February if we have mild weather; for me, though, it's never bloomed till March, and generally blooms mid-April through early May.) Its charming little flowers are tubular with mauve-y pink tips rather like miniature bottle stoppers. Foliage, typically of heaths and heathers, is short and narrow, not unlike hemlock needles. There's an equally hardy white form, Springwood White, on which the mauve tips make a pretty pastel contrast.

I've learned two cents' worth about gardening in the years since then, and think I might have avoided that bitter disaster had I done two things: first, renewed every year the 2-inch mulch around the plants (I use pine needles, of which I have a God-given supply, but wood chips, ground bark or other organic materials are suitable); and second, blanketed the whole planting with evergreen boughs, not only to catch the snow but to give protection against icy winds. White Flower Farm in Litchfield also lost most of its heather plantings that fierce winter and advises the use of an evergreen bough cover, no matter how well the location is protected from unseasonable cold and spring winds. It's worth the trouble.

Before I suggest different varieties, let me state a few tips on heath-and-heather care. Believe me, they know what they like and what they don't. Most of them don't like an alkaline soil. (A few will tolerate it and one or two thrive on it, but don't take a chance.) Make them an acid home. That's generally not a problem here in Connecticut—our soil tends to be acid—but if you have any doubt, buy one of those inexpensive kits that test for pH or send a soil sample to your local extension service. In any case, work a lot of peat into the earth. If you plant near a concrete foundation wall or in between paving blocks that may have some limy cement around them, put in even more peat, and keep adding it every year.

The best planting time is spring so roots can grow strong over summer and fall. They like a moist but not soggy soil. Good drainage, please. If water tends to stand around where you've planted them, add some sand. And give them full sunshine. They'll get sparse and meager in the shade and ultimately fade away. With sun, they'll produce gorgeous growth and bloom. Fertilize in early spring with Holly-tone, cottonseed meal or other food for acid-loving plants.

When you prune, which you will because they get a bit scraggly and out of shape, do it in early spring when you can clip off winter-killed branches and do a bit of sculpturing. Don't prune in the fall or even after plants bloom in later spring and summer. It tends to make them more vulnerable to winter damage.

Now for the good things. Last summer at the great Gleneagles Hotel in eastern Scotland, where the gardens generally are very formal and much too manicured for this lassie's taste, they had several plantings of just heaths and heathers that were lovely indeed. These were large beds, some 20 feet long and 10 feet deep, on gentle slopes alongside the roadways. Only the white varieties were in bloom when we saw them, but the whole was a mass of color from the foliage—soft yellow, bright gold, pink-tipped deep green, silvered green, flame.

It's easy to achieve a similar effect in the home garden. Just pick your varieties for the color scheme you want. I suggest a visit to White Flower Farm, or your local nursery if they're into heaths and heathers. In fact,

I'd advise several visits from spring to fall to choose those that serve your needs and taste. But here are a few personal suggestions for foliage color. The heather Gold Haze, which is 24 inches high and has luminous golden foliage, could bring up the rear in a planting (its plentiful white flowers come in August and September). In front of it might be J.H. Hamilton—a bit shorter variety with rich, deep-green foliage—a strong spreader with masses of dainty double deep pink blossoms that blooms at the same time as Gold Haze. About the same height, Martha Herman has brilliant green foliage that makes an arresting accent point, and white flowers that start in July and go through to September. Another tall variety (about 18 inches), Robert Chapman, has extraordinary foliage that changes from gold to flame to red and stays brilliant through winter. Soft purple flowers come in August and September.

The hairy, gray-green foliage of the heath Mollis—about 15 inches high—can serve to set off the brighter-colored fellows if used in clumps. Ditto Silver Queen, with woolly silver foliage and deep pink flowers in August and September. As a low edging, only 6 to 9 inches high, try Vivelli, which blankets itself in spring with carmine-red flowers followed by deep red foliage that lasts through winter. A lot of people think this is the finest dwarf heath around today.

For gleam and glitter, plant the Irish or Connemara heath *(Cantabrica alba),* which gets to 12 to 18 inches high, and whose shiny leaves are a knockout in the sunshine. But be careful. It's not as hardy as others of the breed, so you might plant it in the protective cover of small evergreens. Wherever you put it, mulch it well and cover it with evergreen boughs. It merits all this fussing for its white oversize lily-of-the-valleylike flowers that start in June and keep coming. It *detests* lime, so take no chances. Add peat, rusty nails or other acidic stuff to the soil.

Although I've emphasized foliage color, all the above have lovely flowers that, as you see, go right through spring to fall. For exceptional blossoms, however, the heath Pink Spangles puts on a splashy show of pink from very early spring (the catalogs say February, but you can't prove it by me) through April. Only 9 to 12 inches high, it's perfect for an up-front edging. C.D. Eason, about 12 inches high, has vibrant crimson flowers all summer long starting in July—and it's fragrant. The heather Kinlochruel, not over 15 inches high, has unusual, fully double pure white flowers in August and September.

Heaths and heathers are overlooked as evergreen shrubs, yet some of them are striking enough to stand alone as handsome specimens and many could be added to a mixed evergreen shrub planting. In his beautiful book *Creative Gardens* (Hamlyn Press, 1986), David Stevens pictures a glorious conifer garden with drifts of heaths set among gray "cobbles" (stones) interspersed with taller evergreens. I like the heath Tib, which grows to 24 inches and has long spikes that flare into a vase shape and are covered with rose-colored flowers from July through September. By itself, or for contrast in the company of rhododendron and azaleas, it's a dilly. The Cornish heath *(Multiflora grandiflora)* also makes a fine specimen shrub—a big one, too. It grows to 24 inches in height, but spreads wide. Flowers are large, pink and plentiful. (It's another lime-hater, so do your acid stuff.)

I've used a few heaths and heathers in the perennial border for different shapes, and also to give me bloom when other flowers are sparse. There's that couple of weeks between the daffodils and the early iris, when the low-growing, spreading heaths Springwood Pink and Springwood White are still showing pink and white for me in small clumps at the front of the border. Then, before the summer-blooming perennials really get going in late June and early July, the Spike Heath, *spiculifolia* (not really a true heath, but a close relation), makes a pretty low shrub covered with pink flower clusters. And in October and November, Mollis and *Cantabrica alba* stretch the garden season with their white lovelies.

Legend has it that there's a lucky white heather which originated in Scotland that Queen Victoria herself brought from Balmoral Castle south to England. Nice thing is that you don't have to be the finder to get the good luck. It will work its magic on you just by being around. Some nurseries in Britain have it for sale for the "luck market." The experts claim what they're selling is not even true heather, but one of the tree heaths. No matter. Put one in your garden for luck—and beauty.

REA LUBAR DUNCAN

RHODODENDRON
AND AZALEAS
MAY 1992

$\mathcal{H}$ere in the Northeast, the most widely used azaleas and rhodies produce their flower fireworks in late May and June. And I certainly wouldn't be without 'em. But why not enjoy blossoms from other species of these shrubs beginning in April—sometimes even late March—through late August? It must be because the early and late bloomers, particularly the latter, aren't well enough known. I can't imagine any other reason for not planting them. They're as easy to grow as others of their breed, they provide the blossom variety we all strive for in the garden, and they're extraordinarily beautiful.

So here's a five-month calendar (six, if you count March), listing a sampling of varieties and telling when

105

they bloom and what they're like. I'm including only *deciduous* azaleas and rhodies, not the well-known broad-leaved evergreen dazzlers with their gorgeous, gargantuan blooms. These deciduous types have a very different kind of charm. Their slender branches and narrower leaves create a graceful, airy form in and out of bloom, their masses of blossom clusters have a delightful delicacy, many are deliciously fragrant, and most are hardier than their evergreen cousins. In the foundation planting in front of our house, I've combined both types, broad-leaved evergreens and the deciduous form. They don't compete—they complement each other.

THE EARLIEST

If you have a rhododendron *mucronulatum,* it's already in bloom, a pink-to-lilac wonder on the gray landscape. In Danbury it came into bloom mid-April. But just a little south, it blossoms earlier. I saw it with my own eyes in Greenwich the last week in March.

For years I knew *mucronulatum* only in its lavender-petaled form, but Carlson's Gardens, the great azalea and rhododendron specialists in South Salem, N.Y., have developed from seed some enchanting pinks. One group, identified simply as Pinks, are just that—a range of lovely, bright pink shades. A very special clone, at least to this pink freak, is a lingerie-pink called, appropriately, Pink Peignoir, which blooms very early, at the beginning of April. An outstanding variation on the lavender of the species is Panzi, with a darker pansylike blotch on the upper petal. Most *mucronulatums* grow slowly (20 years from seed) to 6 or 8 feet, but a dwarf form, called Nana, gets to only 2 feet in height. Clear purple, it would be nice in front of a taller pink or lavender cousin. And there's a very tall variety called Cornell Pink that grows to 12 feet—but in 20 years.

Rhododendron *dauricum* is another species that blooms in April, maybe even a bit earlier than *mucronulatum.* It's smaller and more compact than *mucronulatum,* and leafier, too. The species has lavender blooms, but a variety called Madison Snow has creamy white buds and opens pure white. And a new gentleman, called Adam, is lavender; he is, as his name suggests, the first of all to bloom. His companion, who blooms just a day or so later, is—you guessed it—Eve. She's pristine white.

Both *dauricums* and *mucronulatums* set buds in the summer. Sometimes a late spring frost or a snowfall will make you worry that buds were nipped and you won't have bloom—not so. Just be patient. Many of the buds will open later in the season. Eve, for example, keeps blooming through September, with a lot of flowers. Another bonus from these varieties is that they can be cut and forced, like forsythia. (Put them in warm water and give them a warm-water spritz once a week.) The bouquets are beautiful, especially if you mix colors. They all go together harmoniously.

EARLY MAY

Most azalea petites don't begin to bloom till late May, but one of these low-growing charmers blossoms very early in May, several weeks before any others. Called *kiusianum,* it's a delight for the rock garden or the front of the border. A clump or two in amongst late-blooming daffodils or early tulips makes a charming spring composition. A small, dense plant, *kiusianum* grows to only about 10 inches, with clusters of purple or white flowers. The white species is particularly distinctive, maturing into artful, rather Oriental-looking plants—not unlike bonsai.

A tall species for early May is the native azalea, *vaseyi,* with the common name Pinkshell azalea. Its showy, soft pink flowers have curling stamens that seem to dance in the breeze. Although it hails from western North Carolina, it's hardy to minus 15 degrees, grows 6 to 8 feet tall, and has brilliant crimson fall foliage. A white clone called White Find has clear white blossoms. One of each, pink and white, makes a handsome pair.

One of my best beloveds, the Royal azalea *(schlippenbachi),* one of the finest in the deciduous kingdom, comes into bloom now. A native of Korea, it is one of the earliest of the large-flowered deciduous species. Its exquisite, open-faced, soft pink flowers have charming brown dots in the throat, and seem to float on the bush as if a cloud of pink moths had alighted on its branches. I have three bushes spaced out along the bank of my brook. I wish I had 10.

A beautiful yellow in early May is Yellow Pom Pom, with vivid double flowers in tight round trusses that are delicately fragrant. Early-blooming for the breed, this is one of the famed Knaphill-Exbury azaleas, many of which grow to 8 feet in height. This one stays somewhat shorter and has a compact shape.

MID-MAY

Can't imagine why more native azaleas aren't used in Connecticut gardens. They have such an appealing natural look—and beautiful blossoms to boot. Azalea *nudiflorum,* the Pinxterbloom azalea, for example, which grows wild in the Eastern United States, is sweetly fragrant and bears white-to-pale-pink tubular flowers with long, showy stamens that come in tight clusters. Azalea *roseum,* the Roseshell azalea, also a native of the Eastern United States, has pale-pink-to-light-crimson flowers. Plant one near your deck or terrace or by an open window. Its intense clove fragrance, rather like that of carnations, will perfume house and garden.

A clone of *roseum* developed by the famous hybridizer, Lud Hoffman, pleased him so much he named it for his wife, Marie Hoffman. It has much larger flowers than the species, in a clear true pink. It's also extremely fragrant and very hardy.

Another native, *calendulaceum,* the Flame azalea, generally starts blooming in late May. But again, Carlson's Gardens has developed an earlier-blooming form called Coral Flameboyant with striking large flowers in bright shades of coral that bloom mid-May—'swonderful in the garden.

LATE MAY

Now's the time for more knockout native azaleas, among them the *atlanticum* family, including the Coast azalea of the Eastern U.S. coastal plain, which blooms well into June. A low grower, to only 3 or 4 feet, it has white blossoms flushed with pink set among lovely gray-green foliage. Fragrance? Strong, spicy and delicious.

The Choptank River azaleas, also of the *atlanticum* clan, bloom now, too, with flowers a stronger pink than the Coast azaleas. A particularly beautiful clone, Choptank River Belle, has pink buds that open to very fragrant white flowers flushed with pink—and exquisite, twisty pink stamens.

Now, too, come the rest of the Flame azaleas in a remarkable color range—bright yellow, clear orange, burnt-orange, flame-red. They all last well into June.

A glorious Knaphill-Exbury that blooms now is Sylphides, which Bob Carlson calls "voluptuous." It is. Pale pink and white with a touch of yellow at the throat—and sensually perfumed—it has definite sex appeal. Another extraordinary Exbury is Toucan, which is very tall, with yellow-blotched pale cream flowers and a heady fragrance.

I'm a fan of the low-growing azalea petites, many of which start to blossom now. As an edging for my foundation planting, they provide low mounds of color that complement the taller flowering shrubs behind. Gunrei is one of the loveliest, with ruffled, frilled, showy white flowers, pink-flaked and pink-edged. Kaempo, another little one with big pink flowers, will grow upward to only 2 feet but spread outward to 5 feet.

JUNE INTO JULY

With so many to choose from, where to start? Why, with the natives that were here *at* the start, of course. My favorite from the wilds is *arborescens,* the Sweet azalea, which perfumes the surrounding air with its heavenly aroma and covers itself with good-sized white blossoms from late June well into July. *Viscosum,* the Swamp azalea, lasts even longer. Its white flowers are a bit smaller than those of the Sweet azalea, but there are so many of them it hardly matters. And oh, that rich clove scent! There's also a fragrant pink clone of this species for pink addicts like me. Both species grow to 6 to 8 feet.

Among the ground-huggers, Flat Out, a vigorous spreader, gives out with big white blossoms from late June well into July. Gumpo White is very low and dense with large single white flowers; Gumpo Pink is rose-pink fingerprinted with deeper pink.

Of medium height—growing to 4 feet—are some of the splashiest deciduous azaleas in colors not generally available in the evergreen varieties. Parade, which will bloom much of July, has dark pink flowers with orange eyes and a sweet fragrance. Lollipop has fragrant pink flowers brightened with a light pink-and-yellow flare. Pink Rocket has red buds that open to pink with a delicate fragrance. They're all showstoppers.

Starting again with American natives, there's Hot Ginger and Dynamite, a large-flowered clone of *arborescens,* which, unexpectedly, is delicately colored, white with threadlike pink stamens, but takes its name from its potent scent. The Cumberland azalea *(bakeri)* has vibrant orange and red blossoms. Its horizontal branches give it a pleasingly distinctive shape. This variety is especially shade-tolerant. So is the Plum-leaf azalea *(prunifolium),* which will bloom a month or more—till late August—if planted in the partial shade of a woodland garden or given a bit of protection from hot afternoon sun. Flowers are primarily reds and orange-reds, with occasional pinks, yellows and paler oranges.

Azaleas and rhodies have very definite ideas about the kind of home and living conditions they prefer, but these are easy to satisfy. First and foremost, they like an acid soil that's nice and loose so roots can spread out. No hard clay, no alkali. I suggest a planting medium that's half peat, half friable soil. Feed with half a trowelful of cottonseed meal or Holly-tone when you set out the plant, and every spring thereafter. With established plants, be careful when you scratch in the fertilizer so you don't break the slender surface roots. Half-day sun is best, either morning or afternoon, but most deciduous rhodies and azaleas will tolerate full sun providing the soil doesn't get baked solid.

For heavy bloom next year, pick off all dead blossoms immediately after bloom so as not to damage new growth. Ditto any pruning that needs to be done. Watch out when you snip and shape that you don't cut off buds where you want new growth. Since roots are so close to the surface, a generous mulch is welcomed. Not peat moss—it hardens into a waterproof mat. Use pine needles or buckwheat hulls or other acidic cover. Bob Carlson puts down a heavy layer of newspaper first (it rots), then covers it with pine needles.

REA LUBAR DUNCAN

CHINESE TREE PEONIES
MAY 1994

$\mathcal{O}$K, I'm a chauvinist where Connecticut is concerned—it's where my heart lies—but there's no denying that the state lays claim to some remarkable horticultural treasures. Among others, we have, in Woodbury, the only Gertrude Jekyll garden in America; in Wilton, the only national park commemorating an artist, the Weir Farm National Historic Site; in Hamden, the gardens of one of the world's great hybridizers of mountain laurel, Richard Jaynes, at Broken Arrow Nursery; in New Canaan, the 2,000 azaleas and 300 rhododendron of the Olive and George S. Lee Memorial Garden.

I've written columns about all of these treasures and now am privileged to write about another, a true jewel in Connecticut's horticultural crown, unique not only in the United States but quite possibly in the world—

109

except for China. It's Cricket Hill Garden in Thomaston, where David and Kasha Furman grow the world's most extensive (perhaps *only*) collection of Chinese tree peonies outside the cities of Luoyang and HeZe in northern China, their places of origin, and the palace gardens in Beijing, whose collections are drawn from those cities.

In two earlier columns about peonies, I dealt only with *Japanese* varieties. That's because there weren't any Chinese varieties around in '87, when I wrote the first column, and because David Furman had just begun to sell them in '92, when I wrote the second. In this column, I'm saluting *Chinese* tree peonies—and the Furmans, for bringing them to us.

One of the first tree peonies ever seen by a Westerner was found in 1911 by David Purdom, an English plant hunter. He was seeking Paeony Mountain, Mou-tan Shan, in northwest China, as described in a 17th-century manuscript. It's a place where tree peonies were said to grow wild in such profusion that they scented the air all around and were so big their branches served as firewood. As I noted in writing of that discovery in 1992, "The description so fevered his imagination that at risk of life and limb (he and his helpers were attacked by brigands, his horses were shot and he barely managed to escape), he made his way to that mountain—the first European ever to see it—climbed it and explored it thoroughly, only to find no peonies. Not a one.

"But in that same year, 1911, far west of Paeony Mountain on the border of Tibet, he did find what has become a historic tree peony. It was the red form of *suffruticosa*. And soon after, on an expedition he directed, another Englishman, Reginald Farrer, found the white form. It's hard to believe that virtually all of today's gorgeous hybrid tree peonies derive from those two plants."

So why then, since the tree peony comes from China, do virtually all the hybrids in our gardens come from Japan? Because the Chinese took some of their treasures to Japan, where hybridizers went to town developing what have become today's wondrous varieties. The Japanese, however, like only semidouble flower forms and developed them almost exclusively. The Chinese, on the other hand, prefer many-petaled doubles—"thousand-petal flowers"—as double as our most double herbaceous peonies.

Cricket Hill Garden is the only place where these ravishing doubles are offered, although magnificent Chinese singles and semidoubles, many in shapes and colors new to this country, are also grown there. (You'll also have your pick of the popular herbaceous peonies from China and Japan, and cultivars developed by American and British hybridizers.)

A former advertising manager for Bic Corp. in Milford, David Furman moved with his family from New Haven to Thomaston in 1988 when he retired. The Furmans had bought the hillside property two years before—they chose it because the sloping terrain was precisely right for growing peonies—and camped on the vacant lot while site planning the house and grounds around their dreamed-about peony garden.

Fascinated by things Chinese since childhood (he holds a master's degree in Chinese history from New York University), David had long observed how the tree peony had been, for more than a thousand years, an inspirational motif for Chinese art and literature (paintings, ceramics, fabrics, prose and poetry). The flower remains beloved and revered today. Peony festivals in many Chinese cities, celebrated for hundreds of years, continue to draw hundreds of thousands of visitors each year.

He was hooked. "The beauty of the flowers got to me as no other flower ever had," he explains, "and I set about trying to import some from China with which to start my own nursery.

"It wasn't easy," he recalls ruefully. "It took me 20 years to track down reliable sources, at the beginning for me personally and then for Cricket Hill. First I contacted government agencies and nearly went wild dealing with the bureaucrats. It's the same everywhere, isn't it?

"Many of my letters of inquiry went unanswered. Answers I received promised plants that never came. Others sent inferior stock, dead and dying—there are good and bad people the world over. But five years ago I found two growers who have become steady sources, and although we've never met, we're close friends."

Today Cricket Hill Garden offers more than 60 varieties of Chinese tree peonies, and David Furman hopes some day to grow all 400 of the cultivars that exist in China. Plants are not inexpensive—they range from $50 to $400, with price determined not by the beauty or size of the flowers but by the ease or difficulty of propagation—but all stock is imported directly from The People's Republic of China and is well worth it, considering that all plants are, as David puts it, "Chinese antiques," clones or grafts of plants dating back 1,400 years to the Sui Dynasty (581-618 A.D.). The most favored flowers in the fabled Mandarin gardens of classical China, tree peonies are still regarded as the epitome of Chinese garden culture.

Just the names of these dazzlers—Intoxicated Celestial Peach, Mixing Delicacy with Joy, White Light that Shines in the Night, Jealousy of One Hundred Flowers, Flames Within the Elixir of Immortality, The Blossom that Greets the Day—convey magic.

But wait till you see the flowers themselves. Colors and shapes to dream on. Intoxicated Celestial Peach is a midtone pink that, like its namesake fruit in China, is pink without any yellow tones. A rounded cluster of central petals rides on a flattened ring of outer ones—the legendary thousand-petal shape. Flowers are very heavy and droop languorously on the plant. Thus, intoxicated. Fire in the Stove opens pink-red, changes to peach-pink at maturity, and has a green heart. Eight inches in diameter, the blossoms have 300 petals shaped into a ruffled ball. Peach Blossom Spring takes its name from an old folk tale about a paradise lost and found on earth. The color is apricot, whitened at the edges, and the large stamen cluster is yellow. Pea Green originated in the Sung Dynasty (960-1227 A.D.), has pea-green flowers—yea, verily—that change to white at maturity. Very double. Yao's Family Yellow was once the exclusive possession of the Yao family in Luoyang, and has been recognized for almost a thousand years as one of the finest of all tree peonies. The magnificent 8-inch double flowers have central petals that rise strikingly from an outer ring of level petals. And they're deliciously fragrant.

Want more? A single, Centerpiece of Fruit, has frosted magenta petals charmingly chipped at the edges, and chartreuse center anthers. Twin Beauty is a semidouble with blossoms a good 2 inches deep. As if divided in the middle, half the flower is pink, half red—stunning. A Necklace with a Precious Pearl, one of the great classics of Luoyang, is a ruffled double that opens silver-red, then changes to peach-red with silver frosting at the petal tips.

Oh, wow.

And they're hardy in Connecticut, where winter cold and summer heat resemble their home clime in the mountains of China, and are pretty much pest- and disease-free. If botrytis, a fungus that afflicts all peonies, should blacken the leaves, cut off the sick parts and *burn them*. Some plantsmen advise spraying with Bordeaux mixture, but the Furmans are purists who practice organic gardening.

Plants will live 150 years or more (who's around to count?) and grow to 5 or 6 feet in height, 5 feet in diameter. Kasha Furman, an avid gardener with a background in fine arts, stresses the need for patience. "Growth will be slow the first year after planting, and you'll get only a couple of blossoms," she says. "But after that, up to 75 blossoms on a single bush is not uncommon, 20 to 30 is common—in the best sense of the word."

Cricket Hill Garden sells only bare-rooted plants that should be set in the earth September through mid-October. Some very reliable nurseries do sell peonies—not Chinese, of course—potted up for spring planting. Not so the purists at Cricket Hill. "Maybe when my sons grow up, they will sell potted plants to maximize sales. Not me," says David. "These cultivars deserve the best—and that's bare-root planting in the fall."

Peonies—tree and herbaceous—prefer a neutral or only slightly acid soil, so you may have to add a bit of lime to our sour Connecticut earth. Do *not* plant where water stands. It will kill them. Flowers will last longer in semishade, but not too dense, please. They need sunlight to grow.

Since these are such long-lived plants, give them a home big enough to accommodate them when they grow up, a planting hole 2 feet deep and 2 feet wide. Plant so that the long roots are fully covered with soil up to where they join the stem of the plant. Make sure roots are fully extended, cover halfway with good garden earth, then fill the hole with water, let it all get absorbed, and add earth to fill the hole. No manure, please, and if you use compost, keep it away from the roots.

A thick mulch—even 6 to 8 inches—during the first winter will prevent the earth from heaving. (Wood ashes are a good addition to other mulches.) Remove mulch carefully in the spring. Best to dead-head spent flowers—if you haven't picked them all for bouquets, that is. But don't cut down the branches as you do with herbaceous peonies. These are deciduous shrubs. Their tops do not die back to the ground as the tops of perennials do. And feed with a pound of bone meal every spring—they're hungry critters.

Wonderful news. The Furmans hold a peony festival open to the public from mid-May to late June. (Last year 700 enthusiasts from as far away as Ohio and Virginia came.) The tree peonies are at their height from about May 15 to the end of the month, while the herbaceous types come into blossom at the same time but bloom two to three weeks longer. Any time during this period provides a not-to-be-missed spectacle. But for the Chinese tree peonies, May's the only time, and Cricket Hill Garden the only place to see them in full glory—except for China (lotta carfare).

So *go,* again and again if you can. I'll see you there.

LANDMARKS & BEAUTY MARKS

NICHOLAS JACOBS

A GARDEN WORLD IN AN ACRE

MARCH 1986

*W*hat kind of azaleas are those?" I ask, absolutely dazzled by the solid masses of brilliant bloom—scarlet, pink, fuchsia, lavender, purple, flame, apricot, white—that surround us on all sides.

The answer is refreshingly unexpected. "I don't know," admits Ruth Levitan, whose glorious Stamford garden has been featured in *Architectural Digest* and Europe's top landscaping magazines, and was recently selected as one of the country's outstanding gardens for the book, *The American Woman's Garden.* "Jim and I bought most of them as bargains at roadside stands when they were unnamed peewees. That's all we could afford 30 years ago. That 15-foot magnolia cost only a dollar. It was marked down because it had no buds." She giggles, adding, "It's since bloomed every spring, including the spring we bought it."

By now the peewees have grown into tall spreading trees and bushes. In fact, the shrubs are so high, broad and dense that although I know the Levitan house is immediately behind them and a busy street only three seconds away, I feel we are enclosed by a great garden stretching far and wide around us.

Yet the Levitan property, including both house and land, occupies only 1 acre. For an amateur gardener like me, it is an eye-opener in how to make the most of space. The Levitans' big trick is not having a wide sweep of lawn. Instead, a web of grassy paths wind through the property, so adroitly laid out and so thickly flanked on both sides by shrubs and trees that most are invisible from one another.

Surely a skilled landscape architect conceived the design? Not at all. "What makes our garden so special, at least to me, is that it wasn't laid out according to a master plan," Ruth Levitan reveals. "It grew naturally out of the contours of the land and the way we lived on it. The paths were worn by children's feet—we have three daughters—crossing the woods to play with friends next door or running to the cleared area in the rear where the swing set was."

Ruth and Jim Levitan, then both fledgling attorneys, bought their acre in 1956. A lot that a developer had carved out of old Connecticut farmland, it had reverted to woods and was very shaded, as woods tend to be. "But unhampered by horticultural knowledge, I envisioned a garden-to-be in full bloom among the trees." Levitan laughs heartily. "I never imagined—could not have, possibly—the work involved."

Enormous root systems resisted digging. Underbrush was thickly tangled and infested with poison ivy. The soil, although humus-y, seemed composed mainly of rocks. Towering oaks, some of which Ruth finally persuaded Jim to have cut down, blocked most of the sunlight. Still, they persisted. Each new phase of the garden grew from what was there before. The rocks that they dug up by hand—no bulldozer has ever set wheel on their land—they used to bank new borders or as terraces and retaining walls to protect new plantings.

A little fish pond with fountain and water lilies sits between two centrally located boulders. ("After a trip to the Alhambra, I was convinced no garden could be complete without running water," Ruth relates.) Artfully placed at a wide curve in a path, it seems far removed from the house, a place for quiet contemplation, although it is actually closely surrounded.

Today the Levitans enjoy flowers outdoors from March till October. Their very first effort was an early-spring garden to bloom before the leaves were out. They were so eager to get started that they drove out from Manhattan to plant bulbs while the house was still under construction. Today, March-blooming bulbs come first, snowdrops and early azaleas ("I do know one name, *schlippenbachi*, that heavenly pale pink," Levitan says), and early wildflowers.

But it is the Levitans' late May garden that is most spectacular. The azaleas and rhododendron now resemble the gorgeous catalog pictures that set them dreaming. A big old-fashioned lilac is purpled with flower branches, and white dogwood blossoms arch over all like low lacy clouds against the spring-blue sky. In front of the shrubs, edging the undulating pathways, dense blue carpets of Jacob's ladder and forget-me-nots soften the vibrant colors.

In June come Oriental poppies, peonies and sweet William, and later in the summer, hosta and daylilies, whose fountains of green leaves conceal the yellowing foliage of spring bulbs. Still later, blue balloon flowers and baptisia cool the hot orange echinops and gaillardia. Summer-blooming shrubs such as snowball hydrangea and rose of Sharon mass into leafy green background.

"No exotic flowers for Jim and me," Ruth says happily. "Yes, I do talk to plants. What I say is, 'Shape up or ship out.'"

And now they have a winter garden. To celebrate their 25th anniversary, the Levitans gave each other a lean-to greenhouse that they attached to the south side of the house, with the former playroom next to it converted to an indoor work area. "What a joy to have a proper setup for germinating seeds after all those years of starting seedlings under grow lights among wet towels in the laundry," Ruth says.

"We've been very fortunate," she adds. "Our daughters are happily married with homes and gardens of their own. And Jim has become one of the top tax lawyers in the East. Many of the colleagues who started with him when their law firm—like our plants—was a peewee have since moved into grand mansions with palatial grounds. We'll stay here. The garden is part of us."

For Ruth Levitan, gardening is not only a joy, it is also an essential fulfillment of deep, lifelong needs. From childhood, she wanted to be an artist, a painter. "But my enthusiasm far outshone my accomplishments," she adds ruefully. So, in deference to her parents' wishes, she gave up art for law school, worked at a law firm for a brief period, then gladly gave it up when she moved to Stamford to raise a family—and create another kind of artwork, her garden.

During the "turbulent '60s," gardening answered another crucial need for her. "As a dedicated political activist, I spent endless hours at meetings, marches, vigils and petition drives," she says. "The intense physical work of digging, lifting and clearing gave me a release, and the quiet solitude provided periods of peace I desperately needed. Gardening brought me back to the rhythm of the seasons. And the incredible ability of growing things to survive was, I hoped, a good omen."

Rarely without a smile, Ruth's gaminlike face becomes serious. "May I use the pages of CONNECTICUT Magazine to express a fervent wish?" she asks. "I wish that everyone who reads this article and everyone who visits my garden will feel moved to speak out against man's destructiveness. Our woods and streams are being destroyed by acid rain, which the current administration euphemistically refers to as 'inadequately buffered precipitation'—whatever that means. And our ocean shore is being polluted by indiscriminate dumping of wastes. And our precious wetlands are being paved over.

"So I say to you, readers, don't just thank Jim and me for making a lovely garden. Promise us you will write your congressman about these issues. This is one of the few countries in the world where the individual voice still counts. It isn't too late, although it soon will be."

OLIVE AND GEORGE S. LEE MEMORIAL GARDEN
APRIL 1986

*L*ike great sashes of color unfurled all at once from the top of the sloping terrain, blossoming azaleas and rhododendron spill down the winding paths of the Olive and George S. Lee Memorial Garden in New Canaan. Masses of pale pink, fuchsia, fiery red, white, yellow, peach, orange, orchid and amethyst, they are almost too much for eye and soul to take in.

This spectacular show lasts from mid-May through June. Moreover, it is a *free* show, for it was the fervent wish of the late George Lee, whose gardens these were, to share his Connecticut woodland plantings with all who were or might be interested. There is no admission charge. Together with sightseers and dirt gardeners like me come professional plantsmen from around the world to view the 2,000 azaleas in some 175 varieties, including 1,500 Gable hybrids made up of 40 varieties that represent the only complete collection of the creations of the late great hybridizer, Joseph B. Gable.

It all started when George Lee's brother, Frederic P. Lee, a noted horticulturist and author of *The Azalea Book*, gave Olive and George a housewarming gift of six Gable azaleas. That was the beginning of a lifetime friendship between George Lee and Joseph Gable, during which Lee often visited the Gable gardens in Stewartstown, Pa., and began assembling all the Gable hybrids.

What's your favorite color? Bright red? A rare planting of 125 brilliant red Gable *Stewartstonian* azaleas light up the slope below the house. ("Men like this bright red the best," says "Duffy" Jacobson, who's in charge of propagation.)

Maybe you prefer orchid. Lee considered an orchid-colored Dexter hybrid his "top favorite." Or perhaps you like snowy White Cap from Ilam, bud pinks from Shammarello, or a rich purple from Gable named Olive for George's wife.

The garden's "Rhododendron Walk" provides a simultaneous color explosion in May and June: a quarter mile of sloping path lined on both sides with 300 shrubs, some as high as 12 feet, species and hybrids, large-leaved and small, in every color rhododendron are supposed to come in and some they are not.

Even earlier, an extraordinary number and variety of wildflowers come into colorful bloom, planted beneath and among the shrubs, scattered through the woods and around the granitic glacial rocks that stud the 3-acre site.

I was moved by another feature of the garden, intangible yet all-pervasive, a spiritual quality in the sense that it is born of the spirit with which George Lee conceived and built his garden. The phrase "labor of love" comes to mind, capturing exactly what the garden has been for its 46 years.

Perhaps I should say "labor of loves," for many different loves are involved. The garden is, of course, an expression of George's love of plants. It also embodies his love for his wife, who was ill for a long while and forced to spend much time indoors. Accordingly, George set the house at the top of the sloping site and designed it with bay windows on both the first and second floors, so that Olive could enjoy the gardens.

In a remarkable gesture of generosity and trust, George, who died in 1978, willed both house and garden to the New Canaan Garden Center and also left an endowment for upkeep. His trust has been more than justified. The women of the garden center spend countless hours physically working to maintain the gardens—yet another labor of love.

As important as the physical work the volunteers do, however, is the fact that each seems imbued with George's spirit and goals. Nancy Boschen, who recently relinquished her guardianship as chairman of the garden center's memorial garden committee, set the guidelines: to preserve as much as possible the "natural woodland garden Mr. Lee created."

Open all day, every day, the garden is also an expression of George's love of people. More than 15 years ago, he wrote in the catalog of the gardens, "It is no longer possible for most suburban families to take a Sunday afternoon walk and find violets, bloodroot, hepatica, baneberry, partridgeberry and many other natives growing contentedly nearby." He then added, "Children are always welcome, hopefully to discover that life offers something besides war, pollution and drugs."

"He would be so happy to see how many families *do* come for the Sunday walk he dreamed of," says Susie Stutts, currently memorial garden committee co-chairman.

Although the garden is only five minutes from the center of New Canaan, it seems as remote from civilization as a trail in the Appalachians. That it fronts on a nature preserve accounts for some of this feeling of remoteness. But most of it stems from the way the garden is laid out in paths that wind around for three-quarters of a mile; Lee described it as "a large and complicated pretzel."

"I live nearby, yet I always feel as though I've left town and gone far away when I work here," says Doris Lyman, Stutts' co-chairman. Lucy Garcia-Mata, who is in charge of scheduling volunteers, echoes this sentiment. "Members are required to work three hours a year at the garden," she says. "Many devote 10 or 20 times more. But no matter how much time they give, they all have this feeling of being part of a distant, tranquil place."

"Visitors feel it, too," says Ann Gillerlain, who conducts tours through the garden center for members of rhododendron societies, professional plantsmen and garden clubbers, and groups from the New York Botanical Garden. "People speak softly here, if at all," she says.

Although George Lee's love was for roses and daffodils when he moved to Connecticut in 1940 (he was for many years president of the American Daffodil Society), these are not the stars of the New Canaan garden. The soil is too thin and acid, the land too full of glacial rocks and boulders, and the whole 3 acres too shaded by oaks and other deciduous trees. So instead of changing the land—removing trees, planting grass and making flower beds—George changed his tastes to suit the terrain. "It is not always necessary to cut down trees and grow crabgrass if you live in the woods," he wrote.

Nor did he. In this garden, there's no lawn at all, just plants, trees and shrubs that flank the paths. If a boulder blocked the way of a path, the path took a different direction. Rather than cut down trees, George ribbed the paths between them. In brief, the landscape architect took his lead from nature.

This philosophy still rules today. Plants get very little fussing over. Set out in the acid soil they love, they're fed and mulched by the natural leaf fall. Garden center members work hard and long at clearing the debris of winter off the wood-chip paths, replacing the cord-wood edgings that keep the chips from washing away, transplanting invasive wildflowers, judiciously pruning and propagating when necessary, then labeling, relabeling and re-relabeling. "Labels fade, break, even disappear," says Louise Erb, who handles this tedious task with consummate cheerfulness. Viki Ferreniea, horticulturalist for the adjacent New Canaan Nature Center, assists with the identification of wildflowers.

In mid-May the garden's sea of color stretches beneath the oaks, tulip trees, flowering dogwood and stands of cedar, sweet gum, hemlock and shadbush. And this is when most visitors come.

But a stroll through the paths in late April or early May for the wildflowers and other ground covers is also an enchantment. You will see a positive rainbow of primroses, white and yellow epimedium, oconee bells, trailing arbutus, masses of bloodroot, Dutchman's breeches and columbine.

So come here for a quiet walk whenever you are in need of tranquility and beauty. But don't expect a conventional public garden. This is a "private" garden open to the public. No picnic tables. Not even bathroom facilities. As Lee put it, "It is an oasis in an increasingly bleak environment."

The Olive and George S. Lee Memorial Garden may be reached via the Merritt Parkway, exit 36. Proceed north on Route 106 toward New Canaan. Bear left on Weed Street (before the railroad underpass). Continue north on Weed Street to Wahackme Road. Turn left on Wahackme, then right on Chichester Road. The garden is on your left. Parking is along Chichester Road.

WILLIAM SEITZ

CANDY VOYTERSHARK

MARCH 1987

A woman for all seasons.

    That's Candy Voytershark. And so are the flowers she grows at Painter Ridge Perennials in Roxbury. Here spring, summer and fall are for planting, nurturing, gathering and enjoying blooms, and winter is for savoring their beauty all over again in dried arrangements.

    Candy leads a quadruple life (at least). She's the creative force behind her nursery, and the woman of all work—clearing, digging, planting, fertilizing and propagating. She's also a professional landscape architect—designing, building, planting (always with her own plants) and maintaining gardens big and small in Watertown, Litchfield, Cornwall, Southbury, New Preston and beyond. She also creates flower arrangements

121

for weddings parties and such, "from the bride's bouquet to the church decorations to the table centerpieces" (again, always with her own flowers). And she makes and sells dried flower arrangements and wreaths—*la spécialité de la maison*. The flowers are grown—you guessed it—in her gardens, and hung upside down in her house and barn to dry. No preservatives.

"You have to know when to pick which flowers," Candy tells me. "The secret is to pick the blossoms just before they open fully. That way, they open out wide while they dry. And the drying room has to be *dry*. During a damp spell last fall, I had to move all the hanging stalks from our barn into the house."

"What's special about dried flowers is that they're virtually everlasting," Candy says. So great is her skill that her dried blooms have the color and texture of the fresh, bringing spring and summer indoors year-round. (I couldn't resist buying a charming little wreath of pink strawflowers and white hydrangea florets, dainty enough for Titania, queen of the fairies, to wear as a crown.) Other wreaths are great rounds of hay grasses from her fields, brightened with blue salvia and lavender—as blue as in the garden, silver artemisia, seed pods of allium, and rosebuds heavy with perfume. A highlight of the Roxbury fair in summer is the Voytershark booth, where Candy sits weaving her wreaths. No matter how great her supply, the demand always exceeds it.

Although her gardens have the look of long-established plantings, Painter Ridge Perennials is only six years old. The nursery, the Voytershark house and small barn sit high on a ridge with a glorious view of the Catskill Mountains to the west. Occupying about 2 of the 250 acres of dairy farm owned by Candy's husband, Frank, the gardens were started with leftover plants from Candy's landscaping jobs. Some leftovers! Rare and fragrant old shrub roses, Siberian iris, peonies, sweet William, foxglove.

"I couldn't bear to throw the extras away. I still can't bear to discard babies—new seedlings—so I kept planting them and having to dig up new beds to make room," she says. "It's a good thing. When I started landscaping, I used plants from my own personal garden. But the jobs got so numerous, I would have run out the first season. So I gratefully planted the leftovers customers so generously gave me."

Growth at Painter Ridge is dazzlingly lush. Waist-high Shasta daisies. Thick spreading carpets of ground phlox. Dense thickets of Siberian iris. "That's because of our 'miracle soil,'" Candy explains. "We owe it to the generosity of the cows on Frank's farm. The soil is mostly well-ripened cow manure mixed with sand and earth. Stick in a skinny cutting in the fall and you have a fat clump next spring. And all the gardens are in full sun. That helps, too."

More than 60 kinds of perennials bloom from April to hard frost on Painter Ridge. You name 'em, Candy grows 'em. Columbine, clematis, rudbeckia, feverfew, evening primrose, astilbe, yarrow, phlox, iris, peonies, poppies, roses, delphiniums, coral bells, mums, most in several varieties. And vegetables, too, although these are not for sale but for family consumption (extras are shared with friends). A plume-y hedge of asparagus, fat heads of kale and cabbage, spinach, Chinese cabbage, herbs (parsley as big as a small shrub). On the graded slope slanting from house to gardens, running things like cucumbers, melons, pumpkins and squash trail happily.

To make room for propagating even more perennials, Candy digs up the vegetable plants as soon as they stop bearing, and fills the empty spaces with divisions of perennials. "I just dig up a big clump, tear it apart, put the divisions where the vegetables grew and bingo—next spring, more perennials. It's that 'miracle soil,'" she says with a grin.

Candy's love of growing things extends to fauna as well as flora. Chickens cluck in an enclosure off the barn. "Epic," her white Arabian horse, bangs his hoof on the fence to get our attention. "Eppie is 10 going on 1," Candy laughs, giving him the loving hug he's demanding. "I've had six horses in my life—I ride every morning—and he's the character of the lot. I once tended horses owned by the master of the Fairfield Hunt," she says, "and I'd often ride with them foxhunting. It was wonderful, like acting out a fantasy. But there's no time anymore."

Inside the barn, more animals. Rabbits that the Voytersharks raise for meat. "But these four are pets,"

Candy says, pointing to four huge gray bunnies big as adult raccoons. "They're a cross between chinchilla rabbits and New Zealand whites. Their mother died when they were 10 days old and I saved them, bottle-feeding them by hand till they could manage on their own. They're too fat now, of course. That female can't have babies any longer—too much fat around her ovaries." Like all the Voytersharks' animals—dog, cat, horse, even chickens—these four rabbits are full of affection, lick our hands and cuddle in our arms.

A slim, petite brunette with a short gamine haircut and bangs, Candy is 40, looks 30, and sometimes, with her swift, graceful movements, spirited gestures and twinkling eyes, seems no older than a teenager. She was born in Roxbury, one of six children, grew up in Litchfield and has gardened since she was a tot. "Both my grandmothers and my mother were avid gardeners," she says. "But my mother was too busy raising kids to do all the gardening that had to be done. So I started helping her when I was about 4. I loved it then; I love it now."

Deciding to be an artist and to keep gardening an avocation, Candy attended the Rhode Island School of Design, but only for two years. "I quit because I needed to earn a living," she explains, "but I've never stopped painting or studying." She attended Paier College of Art in Hamden for three years and took courses at the Hartford Art School. "I'm always studying either from books or in class," she says.

Trompe l'oeil, which means, literally, deceive the eye, is a favorite technique of Candy's. And the technique works. Her still life of rosettes and ribbons from a horse show is so realistic that her husband reaches to pick up one of the rosettes. And a mural of black-and-white cows on the wall of the breezeway connecting house and barn looks so much like the real thing that, when the painting went up, Foxy, the dog, growled at the four-legged strangers, and two cowbirds stopped to investigate.

Inside the house, a passive solar structure that the Voytersharks built themselves from a purchased plan is lavish evidence of all the things Candy loves. There are dozens upon dozens of flowers drying upside down from the rafters, art books in profusion, shelves massed with plant encyclopedias and garden books, books on horses, a picture window almost solid green with plants both hanging and standing (a scented geranium is 4 feet high and almost as wide!), and Candy's paintings on the walls, even to trompe l'oeil cows in the bathroom that seem to be drinking from the tub.

Overflowing from a table onto the floor are the makings of dried wreaths—a bowl of little roses, a bunch of white, pink and magenta globe amaranth, perennial sweet pea stems, wild thyme and grasses to shape the base of the wreaths. "I never know how a wreath is going to come out when I start. The material dictates the form," Candy says.

Any advice for gardeners?

"I believe in masses of the same variety—and of the same color—for the most striking garden effects," Candy says. "A wave of blue or white Siberian iris or a golden explosion of rudbeckia or a sweep of pink ground phlox. Even if your garden isn't big, I advise having masses of a few things rather than a 'spatterdash' of many. Look at my 'moon garden.' Everything in it is silvery gray and white—lamb's ears, artemisia, white iris, pansies, allium—luminous in the sunlight and moonlight."

What sells the most at Painter Ridge Perennials?

"Whatever's in bloom," Candy answers. "People see the gorgeous flowers and want them. 'Do you have any in pots?' they ask. I didn't before but now I do. And I'm going to have more. That means clearing out more tangled chokecherry, sumac and wild cherry, rototilling the earth, digging in more 'miracle soil.' Every year means attacking a new area." She sighs, then brightens. "But every year brings more flowers, too."

Painter Ridge Perennials, 35 Painter Ridge Road, Roxbury, CT 06783, (860) 355-3844.

WILLIAM SEITZ

CASTLE GARDEN
OCTOBER 1987

Framed by the blue-green Litchfield hills, its spires looming above them in majestic silhouette against the sky, Cornwall Castle is everyone's dream of what a castle should be—beautiful, mysterious, magical—with turrets, towers and leaded-glass windows. It reigns over a domain of four other buildings and 355 acres of fields, woods, waterfalls, streams and ponds. Built in the 1920s by the late Dr. and Mrs. Walton Martin (he was a noted eye surgeon), the buildings are constructed of native Connecticut fieldstone, now a weathered warm gray, which was cut and fit together to Mrs. Martin's design by Italian stonemasons and other artisans whom she and her husband brought over from Europe.

Owner of the castle since 1983, Joe Cicio is corporate vice president of Macy's and director of visual merchandising, which means he is responsible for the interior design of Macy's stores coast to coast—from creative concept to location of the cheeses in the Cellar—and no slouch himself at construction and craftsmanship. Yet he marvels at the workmanship that went into the castle.

"These were true artists," he says with reverence, "who also made and placed—by hand—the slate shingles that give texture and dimension to the sloping roofs of the buildings. They also hand-forged the exquisite wrought-iron adornments that soften the stone, including 15-foot-high delicately filigreed gates, a molded hanging bell and chain, and the sculptured 8-foot waterwheel above the circular stone well in the main courtyard."

In addition to the 18-room castle, each of the outbuildings is charmingly designed, nostalgically recalling the farms of the Normandy countryside built two and three centuries ago. They include a groundskeeper's house under a big stone barn, chauffeur's quarters to stable a dozen horse-drawn coaches (or cars), and an enchanting guest cottage with its own private stone-walled garden.

Architecturally, the buildings are a subtle mix of Florentine and Norman. (It's said that a cousin of Mrs. Martin was a French princess and that Mrs. Martin wanted the royal guest to feel at home, whether strolling in the gardens or at ease in her private four-room apartment in the castle.) But the pervading ambience is Renaissance, Florentine; it is refined, romantic, elegant. And despite Joe Cicio's modesty, one can see the storied gardens beginning to take shape under his fine Italian hand.

"All the buildings were originally landscaped with elaborate paths, shrubbery and gardens patterned after those in Italian palaces and English great houses," Cicio explains. "It's four years this October that I came to live in the castle and I'm just now beginning to uncover—and discover—all of them. The castle had been empty for seven years when I moved in, and more than being run-down, it was lonely, sad, even bitter. I believe houses resent being deserted and neglected. The grounds were overgrown with dense vines and tangled scrub bushes, and also cluttered with fallen giant trees—some 75 feet long—which took months of work with the chain saw to cut up before they could be removed. In the fields, there was yellowed dead grass as high as an elephant's thigh.

"See that archway?" Cicio says, pointing to the intricately carved, double, wrought-iron gate opening on the castle courtyard, now gracefully vine-covered. "I didn't know it was there for three months. Dense euonymus totally obscured it and also masked the bell and chain just outside. The idea was that when visitors came, they would ring the bell, the gates would be swung open and the Daimlers and Rolls-Royces would drive in, circle the well in the center of the courtyard and deposit their passengers under the portico. In Renaissance times, of course, the cars would have been gilded horse-drawn carriages and the horses would have been watered from the well—which, incidentally, I've put back in working order."

Leading down from the courtyard to the Great Lawn are stone steps that Cicio has restored and relandscaped with low shrubbery. A brook tumbles into a little waterfall alongside. "That brook was so overgrown it had become a bog," he relates. On the Great Lawn itself, leading to one of three large ponds on the property, a sweep of magnificent pink rhododendron has been unveiled. "These bushes are probably 60 years old," Cicio points out, "but I didn't know they were there until the June after I came, when I glimpsed some pink patches under the choking vines. When I pulled the weeds off," he holds out work-calloused hands, "there were the rhododendron, desperately trying to survive. We pruned them, fed them and gave them tender loving care. For two Junes now—they're a late-blooming variety—they've rewarded us with glorious blossoms."

It's a full mile from the massive stone entry pillars and heavy iron gate to the castle itself. One senses the grand design of the original landscaped "esplanade" that Cicio is trying to recreate. He has already cleared the fields alongside the road so that artfully placed groves of trees are once again a design element, and one has been planted with a thousand daffodils that spread a golden carpet last April and May. He's also "unplugged" brooks and freed a series of little waterfalls that highlight the long approach to the castle. Typical of the Cicio touch, a tiny island in one of the ponds is charmingly landscaped with a single miniature weeping willow that drapes over the water.

Twelve ancient apple trees flank the roadway just opposite the castle. "Their gnarled shapes were a designer's dream—once they could be seen," Cicio says. "Grape ivy was choking them to death. But look at them now—gnarled and lovely. We knew we were doing something right when they blossomed frugally two springs ago. Last May they were a pink-and-white vision."

A spreading lilac bush across from the apple trees now softens the side entry to the castle. "That was the original idea when it was planted," Cicio says, "but it took a bit of doing to bring it back to life and health."

Cicio's favorite spot on the grounds is the romantic walled garden outside the stone guest house, where he found traces of three formal terraced gardens. "I've only restored one so far," he says, "a rose garden on the upper level that I've planted with old roses that evoke the romanticism of the castle. Here's Frau Karl Druschki, the grande dame of shrub roses, and *Reine des Violettes*, a lilac-blue that goes back to 1860 and predates all the modern 'blue' roses. I couldn't resist adding a modern-day Princess Grace, a beautiful pink whose namesake seems to belong in this royal setting, and two tree roses that could have graced Malmaison, the home of Empress Josephine outside Paris."

Two enormous espaliered pear trees that climb over the front wall of the house have also been liberated, their gracefully twisting trunks some 6 inches in circumference. "They blossomed lavishly this spring and even produced some pears in August," Joe says happily. "Delicious."

Set outside the stone wall enclosing the guest house garden is a "little bit of old England," a true English country perennial border that magically appeared the first spring Cicio lived at the castle. "Suddenly, orange poppies flamed the 75-foot length of the wall," Cicio recalls with wonder. Then came a long drift of deliciously fragrant pink peonies. Also, of course, the weeds arrived, but even so, daylilies planted close to the wall pushed up among them and bloomed orange and yellow. Later, masses of orange gaillardia and white Shasta daisies bloomed.

With individual plantings uncovered here and there, the full majesty of the landscape scheme has begun to reveal itself. "It's been much easier to renovate the interior of the castle than to restore the gardens," Cicio says. "There are 355 acres here, and while all of them weren't landscaped—dense woods were purposely left circling the property—an overall plan dictated what was to be designed and what left to nature. It will take time to find that out and even more time to emulate it. It's toil and drudgery. I spend every free moment laboring outdoors." He smiles happily. "I guess I must love it or I wouldn't do it.

"Although I want to be faithful to the original concept, I also feel the gardens must answer the needs of people today and accommodate their lifestyle. With my lifestyle," he goes on, "there have to be traffic lanes—invisible, of course—and space to sit, stroll, meditate. Aesthetically, I want shades of light—the dark greens of the hemlocks and cedars enhancing the light green of the apple trees, soul-stirring masses of bright colors where one needs that lift, and soul-soothing pale pastels."

If anyone can bring back the grandeur of these castle gardens, Joe Cicio can. His magic touch at Macy's has won him international awards and tributes. Equally important is his extraordinary expertise for making things work, whether in the kitchen of the castle or the Cellar at Macy's store at the Danbury Fair Mall.

"My dream is of a huge cutting garden full of parrot tulips in spring; then, in summer, zinnias, cosmos, marigolds, anthemis, delphiniums—annuals and perennials. The house demands huge loose French bouquets of them," he says. "So far, most of my flowers come from hybrid lilies, and outside color splashes from potted plants—lots of them. I've hung shell-pink flowering fuchsias in every shady niche of the stone walls and from all the apple trees. In the courtyard, geraniums and impatiens rim the well.

"But someday, someday, there will be a waterlily pool in the pond by the Great Lawn to enjoy from the dining terrace above the courtyard. And someday, all the fine specimen hemlocks and cedars will be contoured into conical Renaissance forms like in the Borghese Gardens, climbing roses will clamber over the stone walls at the entrance gate, holly bushes will provide Christmas decorations. And one meadow will be left uncut for wildflowers."

He looks around. "But first I have to come to know the land and be one with it," he says.

That's good advice even if your home is not a castle.

WILLIAM SEITZ

WALLACE GRAY
OCTOBER 1988

$\mathcal{S}$ ome people tell a story with a novel, some with a painting, some with a symphony. Landscape designer Wallace Gray tells it with a garden, a Japanese garden that artfully uses trees, shrubs, flowers, stones, sand and water to recount a man's life from birth to death.

"When I was 5 or 6 years old, my father took me to see a Japanese garden in Ireland—it was in Kildare and belonged to the National Trust—that had been designed to tell the life story of a man," Gray recalls. "I knew right then I must someday create such a garden. I said so to my father, who laughed at the idea. Well, I have created it."

Gray's Japanese garden in northwestern Connecticut has been more than 20 years in the making. The

127

storybook forms of the shrubs and trees attest to their age—and to his expertise and artistry in giving them traditional shapes. A magnificent weeping hemlock, for example, now 20 feet high, arches into a dense green fountain. "When I bought it 15 years ago, it was a little bush," Gray says. "To buy it today—if you could find one like it—would cost perhaps $2,500. But it's taken a lot of time and attention to shape it just that way. Actually, it requires a full day's pruning and heavy cleaning every spring to maintain its mysterious bower effect."

An earlier visit to Gray's garden, when leaves were not yet fully unfurled nor shrubs in full bloom, gave us the advantage of seeing the overall configuration of the winding paths, seeing how the rocks serve as accent points and the trees and plants as decorative elements. Even the fence, which is cut from maple saplings on Gray's land and entirely hand-meshed, enhances the design.

Gray's garden story opens with the birth of his central figure—"a fictitious person," he carefully points out. A massive hollowed boulder softened with climbing hydrangea *petiolaris* represents "the cave of birth." (The cave fascinates Binnie, one of Gray's two Pembroke corgis, who explores it at every opportunity.) A tall yew on the left and a California privet on the right representing mother and father are both trained to standards so they are, figuratively speaking, in upright human form. "I brought the privet back from California as a tiny bush," he explains. "It does well here in our cold Connecticut clime, and the white flowers have a lovely fragrance."

Starting just outside the cave is the beginning of the gravel path that our hero will follow through life. Small rocks set in it represent his first steps as a child, with a stone bench nearby from which one visualizes his parents watching and guiding him. Soon the path diverges to indicate that his parents are now going their own way. Gray identifies their separate path with smaller gravel than that of his central figure. Following traditional values, Gray's young man still treads "the straight and narrow." Later he will choose his own route.

One of the distinctive features of Japanese gardens lies in their wondrous use of sand or stones to suggest water. The small sand pond that Gray has introduced here shows his whimsical touch through a charming moment in our protagonist's life. Lying off-center in the pond is a small black stone that represents a pebble thrown in to make a wish. Gray has even swirled the sand to conjure the image of ripples moving outward from the stone.

Now begins our young man's upward ascent. "The steep slope of land and rock ledge lend themselves perfectly to the visualization of life's hard climb," Gray explains. Just past a shapely, pink-blooming crab apple tree, placed here as a feminine touch, another path makes its entrance from the left. Aha! A lady enters the picture, crossing a large rock to indicate what a big step she has taken to meet our hero. Getting to know each other, they travel the same path for a little while, then briefly separate while the lady goes her own way to think things over. But she soon rejoins him, crossing a little red wooden bridge that represents the crossover from separate lives to a shared future.

We come now to one of the highlights of the garden, the marriage ceremony, as symbolized by a large round stone with a center hole—the wedding ring. A serene pool of stones surrounds it with an ancient and exquisite stone Japanese lantern nearby to brighten the couple's way, and a magnificent red cut-leaf Japanese maple to adorn the wedding scene. Happily married, the couple now climb together up the stepping stones of life, their path taking a turn to the left, a new direction.

Another chapter begins. A child is born, as tiny stones and gravel indicate. Soon after, another child arrives, which Gray shows us by clustering rocks together into a secluded cave with its own diminutive opening. "The second child is my daughter's doing," he says smiling. "She was 7 at the time and pleaded, 'Oh, please, Daddy, don't make him an only child'—which she is. So there are two children."

Now the upward path is marked with graceful shrubs sculptured into the stylized shapes characteristic of Japanese gardens, each representing another achievement as our couple prospers. At the summit, pinnacle trees and upward-pointing stones poetically signify success. Here Gray has thoughtfully placed a stone bench where our couple can rest and contemplate life. We rest, too, contemplating Gray's marvelous patterning of trees, shrubs and blossoming plants, and admiring a huge spreading Chinese cork tree, which he uses as a focal point of the garden. Around it are tousled carpets of horizontally spreading blue spruce with grace notes of pastel flowers, evocative of the small pleasures of life.

"Each generation must make its own way, so now the children depart," Gray continues. For a departure point, he uses a slim, wooden, pagoda-topped archway through which they enter their own world. From here on, their parents' path takes a gentle descent, ending with a boulder that represents a welcoming tomb and this life's end. A lantern is lovingly placed here to cast light ahead as another lantern did when they married. "It's all meant to be natural and pretty and a happy ending," Gray says. And so it is.

For Wallace Gray, the Japanese garden has been a labor of love ever since he and his wife, Helen, came to live in the house in the early '60s. "The house was built in 1917—it was little more than a cottage—and Helen's mother and father rebuilt it in '39," Gray says. "We've been rebuilding it all over again. Originally, it had no garden, just meadow and fruit trees. I've been planting shrubs and trees since we came. Some I've bought, some were gifts, and some were dumped on us. The Chinese cork tree had outgrown the grounds where my in-laws now live on Long Island, so they brought it here. It was a twiggy mess, but isn't it beautiful now with its strangely spreading branches? I built the whole Japanese garden around it."

Some of the most unusual rocks come not from Japan but from Keene Valley in the Adirondacks, whence Gray has personally lifted and lugged them to Connecticut. He points to a large and lovely egg-shaped rock that he laboriously carried from the bed of a stream and up a mountainside one time while visiting friends. "I was afraid my hostess would think I was stealing," he recalls, "but she was only incredulous that anyone would be crazy enough to go to such trouble for a rock." He has also carried large coral rocks home from Florida. "Not so easy on a plane," he admits, "but worth it for their rough and speckled surface. And many plants manage to take hold in the crevices. That little rosette of hen-and-chickens is right at home."

Gray's plant materials, too, are from all over: from local nurseries, and not so local—Gray gets specimens from Long Island, California, and as far away as England—as well as some wild samples from the Connecticut woods. "This is a plain old Scotch pine that I transplanted from our woods in back of the house," Gray says, pointing to a tree. "I keep shaping it so it will grow tall yet stay horizontal on top. And look at that white pine. It's a native, but it looks as Japanese as you can get. What makes it so splendid is the way it's grown into the rocks surrounding it. Its roots have actually crept under the rocks and the soft branches form a canopy above them."

Born and raised in Ireland, Gray graduated from Trinity College in Dublin, then went to work in London for Angela Saunders, whose famous garden shop was then on Barclay Street. "Much of our work was garden design, particularly terrace arrangements, and we also created flower designs for great parties, including state occasions for Queen Elizabeth at Buckingham Palace," says Gray. "In time I became head buyer and head decorator for the company."

Gray met his American wife in London when she came from the States to visit her brother, who was living there, and she liked it so much she stayed three years. "We met, fell in love and were married in 1961. But we both wanted to live in the States," he says. "So we came to New York, where we expected to stay forever. Unhappily, it didn't work out that way because I simply couldn't find a suitable job. So back we went to London, where Angela Saunders welcomed me with open arms.

"The problem was that we yearned for the States, where we really wanted to live. So once again we made the westward crossing, and this time I was luckier. It was in '65, when artificial flowers were popular, and I began to make and sell them—very successfully, I'm happy to say. Lord & Taylor, Bloomingdale's and lots of private people bought my arrangements for parties and even as objets d'art."

By then the Grays had moved to the Connecticut house. "Helen's parents were eager for the family to keep the house and had generously given it to us," Gray says. "My career as a landscape designer began quite by chance. One day Helen met a friend in the local drugstore who asked, 'Isn't your husband a landscape designer? I need someone to landscape our property.' One job led to another and to a long and happy career designing gardens and landscaping settings for private homes." He smiles and adds, "I consider myself blessed that my work is also what I love most to do."

WILLIAM SEITZ

CAROLINE BRYAN
OCTOBER 1989

*R*ereading *The Education of a Gardener* by the late master landscape architect Russell Page, I came upon a description of novelist Edith Wharton's garden when she lived in Paris in the '20s. Designed around a Louis XV pavilion, its layout was strictly formal, with carefully divided compartments for different plants, a parterre—an ornamental arrangement of flower beds of different shapes and sizes—and 6-foot flowering shrubs clipped into pyramidal shapes.

Caroline Bryan's garden in Bantam is the antithesis of this structured patterning, and yet Page's description of Wharton's design brought it vividly to mind. "She made a garden setting exactly in the spirit of the house," he wrote. And that's just what Caroline Bryan, an artist, has done.

Without artifice, Bryan has created an informal setting that is exactly in the spirit of her house and land. Small islands of miniature evergreens, flowering bushes and blossoming plants form pockets of color that take their place and shape from the meandering nature of the terrain, the wondrous old trees and the character of the house itself.

"This was a farmhouse built in 1787," Bryan says, "a simple two-story wooden square centering around a stone chimney, with ceilings only 6-foot-7-inches high—the heart of a working farm. Certainly, a formal English or French garden was uncalled for. Fifty years earlier," she continues, "in 1737, England bought from the Indians 20 square miles of land in the Bantam/Litchfield area and shrewdly divided it into 100-acre sites that were cleared to entice farmers into buying the parcels. I imagine that's just what our farmer did, although some of the acreage was later sold off."

Early on in the history of this farm, more land was needed for cultivation, so additional meadows were cleared of rocks, big and small. These were left in huge piles at the edge of each field. Bryan and Vaill—mostly Vaill—have laboriously built these into stone walls, steps, rock gardens and other landscape accents, as they, in turn, have cleared more land (about 4 acres) for lawns and planting.

But one massive granite boulder remains where they found it—where, in fact, it has been since the glacial epoch more than a million years ago. Twenty feet long and 5 feet deep, it bears a marvelous likeness to a resting elephant, sloping in height from 8 feet at the beast's head to 5 feet at its rump. And not only is it shaped like an elephant, its color is elephant-gray and its scabby, gnarled surface is a dead ringer for elephant hide.

"We discovered the animal lying in hiding under the shrub trees and tall weeds at the crest of the hill to the south of the house," Bryan relates. "Of course, we immediately named the property for it, 'Elephant Rock.' In the manner of elephants, this one was resting in the shade, under an old cherry. I felt some kind of low greenery was needed to suggest its natural habitat, but a formal planting was hardly appropriate for this creature of the wild. So I transplanted ferns from the woods that have now grown into a lush bed along its flank.

"We now have a second elephant that John gave me five years ago," she adds, pointing to a handsome white sculptured pachyderm set in a square grassy island directly across the driveway from the house. "John found it in an antique shop in New Haven—though it was carved in India—and had it delivered, crated, at Christmastime. I managed to get the crate open for a look inside, but it's so heavy we had to leave it outside in the box till springtime, when it took a crane to lift it out. We found a perfect flat stone for a base among our old rocks. Then, to frame it prettily, I circled it with daylilies. Their arching foliage is a soft foil from spring to fall and their yellow blossoms in summer somehow go with both the Early American setting and the exotic look of India."

Daylilies are, in fact, all over the place, generally in yellow and orange mixed, always in great groupings. "They look best en masse," says Bryan, so she's planted them by the hundreds: in a giant crescent under a Japanese magnolia just as you come in the driveway; circling an aged, spreading, 80-foot maple; in a thick row along the stone wall that separates the property from the road; as guidelines for stepping-stones that ease the way along the sloping terrain; edging the gravel pathways that link the lawns; in waving beds in back of the house; even masking the old outhouse ("a two-seater"). "Daylilies are native to Connecticut and belong here," Bryan says with conviction.

Enormous clumps of dark green hosta also grow in profusion around the house and outbuildings, all offspring of one planting Bryan found on the property 16 years ago. She subsequently divided and replanted the clumps under the big shade trees.

And there are plenty of those. "The biggest were generously bequeathed to us by nature, with some well over a hundred years old," Bryan says with admiration, even reverence. "The old apples are a variety that's no longer raised—although they're good eating. Actually, it's the shape of these old trees that gets me, the thick branches splayed right from the ground and the twisted boughs."

I quote again from *The Education of a Gardener* because this Bantam garden so vividly embodies Russell Page's philosophy. "You design a garden within all the limitations of the site," he writes, "the climate and the nature of the soil, of the local culture and of your own capacities as artist and technician . . . but if your garden is to have magic, you have to give it an extra dimension. I think that awareness of the interplay between objects, whether organic or inorganic, is of major importance if your garden is to be also a work of art."

For all its seeming casualness—perhaps *because* of its casualness—Bryan's garden is as much a work of art as the paintings she creates. Not by chance is there an aesthetic interplay between the house, the sloping contours of the land, the rocks, trees, shrubs and flowers. In composing her plant material, she strives for a unified whole that is more than the sum of its parts. The flowering trees and shrubs she has selected vary in form and leaf yet are compatible with one another and with the land: plum, quince and pear among the fruit trees, a hazelnut tree whose ripening nuts particularly delight Bryan with their fringed, ruffed, thirsty calyxes; native white flowering dogwood; magnolias; oak-leaf hydrangea; yellow-blossoming potentilla; pink flowering crab apple and hawthorns; a spreading, deliciously fragrant mock orange, and more.

"We didn't fight nature," Bryan points out. "If a tree was there before we came, we landscaped around it— the big dogwood, for example. With new trees we tried to create clusters that served a decorative purpose, to fill in swale in the land or soften a rock outcropping or lend interest to a flat spot. But they had to look natural, not as if they were foisted on the land. We also chose trees with foliage in different shades of green— nature's palette is extraordinary—and with different leaf shapes for textural interest."

Among the most striking shrubs on the property are the ornamental evergreens, the biggest of which, two yews, have by now grown together into a hedge 20 feet long, 7 feet deep and 5 feet high. It is the only formal, clipped shrubbery Bryan will allow. "It was planted in 1934 and was kept clipped for almost 40 years till we came along, so we've maintained the tradition," she explains.

Bryan generally defers to nature in her choice of flowers, but sometimes her artist's love of color and form breaks through in her choice of cultivated plants.

Among the "naturals," masses of double white violets, blue violets and lilies of the valley, all Connecticut natives, give early-spring bloom under the maples, oak and evergreens. Islands of Siberian iris, cultivars of the blue flag that welcomed the early settlers to Connecticut, welcome today's visitors to Elephant Rock.

Among the "imports," great clumps of pink peonies front a stone wall. "They're not natives, but I can't resist them," Bryan confesses, then adds, "Neither could the early settlers who brought old-fashioned peony varieties with them from England." In the beds along the front and side of the house, there's a mix of both. Silvery lamb's ears and artemis, yellow feverfew, blue ageratum and forget-me-nots serve as underplanting to tall blue delphiums, warm pink phlox, recurved Oriental lilies and spiky *physostegia*. Zinnias make a bright splash.

Caroline Bryan's love of gardening stems from her childhood. Born in Neuilly just outside Paris, the daughter of a French mother and American father, she grew up in Paris and went to boarding school in England till she was 9. She spent her early summers in Corsica, where her family had a country house. "When we were small children," she recalls, "my father gave one of my sisters—we're three girls—a peach tree, and me, an apricot tree, to tend. I guess that hooked me on growing things." Her interest in art also began at an early age, no doubt influenced by her father and maternal grandfather, both artists.

When the war came in '39, the family fled the Germans, moving first to the South of France, then to Spain, then to Lisbon, and finally to the United States ("As an American, my father—and probably the whole family—would have been imprisoned in a concentration camp"). They settled in Jacksonville, Fla., where Caroline went to prep school. She later attended Vassar, where she studied painting. But during her junior year, she fell in love with Sheldon Bryan, also an artist, and quit school to marry him. Widowed in 1968, she went back to painting once her two daughters were in college.

Her works, which are sold through galleries in New York, Connecticut, Massachusetts and Florida, reflect her love of the New England countryside and of gardens. Soft landscapes and striking florals, they fuse representationalism with Impressionism and what Bryan calls "a touch of the abstract."

"Creating paintings and creating gardens are not dissimilar," she says. "Both require stern selectivity, a sense of space and proportion, a love of color and its subtleties, and a knowledge of form."

And talent.

GEORGE E. SCHOELLKOPF

JULY 1990

*K*nown internationally as a collector and purveyor of Early American folk art and furniture, George Schoellkopf is no slouch as a gardener either. For four years he wrote a regular garden column for a Connecticut weekly, now writes for *House & Garden* and other national magazines, and is busy putting together his own book on gardening in the Northeast. His gardens in northwest Connecticut have themselves been pictured in *HG*, will be featured in *The American Man's Garden* by Rosemary Verey (the follow-up to her beautiful *The American Woman's Garden*), and were one of nine spectacular stops on the recent garden tour held by The Glebe House in Woodbury. Proceeds from the tour are being used to bring to life The Glebe House garden designed by Gertrude Jekyll, the great British landscape artist who changed the look of gardens on both sides of the Atlantic.

"My garden is strongly influenced by Jekyll's thinking—whose isn't?" says Schoellkopf. "It's an English garden, but with a strong Connecticut accent. The first time I went to England, I made up my mind I would someday have an English garden. And at last I have. The layout—three terraced spaces including a brick-pathed parterre, a flagstoned square and a double border surrounding a rectangular pool and fountain—is in the British formal tradition. But when the garden is in bloom, informality reigns, American style. Plants tumble casually, arch loosely, ramble and climb. But don't be fooled. Yes, I let them do their thing, but I've chosen them because their thing is *the thing I want*."

In his mid-40s, Schoellkopf is a native Texan who came to Connecticut when he was 14. He attended Hotchkiss, went on to get a bachelor's degree at Yale and a master's at Columbia, both in art history. The expected next step was a Ph.D., but he chose instead to open an antiques shop in Greenwich Village, where he specialized in Early American folk art. "That was 20 years ago, and you could pick up something wonderful and authentic—a knockout 18th- or 19th-century quilt, for instance, which is what I started with—for a few dollars at a flea market," he recalls. "I guess I had a good eye, because the shop did so well I outgrew it and opened a gallery on Madison Avenue at 81st Street, where I stayed 14 years. Then, five years ago, I gave up the gallery to spend time in Connecticut writing and gardening, and to travel.

"I bought the house here 12 years ago and live here full-time now with Ron Johnson, the landscape painter (and two cats, Louise and Big Blue Cat)," he adds. "Together, we started building the garden 10 years ago. What we had originally was a typical Connecticut steep slope edged north and south by a brook. Slowly and laboriously, we've terraced the hillside into three levels.

"The first garden we built—the topmost level—is a small fenced-in area in an angle of the house that is paved with stones from a street in Brooklyn. One wall of the house is softened by a wonderful old lilac bush

133

that was here when we came, and a gorgeous blue holly—the hardy type. Be careful when you shop for a holly. Ask the nurseryman if it will withstand Connecticut winters. Better yet, ask if it was bred in a cold clime and not imported from south Jersey or Virginia. And of course, plant a male and a female—one male can take care of several females and needn't be immediately nearby. The birds and bees will take care of fertilization."

Diagonally across this little garden is a redbud tree that has *white* blossoms, not red, and a striking tall yew shaped into three tiers with a domed top. "I'm not much for topiary," Schoellkopf admits. "It's generally too formal for my landscaping, but this works."

In the beds facing down the house is an old-fashioned *Rosa alba* ("Do try old roses—they're so fragrant"), some white-flowered angelica *arcangelica* (a wildflower from Europe that reseeds itself generously), and something neither Schoellkopf nor I had ever seen before, a white double trillium loaded with incredibly beautiful gardenialike blossoms.

"They say you can't transplant trillium, but someone gave me this and it's happy here—which leads me to the single most important piece of advice I can give gardeners," he says. "Experiment. If the experts tell you a plant you passionately long for won't make it in Connecticut, try it anyway. Give it a sheltered spot or a ton of leaf mold or a double dose of fertilizer or sing it lullabies, but try it.

"For example, I was cautioned that boxwood wouldn't make it here, but in the formal brick-pathed garden—the second level down—the spaced beds are all edged in English box. Look at it," he says, patting a sprig affectionately. "It's thriving, even after a terrible winter. It's called *Welleri*, and it's a miniature variety of English box that reaches 2 feet in height.

"Of course, it works both ways," he adds. "The Christmas rose *(Helleborus niger)* generally does very well in these parts, but not for me. On the other hand, the Lenten rose *(Helleborus orientalis)* gives me beautiful pink-and-green-tinged white blossoms in late April and May."

A tall, early-blooming flowering quince—another plant that is said to be too delicate for reliable Connecticut bloom—is one of the accents of the box garden. Among the profusion of bedding plants for early-spring bloom are daffodils, tulips and fritillaria from bulbs, lots of white bleeding heart, anemones, *Primula sieboldi* with white lacy flowers (quite different from the usual primrose blooms), and, in clusters everywhere, yellow celandine poppies. "They're not poppies at all," Schoellkopf laughs. "In fact, they're a wild thing. A friend gave me one plant a couple of years ago and it's reseeded everywhere." For summer flowering, peonies, poppies and phlox give a succession of flowers.

In the brook south of the house, Schoellkopf built a waterfall—twice. "Hurricane Gloria washed out the first one, which was entirely put together of natural stones and curved," he explains. "Now the stones are set in concrete and one side of the curve has been straightened. Floods are prone to build up inside curves and destroy them, we've learned." Along the stone path leading from the house to the brook are great clumps of Siberian iris, variegated pulmonaria—spotted lungwort—and very dark purple Johnny-jump-ups. "I was given some unusual, almost black Johnny-jump-ups, and they got together with the usual purple ones so that the offspring are very dark," Schoellkopf says. The shrubbery includes a white *Boule de Neige* rhododendron ("an old variety that still sets the standard for hybridizers") and the tall-growing native rhododendron *maximum*, whose pink blossoms come in July ("wonderful because of its late bloom—I wish they'd develop some hybrids").

To build the next level down, Schoellkopf had to construct an 8½-foot brick retaining wall that encloses a double border of plants with stretches of lawn outlining a rectangular pond. Although the design is formal, the planting is not. Here growing in a charming mix are delphiniums, lilies, iris, astilbe, 4-foot-tall *Crambe cordifolia* ("like giant baby's breath with a cloud of white flowers"), tall feathery pink-flowered filipendula, 7-foot-tall plume poppies, wavy tall ornamental grasses, and *heuchera*—coral bells—that never have bells but have burnished red foliage that gleams in the sunshine.

Climbing the walls are *Actinidia kolomikta* ("a very rare vine with unusual pink, green and white foliage that we imported from the West but is totally hardy here"), euonymus ("God's gift to Connecticut gardeners"), the climber hydrangea *petiolaris* ("a slow starter that's loaded with white lacy flowers once it gets going"), and an old-fashioned *Rosa gallica* climber.

What makes the garden unmistakably Schoellkopf's is the mix of rare plants, familiar perennials, and, yes, weeds. Among the rarities are *Euphorbia graffita*, a red-leaved perennial that is a hardy relative of the poinsettia; the Japanese *Kerengeshoma palmata*, with beautiful foliage and creamy yellow bells in September ("I had it shipped from a grower in England and by a miracle it got through customs"); and allium *bulgaricum*, which gets 2 feet high and has exotic brown and green bells. Among the weeds? Silene, a little thing with shocking-pink flowers that reseed everywhere, Johnny-jump-ups and wild forget-me-nots.

Schoellkopf's 11 acres look north across a brook to a green hillside where he has planted a silver willow that's now 50 feet tall, and where there are also some old apple trees delineating the property. "We fight the beavers to keep part of the brook for swimming," he says. "Our neighbors have problems with deer; with us the enemy is beaver. They ate a half-foot semicircle out of an old apple tree that we've since circled with a high wire fence—better late than never."

Schoellkopf is a down-to-earth gardener who is happy to share his experience and give practical advice. "Don't fight nature," he says. "An architect friend who recently built a spectacular house on a rocky cliff above Lake Waramaug was racking his brains on how to landscape amongst the rock outcroppings. Looking around, I saw that nature had lavished the hillside with mountain laurel and ferns. Plainly, that's what grew naturally there, so I advised him to plant more of the same. What a spectacle! A hillside of pink and white laurel underplanted with ferns. For variety, I advised some of the lovely new laurel hybrids with reddish blossoms, and suggested he intersperse the more common cinnamon and interrupted fern varieties with clumps of the burnished red Japanese painted sword ferns and delicate maidenhair ferns.

"If you want to create a knockout effect," he suggests, "use great clusters of tall plants and grasses—really tall, like plume poppies and filipendula and even delphiniums, which will grow 6 to 8 feet tall if you feed them—and feed them. Once a month is not too much. Another splendid tall grower is artemisia *lactiflora*, which gets to 6 feet and has beautiful white flowers in August. It's not used often enough, probably because it was just discovered in the '20s in China."

Among the tall grasses Schoellkopf recommends are *Misecanthus dracillum*, which waves in the breeze from 6-to-8-foot heights, and, the biggest of all, *Misecanthus giganticus*, which, despite its height, is delicate and graceful.

"For extra foliage interest," he adds, "use plants with variegated leaves—the white lightens and brightens the garden the summer long. And try for different shades of green. Lady's mantle, for instance, has apple-green leaves that contrast handsomely with the different greens of hosta, from yellow-green to an almost black blue-green. Both take shade. I also favor gray-green—there's a beautiful gray lamb's ears with larger leaves than most. It never blooms, but its foliage is a plus all year. Trees with gray-toned foliage, like Russian olives and silver willows, are also lovely for softening effect.

"Flowering trees add grace notes to the landscaping," he says, "but not too many do well for me here in northwest Connecticut. Crab apples are weakened by the weather here and get diseases, and flowering cherries are too often winter-killed. A marvelous flowering tree that's rarely used in Connecticut gardens but should be is the rose acacia *robinia,* which gets 30 feet high and blossoms in June with pink wisterialike panicles. All my visitors are dazzled by it. Me too."

What kind of fertilizer does he favor? "Just about everything," he admits, "though I try to be as organic as possible. The best fertilizer is guano, which the bats in my barn generously give me. Next comes cow manure. Fresh is best; just let it ripen over the winter, covered, or the rain will wash out all the nutrients. But if you don't know a friendly farmer—or cow—dried cow manure is good, too. The important thing is to feed the plant spring and fall—and hungry ones in between."

Last winter Schoellkopf bought a house outside Santa Barbara. "We'll spend a few months there in the winter," he says, "but of course, spring, summer and fall, I couldn't be anyplace but Connecticut."

WILLIAM SEITZ

THE GLEBE HOUSE

OCTOBER 1990

*T*he Gertrude Jekyll garden at The Glebe House in Woodbury gives Connecticut the distinction of having the only Jekyll garden in the country. (There were two others in the Midwest, but they have fall-
en victim to urban development.)

136

That's no small distinction. Miss Jekyll (rhymes with treacle), who died in 1934 at the age of 89, is
acclaimed as one of the greatest garden designers in modern history. Typically, she preferred the more mod-
est "garden designer" designation to the fancier "landscape architect" or "landscape designer," because that's
what she did—design gardens—although with a highly knowledgeable and appreciative eye on both the
house and surrounding landscape. In fact, it was she who, through her long association with the architect

Edward Lutyens, resolved the bitter dispute between architects and gardeners as to who should design gardens, making it unarguably clear that it was not a matter for architects or gardeners, but for architects *and* gardeners. As noted garden writer George Plumptre puts it in his splendid book *Garden Ornament*, "Their work became the primary influence upon the development of English gardens through the 20th century and its influence can be clearly seen in some of the century's most celebrated gardens, such as Hidcote Manor in Gloucestershire and Sissinghurst Castle in Kent."

"It is an old truth that there is nothing new in design, but Gertrude Jekyll brought a unique freshness to the subject," writes David Stevens, founder of Britain's Society of Landscape and Garden Designers, in his informative *Creative Gardens*. Russell Page, in his gardening bible, *The Education of a Gardener*, calls Jekyll a pioneer and notes, "I can think of few English gardens made in the last 50 years which do not bear the mark of her teaching." He could well have included the United States, notably New England.

Jekyll's revolutionizing concept, as realized at The Glebe House, was to *informalize* gardens through the introduction of the herbaceous border—the backbone, one might even say the basic anatomy, of today's gardens. Inspired by English cottage gardens and their "common, no-account flowers," the herbaceous-border approach was in sharp contrast to the prevailing Victorian pattern of gardening "as if it were some sort of military operation in which new recruits were lined up each spring for formal inspection and regiments of scarlet geraniums all in a row were set out next to royal-blue lobelia, while red-hot pokers stood as erect as Her Majesty's household guard" (from "*Earthly Delights*," an article by Paula Weideger in *Ms.* magazine, March '89).

Although a very British lady, Jekyll feistily rejected the geometric rigidity of the Victorians and created instead loose, simply shaped, flowing "drifts" of the same trusty perennials that cottage gardeners had used for centuries and that head gardeners at large estates were then throwing onto their compost heaps by the hundreds (she loved the disdained hollyhocks, for example). Her ideas, as you might imagine, were hardly popular with the emerging English middle class, who wanted to ape the gentry.

But don't get the idea that Jekyll's gardens were casually put together. Her goal of seemingly "haphazard luxuriance . . . comes neither by hap nor hazard, but by careful planning," writes Vita Sackville-West, creator of Sissinghurst Gardens. Jekyll was a trained and accomplished painter long before she turned to gardening—a cheering note to late bloomers like me. She did not take up gardening till her late 40s, when, ironically, it was deteriorating eyesight that forced her to it. Her hand-drawn garden designs, big and small, are said to have reflected the artistry of her paintings. What a shame that none survive. She was also a gifted craftsperson, expert at carving and gilding silver, all of which her fading vision compelled her to give up.

But in many respects, her misfortune turned out to be our good fortune. As Richard Bisgrove of the University of Reading in England writes in the preface to Jekyll's book *Color Schemes for the Flower Garden* (one of 12 she wrote on gardening), "Her greatest contribution to English culture was to reassert the position of gardening as a fine art." He goes on to claim that her skill "should dispel the misunderstanding . . . that [because of] her worsening eyesight . . . she saw the garden only as a vague blur of color. Although her eyesight was both poor and painful, she observed in minute detail and with great accuracy."

To this dirt gardener, what Jekyll writes in *Color Schemes* is inspirational, informative—and daunting. Although her techniques sound easy—simply large beds of one color drifting into each other—my dears, it isn't. And she says so. "To plant and maintain a flower border, with a good scheme for color, is by no means the easy thing that is commonly supposed," she notes. "The duty we owe to our gardens," she goes on, "is so to use the plants that they shall form beautiful pictures . . . and not tolerate bad or careless combination or any sort of misuse of plants." (Can I ever live up to that?)

So how did the Jekyll garden in Woodbury come about? First of all, there was The Glebe House itself, a center-chimney, gambrel-roofed house built in 1690 and considered a superb example of late-17th-early-18th-century Connecticut architecture. The house also figured importantly in the founding of the Episcopal Church in America after its stormy break from England's Anglican Church. The election of its first American bishop, Samuel Seabury, took place here in 1783. Nonetheless, the fate of the house was uncertain until 1923, when the Seabury Society for the Preservation of The Glebe House was formed. Just two years later it was opened to the public.

Soon after, in 1926, a very public-spirited—and wealthy—Fairfield woman, Miss Annie Burr Jennings (whose father, Oliver Burr Jennings, founded Standard Oil Co. in partnership with John D. Rockefeller), took tea with Gertrude Jekyll at her now-famous home at Munstead Wood and, upon her return to Fairfield, wrote to Jekyll asking her to design "an old-fashioned garden" for The Glebe House, for which Jennings would be "responsible for the expense." She sent Jekyll photographs of the house and dimensions of the property.

Jekyll was over 80 at the time, but her directions to Jennings are spirited and precisely to the point. "The first thing that strikes me is the need for enclosure and for this purpose [I suggest] some solid evergreens in the East and West and low hedges to the North and South," she wrote. Also, "What is the usual fencing from the road—nothing shows from the illustrations. The usual thing for this class of house in England for the last 200 years is a fencing of upright slats about 2½-inch thick pointed at the top, either hardwood—oak for preference—or white-painted with posts at intervals of about 9 feet with a gate of the same." And more such specifics.

For one reason or another, only a small part of the Jekyll design was installed in the 1920s—and that was to the south of the house by Amy Cogswell of Norwich, who had been hired by the Seabury Society.

After that, the plan foundered and could well have been lost. It is to Beatrice Farrand, the niece of American novelist Edith Wharton and perhaps the most notable American landscape architect in the first half of this century, that we are indebted for salvaging Jekyll's original Glebe House garden design. Although Jekyll was famous, even revered, in England, it was Farrand, an American, who grasped the full measure of her contribution and bought her drawings and other papers (including The Glebe House design) at auction in England after her death. In 1955 Farrand donated them to the University of California at Berkeley, where they lay unnoticed until the mid-'80s, when a scholar from the university found them and contacted Mary Baker, curator of The Glebe House Museum.

Excited at the prospect of bringing the full design to life, Baker enlisted the aid of Mrs. Nelly Doolan of Woodbury, a native of Britain who vastly admired Jekyll and had contributed to the support of the partial existing garden. "Nelly Doolan has made the project a full-time job—all without pay," says Tony Bleach, associate professor of horticulture at Mattatuck Community College in Waterbury. "The garden would not exist today without her tireless efforts."

Doolan's first step was to organize a group of knowledgeable, highly competent people in the field, including Curly Lieber of New Haven, proprietor of The Garden Container, which specializes in unusual containers and garden ornaments, bookseller Tim Mawson of New Preston, Tony Bleach, and Early Americana and gardening expert George Schoellkopf of Washington.

"Bringing the whole plan to life is the only way for the public to see Miss Jekyll's unique contribution to gardening, and how much our gardens today owe to her glorious vision of plants in harmony with their surroundings," says Doolan. "As Miss Jekyll herself constantly reiterated, 'If something is worth doing, it is worth doing well.'

"We have a long way to go," she adds. "We haven't even tackled the border of conifers Miss Jekyll planned for the back of the house. And many of the plants we have used are temporary substitutions for those she listed. George Schoellkopf, for example, is growing miniature English boxwood for us to replace the germander we have as temporary edging to some of the beds.

"Also, we learned last winter that many plants that thrive in England can't take our low temperatures. Miss Jekyll specified rosemary, for instance, which isn't hardy here. We've tried to achieve the look she wanted with a gray-toned new artemisia called Powis Castle. Also, the foliage of some bearded iris she set forth tends to rot in our dampish soil, so we're planning to substitute a variety of iris *pallida*. And of course, we've had to lime our sour, acid soil heavily to match the sweet soil of England."

Problems notwithstanding, the garden at The Glebe House already captures the great lady's artistry in coloration and form. In late summer, for example, there was a wondrous interplay of pink, blue and white, a favorite Jekyll trio (although she loved hot colors, too, and mixed them in many of her designs—like vivid pink phlox, goldenrod, scarlet penstemon and blood-red dahlias, in one socko combination). The Jekyll magic came from the nuances of each of these colors and the way they were placed to complement one another for their foliage and form as well as blossoms.

Among the blues were spiky periwinkle Veronica, rounded globes of gray-toned blue echinops, velvety-petaled true-blue salvia, lavender lavender ("It's on trial for hardiness," Schoellkopf points out), spires of dark blue-purple delphiniums (in second bloom), low-growing glaucus nepeta, purple-blue heliotrope in shrublike mounds, low tufted rounds of bright blue ageratum, spreading tapers of tiny-flowered sky-blue Russian sage, and clumps of bright-leaved hostas stemmed with pale lavender fennellike blooms.

The pinks blended ever-blooming, red-toned, ferny-leaved bleeding heart *eximia* with clear pink upright-facing zinnias, hot pink stand-up snapdragons, loose groups of pale pink nicotiana, masses of tall spidery pink and white cleome, rosy asters and roses—everywhere roses—the climbing, small-blossomed pale pink Fairy, the rich pink yellow-stemmed single-shrub Frau Dagmar Hastropp, and, in bloom all summer long, the pink form of *Rosa alba*. ("Actually, many roses Miss Jekyll prescribed are not hardy in Connecticut—China roses, for example," notes Doolan, "so we're trying to choose tougher types from gardens she designed or simply those we know will make it in Woodbury and resemble her choice.")

"Jekyll even achieves variety within her whites," Schoellkopf says admiringly. And indeed, there are gray-leaved lambs' ears fuzzed with white, tiny-blossomed white alyssum nestled in apple-green foliage, pristine white dahlias, orange-bearded white iris, green-and-white variegated euonymus—some in tiny-leaved dense mats, others big-leaved and loose—along with little off-white zinnias with yellow centers, floppy nicotiana *sylvestris*, great snowballs of double peonies and orange-anthered Regal lilies.

"Drifts" is the password in this and all Jekyll gardens. No puny cluster of two or three plants for this lady, but a mass of 20 cleome in one place, repeated elsewhere in the border for flow, dozens of ageratum, great clusters of lilies, iris, dahlias, roses. No empty spaces either. Nature and Gertrude Jekyll abhor a vacuum, which accounts for the many annuals that fill whatever large spots perennials might leave.

The design Gertrude Jekyll created for The Glebe House is a rectangle framed on all sides by shrubs and low-growing trees, with lawn space between the house and the 10-foot-deep herbaceous borders to set off both. "Only three sides of the rectangle exist and these are far from finished," says Doolan. "We have an edging of yews to the north and south, but no shrubs yet to the east or west. Also, Miss Jekyll made it plain that a picket fence is required and exactly described it in her letters. Our original timetable scheduled building it in the fall of '91. I hope our budget will allow it.

"We had a wonderful garden tour last June that raised $8,000 for The Glebe House garden," Doolan continues. "We had expected to use the money to install hedges and plant flowers, including hundreds of old-fashioned Pheasant's Eye daffodils naturalized on the hill in back of the house. But then we encountered additional drainage problems in back of the house that will cost $4,000, so things may move more slowly.

"But we'll make it," she insists. "Gertrude Jekyll sought to fashion gardens that are 'a dream of beauty, a place of perfect pictures—a treasure of well-set jewels,' all within a harmonious configuration of house and ground. This is her only existing design in the United States, and we feel it is worth whatever effort it takes to give the public the opportunity of seeing it, learning from it and enjoying it."

The Glebe House, Hollow Road, Woodbury, CT 06798, (203) 263-2855.

WEIR FARM

MARCH 1994

*A*s CONNECTICUT's garden columnist, I'm supposed to write about gardens and, strictly speaking, there are no gardens at Weir Farm (the Weir Farm National Historic Site) in Wilton. There were—you can see vestiges of them—and there will be again. This summer. The Ridgefield Garden Club and the National Park Service are working to restore them. But at the moment, as an old Nutmegger friend of mine says, "Nawthin'."

And yet, the whole place, located on the crest of Nod Hill in Branchville, straddling the border between Ridgefield and Wilton, is a glorious garden. It captures within its 57 acres the beauty, order and disorder of the Connecticut countryside that its owner, the famed American Impressionist J. Alden Weir (1852-1919), portrayed with haunting simplicity in his many paintings of the farm. It's not just the bounty of flowering trees—cherry, apple, crab apple, dogwood—that make it so. Nor the flowering shrubs—lilac, mountain laurel, rhododendron. Nor the artfully placed pond that Weir built. Nor the hundreds of evergreen and deciduous trees in an artist's palette of colors and a sculptor's array of shapes.

It's all of these and more. For it is J. Alden Weir's passionate love of nature and devotion to preserving the humble aspects of country life that pervade the farm—and transcend it. Designated a National Historic Site in November 1990—the first such in Connecticut—the farm and its surrounding wetlands are now open to the public as part of the National Park System. Yet as Connecticut Sen. Joseph Lieberman points out, "This is not the Grand Canyon. The dimensions are very human and very approachable." The leader in the movement to win federal-park status for the farm, Lieberman now is fighting for ongoing federal funding. It was he together with Weir's son-in-law, the sculptor Mahonri Young, who built his own studio at the farm, Sperry and Doris Andrews, the current artists-in-residence at the farm, the Trust for Public Land and the Weir Farm Heritage Trust that eventually succeeded in preserving Weir's "great good place" for posterity.

The farm is the only park ever traded for a work of art. Weir was not only renowned as an artist but also as an expert—"a human divining rod"—at finding buried masterpieces by other artists for museums and collectors. (Manet's "Boy with a Sword," which now hangs in the Metropolitan Museum of Art, is one of his finds.) In 1882, when he was just back from choosing canvases in Europe, collector Erwin Davis offered him his farm in Branchville in exchange for a painting plus $10. As Weir's friend, C.E.S. Wood, wrote, "Mr. Davis, judging by the rocks, thought he had the better of the artist, and Weir, judging by the inexhaustible beauty of woods, fields, hills, pond . . . knew that he had the better of the man of business."

Weir would probably have been amused by his place being called a National Historic Site. To him it was home, a working farm for him and his family, as well as an outdoor studio where he and his artist friends could capture the beauty of the Connecticut countryside. In fact, it was the farm that shaped Weir's mature style of painting, moving him to reject formal portraiture and still lifes (although his paintings of flowers are acclaimed as among the masterpieces of still life produced in this country) in favor of landscapes in the Impressionist style.

In 1890 he began painting out-of-doors in earnest, using pure, prismatic colors, unmixed on the canvas to create effects of intense coloration and flickering light. The farm became his inspiration. His paintings range from homely country scenes—laundry lines in the back yard of his studio, a barnyard, workers resting—to intimate landscapes. In a sense, he was one of America's first environmentalists, preserving a natural American landscape "free of bombast and commerce." He also produced a series of industrial landscapes of historic as well as artistic significance depicting the textile mills around Willimantic, which was his wife's family home and his "other Connecticut studio."

(His grandson, Charles Burlingham Jr., notes that Weir often "fine-tuned the landscape with his brush." Weir called this "hollyhocking." If he felt a few extra flowers—even a tree in an otherwise flat field—were needed for aesthetic reasons, he would paint them in. It's said that he built the pond on his property as much for a setting to paint as to fish—and he loved to fish.)

The farm also became a studio and meeting place for artists Childe Hassam, John Twachtman and Albert Pinkham Ryder, whose Branchville-inspired landscapes rank among the finest paintings of the American Impressionist movement. "All of these artists painted gardens," writes University of Connecticut Professor Emeritus Rudy J. Favretti, a landscape architect and historian who in 1990 was commissioned by the Ridgefield Garden Club to prepare the initial restoration plan for the Weir Farm garden. "As with Monet and the European Impressionists, gardens were an integral part of their lives and had a profound effect on their work," notes Favretti in his study.

Favretti describes the Weir Farm garden itself as "not large—only 68 feet by 48 feet." But, he adds, "The whole landscape was a type of garden; the cultivated flower garden was just an accent on the whole, a place to enjoy concentrated nature and to observe the hand of man upon it.

"Its location suggests a knowledge of horticulture on its builder's part," Favretti continues. "It was situated on the highest part of ground within the 'house lot' of the farm, thus providing the best drainage . . . where it would receive full sun—no shade from the studio or the large ash tree at its northeast corner . . . [with] a hedge of deutzia to provide protection from the winds of winter and act as a 'snow fence' to prevent huge drifts of snow. Yet air could circulate through its branches . . . . On the south side was a rustic fence, very much in style during the turn of the century but also practical enough to allow for maximum penetration of sun and air."

Because it was the natural setting of the farm that sparked Weir's life and work, the National Park Service is painstakingly working to "retain the site's feeling, character and sense of place." Says Susan F. Anjevin, executive director of the Weir Farm Historic Trust, "The treatment of the landscape is an integral part of the understanding of the site." A detailed mapping project of the garden is under way, she says, to determine "patterns of use and help guide the future restoration."

"It is richly rewarding to be in on the ground floor of so historic a project," says Lillian Willis, president of the Ridgefield Garden Club, "but it is a tremendous job and a costly one. In 1992 our club won a $5,000 Founders Award from the Garden Clubs of America for the project. That's only the beginning; additional funding is necessary, not only for our efforts but for the whole gargantuan project. In addition to research, serious hands-on labor is demanded. The garden is wildly overgrown—the poison ivy is so rampant, for example, that for the first time in my life, I have seen its berries. Our full membership of some 70 women will be involved in one or another phase of the work. Plainly, for us it is a true labor of love."

To introduce Park Service techniques for landscape restoration, an on-site workshop was presented by experts on horticultural historic preservation from the National Park Service's Olmsted Center for Landscape Preservation in Brookline, Mass. Ridgefield Garden Club members took it all in—and are now applying what they learned about restoration procedures, rejuvenating and renewal methods to the farm.

"The first job," explains Willis, "was inventorying plants—what the experts call plant identification and mapping. That means finding out what's there and where. Then comes pruning. Whew! The privet is so big, pruning doesn't describe what has to be done to it. The experts call it 'rejuvenative pruning.' I call it shearing. The existing boxwood may be too far gone for restoration so our members have taken cuttings from the existing shrubs—hopefully, for future planting. Deutzia is also being rooted. The lilacs are so overgrown, we only hope we can save them. Although the flowering trees look marvelous, they all need loving care—pruning, shaping, feeding. Also, existing perennials like daylilies, peonies, lily of the valley and roses must be dug up and heeled in for later use."

Helping the garden-club members with their mapping and planting has been an unexpected find—a treasure trove of garden photographs, taken around 1915 and discovered just last year in an old Weir family album. (Weir, that master at finding buried works of art, would no doubt approve.) Says Sarah Olson, superintendent of the Weir Farm National Historic Site, "They show the *whole* garden as it was, revealing perennial borders we didn't know existed, and a second gate in the fence, so they're a welcome addition to Professor Favretti's studies. Also, a Park Service archeological survey has turned up fascinating information about the lay of the land, even revealed the complicated workings of the fountain—of which only the base remains. Although restoration of the entire site is an ongoing project that will take years, thanks to the information we have now—and the work of the Ridgefield Garden Club—we expect to plant the garden this spring for summer viewing."

"This garden, when restored, will be a rare piece of art," Favretti predicts, "and will rate along with Church's garden at Olana, Thaxter's garden often painted by Hassam on Appledor Island in the Isles of Shoal, and Monet's garden at Giverny."

So go soon: in May, to see the spectacular flowering trees; in summer, the marvel of the restored garden and the whole green landscape; in October, the dazzling foliage—and all year-round to enjoy this national treasure fusing art and nature.

Weir Farm, 735 Nod Hill Road, Wilton, CT 06897, (203) 834-1896.

KAREN BUSSOLINI

KATHLEEN NELSON

OCTOBER 1994

Z oologist, biologist, teacher, wife, mother, plantswoman—all these meet and fuse in Kathleen Nelson, and are reflected in her highly personal and charming nursery in Gaylordsville.

Nelson came to her nursery in roundabout fashion—and so must you to get there. In fact, it's testament to her extraordinary plantsmanship that customers come at all. Crookedly west of Route 7, Mud Pond Road, where Nelson lives and works, is a one-lane dirt road. But it's worth the trip. The house sits high above the road and the nursery climbs upward to it, then sprawls northward in an informal series of terraces contained by stone walls, some of them built by Nelson's husband Randolph, a retired professor of counselor education at the universities of Connecticut and Bridgeport.

143

Born in northern Minnesota and proud of it ("All Minnesotans will find a way to sneak in where they come from," she laughs), Nelson earned her bachelor's degree in math and master's in zoology at the University of Minnesota, then studied a year toward her doctorate in human anatomy at Columbia, but left to take up teaching. She continues to take courses in a variety of subjects from chemistry to landscape gardening. "I love to learn and keep studying for that purpose," she says. "It all comes together somehow in my nursery work."

"I came to New York in '63 when I was 24, because someone told me it was an interesting place, but the city was not for me," she explains. "I stuck it out for 14 years and taught biology at City College and the Manhattan Community College, but I desperately missed the country."

Twenty years ago, she bought a couple of acres and a tiny one-person house on Mud Pond Road in Gaylordsville, both of which she's added to. "There was no running water, no electricity then," she recalls. "I loved it."

She also passionately loves to teach and, she says, "only stopped when, at age 40, I was lucky enough to give birth to our son, Tom. The baby was the best thing that ever happened to me and I didn't feel I had the emotional energy to be the kind of teacher and mother that I wanted to be."

Now that Tom is 14 she has begun to teach a few classes, when time permits, at the Institute of Ecosystems in Millbrook, N.Y., an outpost of the research program of the New York Botanical Garden. Her subjects are perennial plants and ornamental grasses. She also lectures to garden clubs and other groups and does landscape design and garden installation.

An attractive, slender woman with graying blond hair pulled back from her face, Kathleen Nelson is gentle-spoken but has very definite ideas. She has a deep understanding of the needs of plants—and people—and their interdependence. "I'm pessimistic about how overpopulation is causing chaos on our planet," she says. "People simply don't realize how any small changes in an ecosystem can alter or destroy an entire habitat for humans, animals and plants. This tragedy is unfolding everywhere on our planet. We violate the land out of ignorance and greed, yet we are totally dependent on our ecosystems.

"So when I teach," she continues, "I try to convey the whole picture, paring down to what's important to people and their needs. I strive to create some understanding of the interplay of evolution and genetics and the complexity of the ecosystems that contain—and sustain—all life. It's the reason I'm so active on the Wetlands Commission of New Milford. That's one ecosystem I can help to preserve."

So how did she come to run a nursery?

"Ever since I was a little girl, I was interested in plants and was forever collecting them, and identifying them, then pressing them," she says. "Northern Minnesota is too cold for most gardening but the wildflowers in the woods are wonderful. So, when we bought this land—it has basic gravel conditions—I started growing things. First I gave top priority to vegetables and just stuck the flowers in the gravelly earth. The result, of course, was more weeds than flowers.

"Then," she says excitedly, "I discovered mulch. First I used mulch from the electric company, which was full of poison ivy and other unwanted clippings, but over the years I found that the best mulch for me is bark-free wood chips, which we buy by the truckload from a sawmill. It will last three years.

"But I'm getting ahead of my story," she says. "When I bought the house, I had the flu the very week the seed catalogs arrived. I chewed them up and by week's end I had ordered dozens of seeds. They turned me into a perennial addict. So I started planting perennials. When my son was a toddler, I tried to sell them at wholesale. But I soon learned that a wholesale business was not a one-person operation. So nine years ago, I began selling at retail. It's right for me. I love the mix of plants and people, working outdoors spring, summer and fall, indoors with my books and computer in winter."

Nelson studied everything she could about perennials—the nature of plants, of soil, how to propagate, how to fertilize—and the interdependence of all of them. "Having studied biology, chemistry, zoology made it easier for me to learn," she says. "I knew how and where to acquire information and how to synthesize it meaningfully. I continue to do research into the nature of different plant materials and still learn every day.

"I'm a very opinionated gardener," she admits. "I like tough plants, those that thrive naturally in our soil and climate. Oh, I have a small space where I fuss with delicate types, but in the main, the plants I offer are stalwarts. I favor native plants, but also enjoy discovering new and unusual plants that will grow here—good tough ones—and I am adamant about avoiding invasive plants, especially those that aren't native. I also love architectural plants and enjoy playing with contrasting and complementary foliage, color and texture."

What's particularly interesting is that some plants that are generally considered not hardy or otherwise right for Connecticut are happily at home in her Gaylordsville nursery. Redbud, for instance, ordinarily given up as a flowering tree of the South, thrives here. "It depends on the seed source," Nelson explains. "If you get seeds that originated in Georgia, for example, they probably are not going to grow here. But seeds from Wisconsin are likely to take."

On my midsummer visit, I saw an enormous clump of sky-blue balloon flowers *(platycodon)*, the tall variety, bigger and better than any I've ever seen; tall, handsome white coneflowers *(echinacea)*, which, for me, have always been sickly types compared to the pink; masses of shade-loving hosta—blue-green, forest-green, apple-green, gold-green, variegated, narrow-leaved, broad-leaved—artfully used together in monochromatic shadings as well as separately for a dramatic single statement; great white spires of native meadowrue in dense plume-y clumps; clusters of flowering sage thick with blue flower spikes.

And grasses, ornamental grasses! The specialty of the house, they are dazzling in beauty and diversity. Nelson offers more than 40 different kinds of grasses with different varieties within each group. "Grasses provide marvelous material for landscaping," she explains enthusiastically, "both en masse or in specimen clumps. Plus they're great low-maintenance plants. Most prefer good well-drained soil and sun. So far mine haven't been troubled by pests, including deer." The varieties she lists are generally "clumping" rather than invasive types, and hardy in our Connecticut clime.

What will you have? Short, tall, towering; green, yellow, blue, pink, solid, variegated.

Maybe Wild Oats *(Chasmanthium latifolium)*, 3 feet tall, with dancing seed heads formed in summer that last all winter.

Or the many cultivars of *Miscanthus sinensis*, a group of particularly easy and varied grasses, many with variegated leaves, which bear purple plumes in late summer and fall that turn silver, then pale gold in winter.

Or the spectacular *Molinia caerulea* (Skyracer), with open arching plumes that rise high above a 3-foot fountain of foliage.

Or *Molinia caerulea* (Variegata), a neat low mound of softly flopping green-and-cream striped leaves above which floats the delicate purple inflorescence in summer, a choice specimen as an edging plant ("nice with hosta").

Or the native *Panicum virgatum* (Heavy Metal), with its glorious vertical blue foliage.

Or the unusual *Carex nigra*, a lovely low sedge that serves delightfully as a ground cover, particularly with blue and gold hostas.

Or Little Bluestem *(Schizachyrium scoparium)*, a native for massing and naturalizing on poor dry soil, which gets to 3 feet and is bluish in summer, brilliant orange in fall.

And more.

Nelson also offers some 400 varieties of perennials, including both rare species and "regulars." They range, alphabetically, from *achillea*, the fernleaf yarrow, to *Waldsteinia ternata*, a ground cover for sun and shade. Among her favorites are a large selection of native yellow daisies; the hard-to-find, gorgeously colored Korean angelica *gigas* with large burgundy dome-shaped flower heads and maroon stems, which blooms summer through fall; *Aralia racemosa*, a large architectural plant with arching stems spaced with spheres of green-white flower clusters; many wetland natives and plants with fragrant leaves that deter furry creatures.

She also grows a few carefully chosen shrubs, trees and woody vines, and a small assortment of annuals, non-hardy perennials and biennials.

I asked for simple pointers on growing perennials.

"First and foremost, analyze the site and prepare the soil," she replied. "Then learn the needs of individual plants—which like sun, which shade, which dry soil, which moist, and so on." (Her catalog spells all this out clearly.) "And remember, most plants want good drainage—even most moisture lovers don't want to stand in water.

"About deer," she added, changing the subject, "try to plant things they don't like to eat—for example, plants with fragrant foliage. But since that leaves out so many lovelies, I have used Hinder, which has a scent most deer find offensive. Happily, it can be used on vegetables and fruit. Some people also spray ornamentals with a systemic repellent, which, however, can't be used on edibles because of the bad taste. Trouble is, each deer has to sample each plant to find which taste bad. If you have a large flock, damage can be considerable."

October is a particularly good time to visit the nursery because so many of the grasses come into spectacular bloom. But call for an appointment. "Truth is," Nelson says, "we welcome droppers-in, but we're not always here. And, as you know, it's not easy to get here and finding no one at home is frustrating.

"Best time to telephone," she adds, "is after dark—pitch dark, that is. It's amazing how much you can get done in those last rays of light. And do let the phone ring. I have an outdoor ringer but sometimes I'm at an unstoppable task or I just can't get there fast enough." You might also write for her catalog. Like her, it's warm, welcoming, opinionated, and wondrously rich in helpful, to-the-point information.

Kathleen Nelson Perennials, 55 Mud Pond Road, Gaylordsville, CT 06755, (860) 355-1547.

WILLIAM SEITZ

SUSAN AND ROBERT BEEBY

MARCH 1995

The gardens at Susan and Robert Beeby's home in Greens Farms, Westport, are at once a *recreation* and a *creation*, fusing elements of past and present into a delightful and harmonious whole.

What the Beebys have *recreated*—indeed, brought from darkness to light—is a key part of the historic Bedford Gardens established in 1912 by local philanthropist Edward T. Bedford, one of the founders of Standard Oil, who lived in Westport from the mid-1860s until his death in 1931. The gardens were just part of the substantial Bedford estate, which stretched on both sides of the public highway, overlooking Long Island Sound on the shore. What the Beebys have *created*, in collaboration with landscape designer James Bleuer, principal of Casa Verde Florist and Gardens in Southport, are new gardens that are a personal expression of

147

a gracious lifestyle enriched by world travel and a passionate love of growing things.

The restoration of the old gardens is a saga of discovery. As Bob Beeby tells it, "Astonishingly, the gardens were invisible when we bought the property 15 years ago. Not a vestige could be seen, neither of plantings nor stonework. Like buried treasure, all lay submerged beneath a sea of green—dense weeds, scrubby trees and rampant ivy. I'm not talking about little patches of flowers, or an occasional piece of sculpture," he continues, "but hundreds of feet of shrubbery—rhododendron, andromeda, boxwood—a large terraced garden and more. As for the stonework, including walls, stairways, walkways, pools, fountains and, most remarkable, an entire neoclassic channeled watercourse some 50 yards long and 3 yards wide, all was totally hidden from sight. Even the lawn—a full acre-and-a-half of it—was blanketed by brush."

It's hard to grasp the full measure of the transformation between the 1930s, when the Bedford Gardens were a showplace for the public, and 1979, when the Beebys bought their 3½ acres. "Thousands Visit Beauty Spot in Greens Farms," proclaimed the *Bridgeport Sunday Post* in 1932, and continued, "The late Edward T. Bedford created the gardens because he loved flowers and trees and nature. But when he beheld so much beauty around him, it was the natural instinct of a fine and generous nature to share it with his fellow man. Every day the great gates to his estate are flung open for all who wish to feast their eyes on nature in her loveliest."

Sadly, seven years later, in 1939, the *Post* pictured a bleak sign bluntly warning, "Gardens Closed. No Admittance," with a caption explaining, "Because the U.S. government's demand for detailed accounting of the cost of maintaining the famous Bedford Gardens, Greens Farms, makes it impossible for the late Edward Bedford's heirs to keep the gardens open, the 'no admission' sign has been at the entrance since last fall and will remain there despite the ruling of the U.S. Board of Appeals that they were maintained as a local benefit."

The gardens' history during the next half century is fuzzy. One gathers that they never were reopened to the public, and that the Bedford heirs sold the vast acreage with greenhouses, a huge stone windmill and a house—all of which were apparently taken down over the years.

It took the Beebys a year of non-stop work to clear the land. "I used high-school kids to help me cut and stack the brush. Sixty truckloads full were carted away!" Bob recalls. In a feat of detection worthy of Sherlock Holmes, Susan unearthed the top step of the stone pathway edging the terraced plantings that had been the heart of the gardens. "I figured the Bedfords had to have had a pathway of stepping-stones leading from the top of the terrace to what was—and is again—the lawn. Those steps haunted me until, finally, I lay down on my back where I surmised steps might be, spread my arms wide, scrambled with my fingers among the weeds, then dug in my nails. Ouch, they hit rock. But that was only the beginning," she says, adding, "I spent the entire summer of 1980 unearthing that staircase, and the whole next summer clearing the lower walk."

Bob and Susan have also resurrected the lush bank of rhododendron and andromeda in the terraced gardens, and, with Jim Bleuer, replanted the entire slope with dwarf junipers, mugho pines and other low conifers interspersed with pockets of ground-hugging *mazus* for sky-blue carpeting in spring, ajuga for more blue in summer, and variegated lamium. They have also restored two stone-rimmed pools set into the terrace, with fountains plashing from above to below in a graceful waterfall. A pair of ornamental cranes from Thailand stand as sentinels, one at each pool. "I couldn't figure out how the old piping system worked," Bob confesses, "so I devised my own system and installed a pump to recirculate the water back up to the top pool."

At the base of the slope, Susan found a great drift of wild orange daylilies to which she has added 200 more shaded apricot to lemon-yellow. She has also planted an evergreen sash of pachysandra at the base of the slope, setting it off from the lawn. "Pachysandra!" she exclaims, flinching a little. "I dug up hundreds of plants from a long vacant house, lugged them home in wash baskets, and planted them while our house was under construction. I've used them wherever a ruffled green ground cover was needed at the front, side and rear of the house."

At the very front of the property, the Beebys have also uncovered the channeled stone watercourse that originally consisted of an elaborate series of pools with fountains and waterfalls splashing from one to the other, spanned by an arching metal bridge modeled after the bridge over the famed water-lily pool in Monet's gardens at Giverny. Although they have not restored the structure to working order, they have gracefully edged it with thick plantings of yew and juniper.

Before he retired three years ago, Bob was president of Frito-Lay; before that, he had been president of Pepsi-Cola International (both are subsidiaries of Pepsico Inc.). The international post entailed extensive travel to Asia, Europe and South America. Susan, a retired teacher (and a master calligrapher with an artist's eye for objets d'art), accompanied him whenever possible. As might be expected, their home is full of treasures found abroad.

More than that, both house and landscaping reflect architectural and decorative inspiration from the different lands they have visited. The house itself brings a touch of Provence to Westport. "We love the French countryside and were charmed by the farmhouses nestled in the rolling fields and hillsides," Susan explains. "So when we came to build this house 15 years ago, we, together with architect John Houk of Wilton, looked through dozens of books picturing houses in the South of France, and finally created *the* design that best suited the contours of the land and our needs."

Made of white stucco, the two-storied house sits far west of the street at the back of the property, against a backdrop of towering old trees. Level with the top of the hillside plantings that climb upward from the lawn, it looks for all the world as if it "grew there," says Bob contentedly. Along the driveway approaching the house are living memorabilia of the past: a 100-year-old purple beech whose leaves are burnished amethyst to copper from spring to fall, a grove of sassafras, and a clump of white birches.

Espaliered the height and width of the walls on both sides of the front door—which is really the back of the property—hydrangea *petiolaris* is dense enough to accommodate several birds' nests and is, as Susan describes it, "dazzlingly tiered with layers of white lace in June."

Although the views of the gardens from every room are beautiful, the vista from the dining room is *spectacular*. Here is a new garden that is the joint creation of the Beebys and Jim Bleuer. "The feeling we wanted was of an English garden, more formal than elsewhere but not overly so," Bob explains, and Bleuer obliged. Not only a master plantsman but a superb colorist and something of an architect and sculptor, Bleuer has designed a large garden (80 by 250 feet) that is basically biaxial—one axis running from the western end of the property eastward to the beginning of the terraced slope, the other from the house to the northern boundary of the land—but so gracefully planted that the geometry of it is masked.

Using a glorious mix of flowers, flowering trees and shrubs and setting them in artful irregularity among stone and grassy pathways, he has indeed achieved a look reminiscent of the "natural" landscaping of an English country estate. Rimming the entire north side of the garden, a 7-foot stone wall is embellished with a Medusa head set within a faux-copper door the Beebys found in France. The wall forms a handsome background for a large water-lily pond, installed by Bob, which lends shimmer and serenity to the whole.

Leading west from the pond, Bleuer has designed a miniature allée of *fastidia* cherry trees, columnar in form and grafted on standards (he loves standards for the dimension of slim height they provide), which beckons toward the terraced slope at the front of the property. In between is a glory of blossoming shrubs and plants and an occasional piece of delightful ornamental sculpture that expresses the Beebys' classic taste: a beguiling cherub spouting a fountain that serves as a grace note for the lily pond; a handsome sundial that lends contrasting texture to flowers and foliage.

One steps from the house into a patio paved with randomly placed flagstones that the Beebys have transformed into an "outdoor room" which provides a convivial yet private setting. Overhead is an arbor that duplicates one they saw at a hotel on the Costa del Sol in Spain. Made of huge cross-sawn cedar beams that they obtained "with difficulty" from California, it is thickly intertwined with the climbing Fairy Rose that blooms all summer in pink profusion. Indeed, there are roses, roses everywhere: a bounty of them in the whole inner portion of the gardens—Mary's rose, the Heritage rose, *Rosa bonica*.

As a plantsman, Jim Bleuer believes in low-maintenance, carefree gardening, and for all the seeming splendor of his plant material—some 50 varieties of flowering trees, plants and shrubs, as well as ornamental grasses and ground covers—he has achieved his goal. "All the roses are pretty much trouble-free and are either ever-blooming or repeat June bloom with a great burst in September," he says.

"The lilacs are also easy to grow," he adds matter-of-factly of a positively dazzling planting of four *Syringa palibiana*, the dwarf Korean lilac, set on his favored standards, which form an amethyst cloud of bloom in June, "a week later than most lilacs and with a heavenly fragrance."

Some of the most striking effects in the garden are achieved with "familiars" that Bleuer treats as if they were exotica. *Eupatorium* (plain old Joe-Pye weed) bears masses of fluffy pink blossoms and reseeds into great clumps. Silver-gray *Tiarella cordifolia* (native foamflower) grows into snowy drifts. Grassy *Liriope muscari* (lily turf) blooms blue in August, then rims the bare branched patio roses with green all winter long. Among the native shrubs, *Hammamelis intermedia* (witch hazel) explodes with "yellow firecrackers" in February and March; new hybrids of *Kalmia latifolia* (mountain laurel) bloom pink to bright red; *Ilex verticulata* (winterberry) bears bright-red fruits that bring birds all winter; *clethra* (pepper bush) stretches its fingerlike pink flowers in summer and ornaments the winter landscape with black peppercornlike seeds; and dwarf forms of weigela bear delicately spurred pink "flutes" both spring and fall.

Originally from the Chicago area, the Beebys first came to Connecticut in 1966. "This is our third house in Westport," Susan explains rather ruefully. "Because of Bob's job, we had to pick up and move twice to Dallas. But Greens Farms is now home for *good*. Our children, a son and daughter, now all grown-up, live with their families less than half an hour away.

"Despite all the work involved—or perhaps because of it—it has given us enormous pleasure to have restored to bygone beauty some of the fabled Bedford Gardens. I like to think that, like Sleeping Beauty, they were waiting to be awakened and loved."

SOURCES

Broken Arrow Nursery
13 Broken Arrow Road
Hamden, CT 06518
(203) 288-1026

Carlson's Gardens
P.O. Box 305
South Salem, NY 10590
(914) 763-5958

Claire's Garden Center
Haviland Hollow Road
Patterson, NY 12563
(914) 878-6632

Cricket Hill Garden
670 Walnut Hill Road
Thomaston, CT 06787
(860) 283-1042 or (860) 283-4707

Thompson & Morgan
P.O. Box 1308
Jackson, NJ 08527
(908) 363-2225

Van Bourgondien
P.O. Box 1000
Babylon, NY 11702
(800) 622-9959

Venamy Orchids
Route 22
Brewster, NY 10509
(914) 278-7111

Wayside Gardens
1 Garden Lane
Hodges, SC 29695
(800) 845-1124

White Flower Farm
30 Irene Street
Litchfield, CT 06790
(860) 496-1661

Winterthur Gardens
Winterthur, DE 19735
(800) 767-0500

INDEX

157